... performers ... the politics are ...globalisation. Here's a book that explains how the we're in really works and how some of us try to get a ... the system. Without question an enjoyable and stimula...

> – Ed ... Emmy-winning star of *Lou Grant* and former President of the Screen Actors' Guild

'Ben Dickenson bypasses clichés about the politics of Hollywood to probe some key underlying realities. The customary movie focus on individuals – while seemingly essential to storytelling – is apt to provide more evasion than clarification in a world that cries out for collective action and social remedies. While economic injustice is the rapacious elephant in the living room, the media generalities about movie-biz liberalism are masking the differences between mild complaints and fundamental critiques. *Hollywood's New Radicalism* takes a discerning look at the commercial film world's political and social messages, on and off screen. This book is especially valuable because it raises pointed questions that can puncture complacency and spur us on toward a deeper exploration of how creative talents could be serving humanity instead of boosting corporate profits.'

> – **Norman Solomon**, Executive Director, Institute for Public Accuracy and author of *Target Iraq: What News Media Didn't Tell You*

'*Hollywood's New Radicalism* is ambitious and refreshing. Ben Dickenson displays a rare and welcome use of political ideas to make sense of Hollywood, beyond its trivial surface.'

> – **Tony Garnett**, director and BAFTA-winning producer

Cinema and Society Series
General Editor: Jeffrey Richards

'Banned in the USA': British Films in the United States and Their Censorship, 1933–1960   Anthony Slide

Best of British: Cinema and Society from 1930 to the Present   Anthony Aldgate and Jeffrey Richards (revised edition)

British Cinema and the Cold War   Tony Shaw

Christmas at the Movies: Images of Christmas in American, British and European Cinema   Edited by Mark Connelly

The Crowded Prairie: American National Identity in the Hollywood Western   Michael Coyne

Distorted Images: British National Identity and Film in the 1920s   Kenton Bamford

An Everyday Magic: Cinema and Cultural Memory   Annette Kuhn

Epic Encounters: The Films of David Lean   Michael Coyne

Film Propaganda: Soviet Russia and Nazi Germany   Richard Taylor (revised edition)

Licence to Thrill: A Cultural History of the James Bond Films   James Chapman

Propaganda and the German Cinema, 1933–1945   David Welch

Spaghetti Westerns: Cowboys and Europeans from Karl May to Sergio Leone   Christopher Frayling (revised edition)

Spectacular Narratives: Hollywood in the Age of the Blockbuster   Geoff King

Typical Men: The Representation of Masculinity in Popular British Cinema   Andrew Spicer

The Unknown 1930s: An Alternative History of the British Cinema, 1929–1939   Edited by Jeffrey Richards

Hollywood's New Radicalism

WAR, GLOBALISATION AND THE MOVIES FROM REAGAN TO GEORGE W. BUSH

Ben Dickenson

I.B. TAURIS

LONDON · NEW YORK

Published in 2006 by I.B.Tauris & Co Ltd
6 Salem Road, London W2 4BU
175 Fifth Avenue, New York NY 10010
www.ibtauris.com

In the United States of America and Canada
distributed by Palgrave Macmillan a division of St Martin's Press
175 Fifth Avenue, New York NY 10010

Hardback   ISBN 1 84511 025 0
             EAN 978 1 84511 025 3

Paperback   ISBN 1 84511 103 6
             EAN 978 1 84511 103 8

A full CIP record for this book is available from the British Library
A full CIP record is available from the Library of Congress

Library of Congress Catalog Card Number: available

Typeset in Book Antiqua by JCS Publishing Services
Printed and bound in Great Britain by MPG Books Ltd, Bodmin

Contents

List of Illustrations

Acknowledgements

I remain in the debt of those who have contributed time, insight and intellect to assist me over the last two years. Thanks go to: Bruno Chatelin, Dana Polan, Danny Schechter, David Garte, Ed Asner (and Patty Egan), Ed Begley, Gary Morris, Haskell Wexler, Ian Green, Kate McArdle, Michael Albert, Nina O'Farrell, Norman Solomon, Paul Buhle, Philippa Brewster, Saul Landau and Tony Garnett. If your name is missing, I apologise, but you know who you are and what you have done.

Special thanks go to those with whom I've shared some difficult times of late: Howard, Luke, Siobhan, Shereen, Yuri, Beccy, Rosie, Eden and Viv. Finally, life would not be worth living and books not worth writing without the daily inspiration given to me by Sara.

General Editor's Introduction

Given the much-trumpeted box-office success of Michael Moore's anti-Iraq war polemic *Fahrenheit 9/11*, the popularity of the television series *The West Wing*, with its impeccably liberal president played by Martin Sheen, and the high profile of the left/liberal/progressive Hollywood aristocracy (comprising the likes of Tim Robbins and Susan Sarandon, Tom Hanks, Sean Penn, Danny Glover, George Clooney and Martin Sheen), it has sometimes seemed as if liberal Hollywood represents the whole of present-day America. The re-election victory of President George W. Bush, when it emerged that moral values played a greater part in determining voting intentions than the economy and the war and that the difference between the two candidates was essentially the support of nearly four million conservative Evangelical Christians for Bush, points to the limited extent to which the message of liberal Hollywood has penetrated the American heartlands.

Exploring the relationship between filmmaking, society, politics and the movies over the past 25 years, Ben Dickenson in his timely and cogently argued book demonstrates how difficult left-wing filmmakers have found it to get their message across through the movies. He shows how, following the take-over in the 1970s of the old studios like Paramount, Warner Brothers and MGM by corporate big business, Hollywood's output in the Reaganite 1980s was dominated by right-wing pictures of the *Rambo/Die Hard/Lethal Weapon* school. Just as in the McCarthy-dominated 1950s, radical messages often had to be smuggled into genre pictures like the sci-fi dramas *Aliens*, *Blade Runner* and *Robocop*. Even when a mainstream film like *Wall Street* criticised corporate capitalism full on, its leading figure Gordon Gekko became a hero to those who shared his creed that 'greed is good'.

The advent of the Clinton presidency created great hopes on the left and a growing independent sector of filmmakers took up radical themes. But there was always an inherent tension between the desires of individual filmmakers and the demands of big business corporations controlling the industry. Successful films critical of capitalism and globalisation were produced (*American Psycho*, *American Beauty*, *The Truman Show*), but they tended to individualise and thus blunt the message. Then disillusionment set in when Clinton failed to deliver the radical agenda and critiques of Clinton's regime appeared in *Bulworth*, *Primary Colours* and *Wag the Dog*. But at the same time, the mainstream industry was absorbing the adventurous mavericks like Steven Soderbergh, who had been thrown up by the independent sector.

The George W. Bush presidency, the Iraq war and the corporate scandals like Enron reinvigorated the independent sector, and leading Hollywood figures threw themselves into political activism. Dickenson traces the various manifestations of radical filmmaking that have emerged as a response to these political developments. Only time will tell if they will prove enduring or influential.

Jeffrey Richards

Introduction

Haskell Wexler is popular in my family home. He created an original and powerful film in the 1960s called *Medium Cool*. Wexler skilfully combined footage of American police clashing with anti-Vietnam War protesters outside the 1968 Democratic Party Convention, with dramatic scenes where characters discuss the role of the artist in modern society. He shot the action at the Convention himself, capturing the immediacy of the moment with tenacious camerawork. He gently directed and edited the fictional sequences so that both dialogue and performance conveyed an overbearing dissatisfaction with the harsh realities of the contemporary world. Wexler's film encapsulated the tensions of a situation in which ordinary citizens are at odds with the people who hold the reins of social and political power. My father had protested with tens of thousands of others in London against America's war with Vietnam. Consequently he raved about *Medium Cool* and I became fascinated with the way that social and cinematic worlds could interact.

When I interviewed Wexler for this book he opened with a humorous but revealing turn of phrase. 'I don't mean to be difficult … but I am', he said. He was referring to the minor problem we'd had in scheduling a convenient time to speak, but I felt his statement conveyed a much deeper understanding about his position in the world. Actor, director and political activist Tim Robbins has repeatedly stated that 'Hollywood is not a liberal town'. It is not even a town in the context that this book discusses filmmaking. Hollywood today is a set of multinational entertainment conglomerates, with outposts in Los Angeles, that are engaged in the business of buying, making, distributing and exhibiting films. Inside that profit-driven system a small minority of writers, directors, producers and actors make both big-budget commercially successful movies and create films exploring the social problems that confront humanity. In this environment a filmmaker with a left-wing worldview may set out simply to make good cinema. Yet the world around them throws up countless examples of division between the haves and the have-nots, compelling socially conscious Hollywood talent to respond both as activists and artists. Being 'difficult', as Wexler's words imply, goes with the territory of living as a politically progressive person in Hollywood.

This book is a journey into the contradictory relationships between filmmakers, society, politics and movies. The three sections of this book chart the advancement of the American cinema industry over the last 25 years, as well as revealing the tumultuous path taken by those in Hollywood who are committed to social justice. This book does not survey the entire history of American cinema. That task has been successfully completed many times before, and important trends such as American populism and the liberal movies of the 1930s – whilst being relevant context – are not the main subject here. Neither is this book confined to a study of electoral politics and its relationship to Hollywood. Wider social situations are this book's terrain. Formal debates in film or cultural studies, critiques of approaches taken by academics to cinema are factors in this book's exploration, but they are not the main focus. In these pages you will find an account and analysis of late twentieth- and early twenty-first-century economic, aesthetic and socio-political phenomena in American cinema.

Part One reveals how, in the 1970s, capitalists trained on Wall Street began buying up American film production studios like Warner Brothers, MGM and Twentieth Century Fox. These new Hollywood owners undertook a re-structuring programme founded on their ethic of gross financial accumulation. In the 1980s President Ronald Reagan's fiscal policy supported these businessmen, through cutting their taxes and changing legislation to suit their needs. In this climate left-wing Hollywood talent soon became marginalised. Hollywood activists demonstrated their recurring disgust with war, by organising protests and publicity stunts against Reagan's divisive foreign policy in Central America. Consequently, leading activist and television actor Ed Asner lost his job on the hit NBC series *Lou Grant*. Films challenging Reaganite ideology were rare, but savage critiques occasionally broke through, such as Oliver Stone's stock-market drama *Wall Street*. In this difficult period avenues of collective organisation were limited, and anti-Reagan resistance both on and off screen developed an individualistic tone. Thus Asner waged a lone war against NBC, and *Wall Street*'s central character, Gordon Gekko, channelled Stone's disgust with the entire project of Reaganism into a single fictional persona.

Part Two of this book explores how this tendency to individualise complex social situations laid the Hollywood left open to manipulation. When Democratic President Bill Clinton arrived on the political scene in the 1990s his personal charisma seduced many Hollywood activists and filmmakers. Clinton's liberal rhetoric encouraged the production of several movies featuring presidents with panache and compassion. Michael Douglas, who had played Gordon Gekko in *Wall Street*, now became *The American President* with a twinkling eye and a passion for the average citizen's welfare. The reality of Clinton's policies was very different.

Globalisation became the order of the day and trans-national corporations took a grip on the global economy. International media giants like Vivendi and Sony moved into Hollywood. The multinationals rapidly bought up the independent American film industry, which had been thriving since the success of Steven Soderbergh's award-winning relationship drama *sex, lies, and videotape* (1989). Gradually, stories of suffering caused by the same business interests in Latin America and Africa began to filter through to Hollywood. Alternative media producers, like Globalvision's Danny Schechter, began to find a new American audience for their anti-business message. Indeed, in the USA the urban poor saw no practical benefit from Clinton's administration. Consequently, movies produced by Hollywood left-wingers in the late 1990s became focused on the failure of the American liberal agenda. Warren Beatty weighed in with *Bulworth*, a portrait of a chronically failed Democratic politician.

Part Three examines the emergence of collectivist grass roots activism in the wake of the failure of the Clinton presidency. In November 1999 hundreds of thousands of people demonstrated against corporate power outside the Seattle summit of the World Trade Organisation. A half-decade of worldwide anti-capitalist protest was ushered in, which rolled over into anti-war protest in 2003 when Clinton's successor – Republican George W. Bush – went to war with Iraq. A fresh generation of Hollywood progressives became engaged in the new activism and helped to mobilise for the protests. During the Iraq war Hollywood personalities, like actors Martin Sheen, Danny Glover and Sean Penn, were identifiable figures in protest movements.

The talent that had emerged from the early 1990s independent scene was also infected with the spirit of the protests. These filmmakers tended to produce films that prized individual anti-corporate heroes, such as Steven Soderbergh's 1999 hit *Erin Brockovich*, in which a working-class mother takes on a major corporation. The Hollywood corporations were keen to exploit the new political mood themselves, and produced confused, violent movies that had a veneer of anti-capitalism. *Fight Club* (1999), with its visceral fury at consumerism, is one such example. However, those in Hollywood who were directly involved in the anti-capitalist movement began making niche-marketed films that represented moments of collective resistance to social oppression. Tim Robbins's directorial effort *Cradle Will Rock*, for example, parallels modern protests with those of 1930s America.

Finally, this book discusses how such developments prepared both Hollywood business and talent for the second term of President Bush's government, and beyond. Hollywood has been through a process of change in the last three decades: from the first corporate invasion in the 1970s, through Clinton's support for globalisation, to the multinational media conglomerates that today own American cinema. Those developments have run alongside a re-shaping of the Hollywood left: from individualistic anti-Reagan opposition, through manipulation by Clinton, to engagement with mass anti-capitalist and anti-war resistance. The people who make up this left desperately hoped for an end to the Bush presidency in the 2004 elections. His return to office with more than 50 per cent of the popular vote left them with a bitter dissatisfaction at the weakness of the Democratic alternative, and an even deeper anger that a right-wing president, who fully supported the global capitalist orthodoxy, was bedding down for four more years in the White House.

This book analyses these dramatic developments, hoping to fully explain Haskell Wexler's intuitive remark above. The people who make movies are by no means the main drivers of social change, but the idea that progressive filmmakers are by their nature 'difficult' people is more relevant today than ever before. The fruit of the last 25 years of activist and ideological battle in the arena of American cinema is the emergence in the twenty-first century of a new radical Hollywood left. How difficult they become in an era when the American right wing continues to run the most powerful government in the world, will depend largely on how far they can understand the recent social, political and economic history that shapes their position as artists and activists.

PART ONE:
The Inheritance

The key character in writer and director Oliver Stone's 1987 film *Wall Street* is the slick, avaricious businessman Gordon Gekko. Gekko turns ordinary Americans into victims by buying up companies on the stock exchange and laying-off their employees, to make a quick profit. Gekko's ruthless and uncompassionate pursuit of personal gain is a reflection of life in President Ronald Reagan's America, as Stone saw it. Speaking to the American Civil Liberties Foundation, shortly after *Wall Street* was released, Stone suggested that his country had become a slave to the ambitions of big business. He argued that 'war ... poverty ... Moral Majorityism [a right-wing campaign group aiming to censor the media industries]' were 'converging to diminish and repress man'[1] in 1980s America.

The story of Reagan's presidency was one of economic and political polarisation. An already wealthy American elite grew their income tremendously, whilst a combative and manipulative foreign policy earned the USA an aggressive reputation abroad. Hollywood personalities who shared Stone's social perspective sought to make the American cinema industry a site of anti-Reagan opposition. Loose coalitions of Hollywood talent successfully organised protest events during the 1980s, but their activism was rarely reflected on the movie screen. *Wall Street* was an uncommon example of cinematic anti-Reagan resistance in a decade where powerful multi-media corporations, run by men not too dissimilar from Gordon Gekko, became the dominant force in Hollywood. It was this context of rampant individual profiteering that led Stone to represent the fault lines of American society through a single dislikeable character in *Wall Street*. However, by reducing complex social situations to the actions of individual personalities, Hollywood progressives would come to find a fundamental flaw in their anti-Reagan project.

The creation of modern Hollywood

Gordon Gekko swaggers in pinstripe suits, smiles with a thin flash of pearly white teeth and rides in chauffeur-driven limousines as if he's done so his whole life. This was a performance for which Michael Douglas – a man involved with anti-Reagan protests during the 1980s – won an Oscar. However, Gekko is significant not only because of the quality of his portrayal but also for the way he reflects the situation in which *Wall Street* was produced. Consider that Oliver Stone organised the production from an office on Twentieth Century Fox's Hollywood site during 1986. Less than a decade earlier Fox had been acquired by Marvin Davis, a millionaire who had made his fortune speculating on the stock market and buying up businesses that he could re-organise for maximum profit. By the time work on *Wall Street* was underway Davis had re-shaped Fox into the model of a profit-hungry late twentieth-century corporation. After purchasing Fox for $700 million in the late 1970s, Davis immediately sold off its drinks-bottling operations and beach resorts. He cleared out existing executives and replaced them in 1979 with Chief Executive Officer Alan J. Hirschfield. Hirschfield shared Davis's Wall Street training ground, having been a successful stockbroker. Neither Davis nor Hirschfield paid much respect to the history of Fox, which had been making movies since 1919.

Hirschfield went so far as to state he was a 'financial consultant – not a movie executive'[2] and helped Davis reduce film output by a quarter whilst expanding home video operations. Hirschfield argued that home entertainment was a 'market [of] extraordinary change and growth'.[3] Fox pursued video distribution over and above other areas of work in order to try and monopolise this emerging source of income. Via a heavy advertising campaign, the company set sales records with the home rental release of futuristic outer-space adventure *The Empire Strikes Back* (1980). This business strategy of downsizing existing operations and exploiting new markets came to dominate Hollywood in the 1980s. Paramount, for example, stripped out high-cost activities in heavy industry and expanded book, music, television, video and cable television arms. Meanwhile at Disney, in 1984, executive Michael Eisner and production chief Jeffrey Katzenberg auctioned off libraries and sound stages. They then opened high-street stores, bought television advertising to promote an endless stream of merchandise and created multifarious video products. In addition they developed technology to make cartoon features cheaper and they expanded theme parks. As a result, Disney's market share of cinema exhibition climbed from 4 per cent in 1980 to 20 per cent in 1988.[4] This was the specific context in which *Wall Street* was made: the development of a ruthless modern corporate Hollywood, led by Wall Street financiers. Indeed, *Wall Street* is a negative comment on this state of affairs.

Gordon Gekko could have been modelled on Hollywood business-men like Davis and Hirschfield. When Gekko wins a controlling stake in ailing corporation Teldar Paper, for example, he promptly liqui-dates the least profitable sections of the business. In the process he sidelines the ageing executives who run Teldar, explaining to his prod-igy – coincidentally called Bud *Fox* – that there is no room in business for stuffy old men. This removes any pressure on Gekko to bolster the company with his own money and he is able to profit handsomely from the re-organised enterprise. Moreover, Gekko is a thoroughly dislikeable character. He is king of his New York skyscraper office. Minions hang on his every word and he lambastes them into submis-sion when they fail him. He tosses birthday gifts into a waste-paper basket, forgets the names of visitors and hires prostitutes as a reward for junior stockbrokers who break the law. Whether Gekko is based directly on Stone's experience of Davis or Hirschfield is hard to ascer-tain, but the stinging criticism of their business method, in a film produced on the Fox lot, is glaring.

Wall Street cost $15 million to produce – a budget equivalent to the average cost of a blockbuster movie in the mid 1980s. The money came directly from Twentieth Century Fox and the film boasted one of Fox's most experienced producers – Ed Pressman – on its credits. Stone's office, used for pre- and post-production activities, and his locations were bought and paid for by Fox, as was his entire crew. The fact that the film was a Fox production from start to finish might seem to con-tradict the ruthless approach of men like Davis and Hirschfield. They could not have failed to recognise that Stone's work exhibited progres-sive, or liberal tendencies. He had exerted formidable artistic control over his previous two directorial efforts, acting as not only director but also writer and co-executive producer. These films were expressions of Stone's disquiet with the decisions made by the leaders of American society, and his keenness to expose the suffering of the average citizen at the hands of such decision makers.

Salvador (1986) had been a chaotic exploration of US foreign policy in Central America. The film pictured American officials assisting in the murderous actions of local right-wing military forces in El Salva-dor. Scenes depicting brutal deaths of innocent civilians, in which the American representatives are complicit, clearly demonstrated that Stone's sympathies were not with the American authorities. *Platoon* (1986) had the same sensibility. It is the story of a young man's physical and moral education in the bloody Vietnam War. Chris Taylor and his compatriots are thrown into a violent war for which none of them can explain the cause and in which countless lives are destroyed. Not once does a senior American representative suffer in the violence, nor can they justify sufficiently the reasoning behind the conflict. Both these films were also critical successes.

Variety called *Salvador* 'raw, difficult, compelling, unreasonable, reckless and vivid'[5] and said that *Platoon* would 'grab the viewer by the collar'.[6] Such praise made Stone hot property, as did his Oscar-winning script about the mistreatment of an American youth arrested in Turkey for carrying hashish – *Midnight Express* (1978). However, the aesthetic qualities of Stone's movies were not completely original. Stone borrowed from a gritty, realistic and technically inventive body of films that had come to prominence in American cinema two decades previously. It was those earlier efforts that raised the flag of social critique in Hollywood, creating a tradition for *Wall Street* to follow. Ironically it had been men from Wall Street, forerunners to Marvin Davis and Alan Hirschfield, who opened the doors of Hollywood in the late 1960s to a socially engaged aesthetic. Ambitious Wall Street financiers making their first forays into the industry had looked around for a product with which to make their mark. A set of films inspired by the social and political upheavals of 1960s America were the freshest things around and presented a way to connect with a contemporary audience. The shape of Hollywood business and progressive filmmaking in the 1980s developed out of trends that had emerged in the 1960s and 1970s.

The movement last time

The guardian of Hollywood's fiscal security is the Motion Picture Association of America (MPAA). Since its inception in the 1920s the MPAA has developed many ways of protecting the profit margins of American cinema. For example, the MPAA demands that the titles of all potential releases are registered with them. The Association avoids registering films with similar titles, hoping to stop one product undermining the success of another in the marketplace. Such a set-up favours corporations, who can organise and pay for the registration of multiple titles. Among other pro-business functions the MPAA performs are its advocacy on the industry's behalf to government, its ability to draw in new finance to Hollywood corporations and the dishing out of advice on where the emerging markets for movies are to be found. In 1968 Jack Valenti, who has now been MPAA chief for 40 years, made a speech to a Federal Communications Commission hearing that neatly achieved all three of these missions.

Valenti talked about 'a new breed of filmmaker … an extraordinary fellow … dedicated' to his work, who was 'reaching for new dimensions of expression'.[7] The Commission should not try to censor these filmmakers from making challenging, even violent, films. Besides which, a contemporary audience was lapping up the fruits of their labour. The message to businessmen willing to explore the box-office dollar was implicit: Hollywood's products were changing and there was a marketplace to be exploited. Valenti's message seemed to get through and from 1968 onwards millionaire stock-market gamblers moved into Hollywood. Steve Ross, who owned the Kinney parking-lot corporation, took control of MGM. Kirk Kerkorian, who made his fortune as a Las Vegas casino owner, bought Warner Brothers. What opened up the new market that these millionaires aimed to exploit was social disaffection. Valenti's 'new breed of filmmaker' was being invigorated by immense social upheavals that had begun in the African-American community and spread across the country during the Vietnam War.

African-American families were dissatisfied with a situation in which they occupied 70 per cent of blue-collar jobs[8] but had an income averaging just 55 per cent that of white families.[9] Frustration with a gradual battle for equality, led by the National Association for the Advancement of Colored People and its figurehead Dr Martin Luther King, boiled over in riots in Harlem in 1964, Los Angeles in 1965 and in 13 other locations in 1966. Then in Detroit in 1968, where car-production giant General Motors had most of its plants, mass strikes erupted. Eyewitnesses Dan Georgakas and Marvin Surkin describe the situation that unfurled: 'on May 2 … workers shut down Dodge Main [a General Motors plant] in the first wildcat strike to hit that factory in 14 years … the black revolution of the sixties had finally arrived … at the point of mass production … the Great Rebellion.'[10] In 1969 wildcat strikes across the USA doubled. White urban poor joined the disputes, and were especially prominent in a prolonged New York postal strike. In Oakland, California, a new radical organisation called the Black Panther Party called on African Americans to take up arms against police brutality and rallied crowds against the segregation policies of the state governor. That governor was Ronald Reagan, who argued that America was being held to ransom by the riots and walkouts. As a Republican and a believer in the iron rule of law, as a supporter of business and of the segregated school system, Reagan was out of touch with the social ferment. The arrival of the Vietnam War, which Reagan fully supported, only served to distance him further.

From its start in 1964 up to 1968, the war required 470,000 US troops and cost $27 billion. In December 1965 students and manufacturing workers were told they could be drafted into the military and 400,000 hit the New York streets in protest, a further 100,000 in Washington and another 30,000 challenged armed troops outside the Pentagon. The Tet offensive and General Westmoreland's demand for another 206,000 troops in March 1968 fuelled further protests. It was in this context that the first Wall Street financier to heed Jack Valenti's call, Charles Bludhorn, recruited film critic Peter Bart to identify up-and-coming filmmakers for Paramount Pictures. Bludhorn, owner of industrial giant Gulf & Western, bought Paramount in 1968 and Bart, today editor of *Variety*, was tempted to join him because it 'seemed a fascinating moment of transition'. Bart rightly predicted that the changing social picture in America and the arrival of new marketers in Hollywood would afford him enough space to shepherd through some 'boldly innovative films'.[11]

One of those films was a cocktail of documentary realism and social commentary called *Medium Cool* (1969). Although not a significant commercial success, the aesthetic qualities of *Medium Cool* laid the foundations on which Oliver Stone's cinematic attacks on Reagan's America would be built. *Medium Cool* features naturalistic scenes involving the film's central character – a cameraman – and his pals, discussing the relationship of filmmakers to social events. These are interspersed with footage of army riot-control manoeuvres, ghetto life, police officers attacking political demonstrations and a riot of anti-Vietnam War protesters at the 1968 Democratic Convention in Chicago. The film is a disconcerting edit of dramatic scenes and frighteningly immediate sequences of real-life social unrest.

Director Haskell Wexler himself shot the footage at the Democratic Convention. As if to prove this fact, a voice shouts 'look out, Haskell' as tear-gas canisters are fired just out of shot. Through taking such risks Wexler has become an esteemed Hollywood talent over the last 40 years. In 1976 he won an Oscar for cinematography on *Bound For Glory*, the life story of depression-era folk singer Woody Guthrie. On the *Bound for Glory* set he invented the steady-cam, experimenting with weights to balance the movement of hand-held cameras and remove the jagged motion of the cameraperson's walk. His commitment to social causes has been equally significant and in the 1960s he presented

1. Riot police attack protesters in Haskell Wexler's politically charged *Medium Cool* (*courtesy of Haskell Wexler*).

a shining example of how to combine activism and filmmaking for future talent like Oliver Stone. One marker Wexler laid down was on the subject of American action in Vietnam that Stone would subsequently explore in *Platoon*. Wexler approached the Vietnam issue by helping director Joseph Strick to interview soldiers involved in an incident in the Vietnamese village of Mai Lai. In *Interviews With Mai Lai Veterans* (1970) American infantrymen explain how they killed innocent civilians because senior officers directed them to do so. Wexler was also keen to tackle domestic concerns, such as racial discrimination. In 1967 he worked on the multi-Oscar-winning hit *In the Heat of the Night,* which featured distinguished black actor Sidney Poitier as a Philadelphia policeman battling racist thugs to solve a murder in a small southern town. Wexler exemplified the kind of filmmaker Jack Valenti had described, but there are other examples.

Martin Scorsese reflected on debilitating urban poverty in *Mean Streets* (1973), which trails four working-class Italian Americans as they sink into drinking and brawling in New York. Dennis Hopper wrote, directed and starred in *Easy Rider* (1968), a road movie featuring Hopper and Peter Fonda as motorcyclists travelling across America. A strait-laced Jack Nicholson is drawn into their alternative and liberated lifestyle, which involves rebelling against the rule of the state by smoking pot. Robert Altman's *M*A*S*H* (1970) tackles the theme of war, featuring a cast of misfits employing gallows humour to survive a dirty conflict in Korea, and slipping into conversation about the pointlessness of the conflict. *Easy Rider* was also a commercial success, on release for 10 months across the USA and making $90 million worldwide. *M*A*S*H* made $73 million in the USA alone, prompting a successful adaptation to television, where a series featuring the same cast of characters ran from 1972–83 on the CBS network.

Wexler, Altman, Hopper and Scorsese set out to make movies that reflected the social circumstances in which they worked. These movies also returned a healthy box-office profit to the corporate entrepreneurs taking root in Hollywood. There were, however, significant differences between the historical period of unrest in which these directors cut their teeth and the decade in which Oliver Stone cut his. Throughout the 1970s the new Hollywood capitalists extended their tentacles into television corporations, publishing businesses, theme parks and music companies. By the mid 1980s Hollywood corporations were setting up limited partnerships with other investors. These partnerships were, under President Ronald Reagan's ruling, exempt from taxation. A limited partnership was essentially a holding account for studio money tied to a particular project or set of projects. Studio money was matched by at least equal, and in most cases considerably greater, funding from external investors. The studio shifted the burden of production costs to others by engaging them in deals for particular films. The Hollywood corporation, however, retained the distribution rights for the movie and awarded itself the lion's share of the box-office profits. Developments like these helped the stock-market speculators in charge of Hollywood make profits without needing to rely on the 'extraordinary fellows' that Jack Valenti had identified. Furthermore, the social and political movements that had risen up in the late 1960s evaporated within 10 years. The arrival of Ronald Reagan in the White House in 1980, a man who had seemed so out of sync with the political context 15 years earlier, must have seemed the ultimate affront to the generation of Hollywood talent inspired by the 1960s experience.

Whilst the economic re-formation of Hollywood was advanced by Reagan's arrival, the trajectory of progressive filmmaking was interrupted. The raw social material of collective action from which *In the Heat of the Night*, *Medium Cool*, *M*A*S*H* and *Easy Rider* were modelled was denied to the 1980s generation of Oliver Stone. While the legacy of such socially engaged movies would live on, leaving a space in Hollywood for Stone's social critiques to occupy, the 1980s would generally become a far more difficult time for Hollywood progressives.

'Greed is good'

Wall Street's most memorable scene pictures grey-haired, grey-suited middle-aged men sitting in neat rows at an annual shareholders' meeting of fictional business Teldar Paper. The company's logo festoons the walls, and executives read excerpts from financial reports that detail how the corporation makes and spends millions of dollars. With greased-back hair and an expensive pinstripe suit, Gordon Gekko grabs a microphone. He glides through the aisles of the conference hall. Only his head and shoulders are visible, granting his movement a smooth quality reminiscent of a slithering snake. He speaks with self-assurance, smoothly persuading the shareholders to let him buy a controlling stake in Teldar. 'Greed, gentlemen, is not a dirty word', Gekko argues. It is the motor that drives modern society, he asserts, 'greed is good'.

In Gekko, Oliver Stone created an iconic representation of what he thought was wrong with 1980s America. This was a time when individuals like Gekko took pride in their personal quest for wealth, regardless of the detrimental effect their profit-making may have had on others. Gekko is charismatic, with a glint in his eye and a rasping chuckle. Just being associated with Gekko opens doors for his protégé and the film's central protagonist, Bud Fox, played by Charlie Sheen. Bud quickly gets promoted after he works with Gekko, is given the best office in his own building and is invited to the most exclusive parties. Consequently Bud transforms from a hard-working loyal son into a deceitful stock trader with a rampant desire to 'own' the best of everything, including an attractive girlfriend. Bud winds up souring old friendships and risking a prison sentence to obtain information about corporate deals illegally. What drives the film on through these developments is the action that Bud chooses to take, or that he is encouraged to take by Gekko. *Wall Street* is a film shaped by individual choices.

Even when Bud's partnership with Gekko seems likely to result in the firing of workers at Blue Star Airlines, the film avoids exploring the collective consequences of this possibility. We do not get to see the experience of the Blue Star workers. Instead the vehicle for looking at the Blue Star situation is Bud's relationship with his father Carl – played by Charlie Sheen's real-life father Martin Sheen, a time-served left political activist in Hollywood. Carl works as a construction fore-man at Blue Star and has an honourable history of organising union disputes to defend co-workers. He argues that a rewarding job is not one where money is the primary motive to turn up to work. He refuses to buy into a proposed – and illegal – deal with Gekko that will sup-posedly save Blue Star from financial trouble by handing its ownership to the stock exchange. Carl is a positive moral counterweight to Gekko, a man who is concerned with the welfare of blue-collar buddies and not with personal profit. Carl has a straight-talking approach that seems to disarm Gekko, and a squint that implies he sees through the veneer of Bud's exclusive lifestyle to the decent boy underneath. Carl is a creation that suits Stone's proclaimed mission to go 'back to those movies I believed [and watched as a kid with his dad, who took him to the movies every Saturday] ... where my hero ... by some shining light of inner force ... triumphs.'[12]

When Carl walks out on Gekko's deal, Bud is forced to choose between his mentor and his father. In the end he follows the 'shinning light' of Carl's integrity by exposing Gekko's illegal stock trading and bringing an end to the lizard-like businessman's career. In this way Stone's film focuses the viewer's attention on individuals within Rea-gan's America. This individualised perspective was a common thread among progressive personalities in 1980s Hollywood. Indeed, socially conscious talent in Hollywood seemed fixated with Ronald Reagan, in the same way that *Wall Street* is fixated with Gordon Gekko. 'Reagan ... obsessed us',[13] says Ed Asner, a popular television actor during the 1980s and a key figure in several campaigns against the Reagan gov-ernment. Hollywood progressives held Reagan personally responsible for the creation of a super-wealthy elite of real-life American Gekkos. The 1986 Tax Reform Act, for example, reduced the burden on the top fifth of American corporate earners from 70 per cent to 28 per cent. Previously, in 1982, Reagan's government had deregulated the savings and loan industry. Federal insurance was then provided for every investment of $100,000 or less. If any savings were loaned to a stockbroker and lost in a bad deal the federal government would refund the original $100,000. Policies like these helped American millionaires collectively increase their wealth by 1,630 per cent between 1980 and 1989.[14]

In the early 1980s Asner starred as a newspaper editor in hit show *Lou Grant*, a drama series produced by the CBS television network. Simultaneously, Asner was a high-profile participant in several campaigns against Reagan's administration. One action, seeking to draw

2. Ed Asner: a leading Hollywood activist throughout the 1980s, something that lost him his part as newspaper reporter Lou Grant in the hit television series of the same name (*courtesy of Ed Asner and Patty Egan*).

attention to Reagan's foreign policy misdemeanours, was a press stunt launching medical aid for victims of corrupt administrations in Central America. In front of several newscameras Asner tossed $52,000 on to the steps of the State Department, and damned the officials there for backing what he called 'dictators and murderers' in foreign governments. That action convinced CBS to sack Asner from the title role in *Lou Grant*. Reflecting on such activities Asner comments, 'when I became involved in these issues nobody knew a damn thing about the politics of the situation, people did not recognise the integration of the government'.

When Asner 'couldn't find enough people around to help me' after his *Lou Grant* sacking he came to believe that to resist Reagan's government needed a mass movement of Americans. It was 'in everybody's interest' to take a stand, points out Asner, as wealth creation at the top of American society resulted in cuts to the resources that government allocated to the poorest American people. Take the federal Food and Nutrition Service, set up in the era of President Franklin D. Roosevelt to ensure that America's poorest citizens could eat healthily. By 1988 this scheme had almost closed down. Meanwhile, the spending of Reagan's government on education and welfare schemes shrank by 8 per cent over the first six years of his administration, a figure equivalent to tens of millions of dollars.[15]

Asner describes his own learning curve about American society and politics as being several steps in advance of most people around him in Hollywood.

> I narrated a couple of documentaries … that dealt with the trage-dies in El Salvador and Nicaragua [where US money and troops backed repressive military forces in bloody civil wars]. I discov-ered that the 'cause, dear Brutus, lies in ourselves'. It was a collective responsibility of the American people that we shirked or ignored and that allowed the government [not Reagan alone] to continually impoverish the Central Americans.[16]

It would not be until the late 1990s that Oliver Stone would begin making films that, unlike *Wall Street*, explored this collective nature of modern society. When he did so, his films would largely focus on pre-senting a more complex picture of corporate power than Gordon Gekko had given.

Any Given Sunday (1999), for example, is a film in which American football coach Tony d'Amato finds his long and successful career undermined by the movement of corporate interests into his sport. This film pictures a board of executives, their corporate lawyers and an integrated corporate media working against Tony's objectives for his team. As Tony tries to galvanise his players into a winning unit various corporate flunkies issue orders that change his plans. Repeatedly Tony has to stand up to the flunkies and corporate chiefs, eventually deciding to leave the club where he has coached for many years and take the team's best player with him. This representation of a whole social structure, and of Tony's resistance to it, is a reflection of the anti-capitalist movement of the late 1990s. This movement sprang to life in November 1999 as activists protested in hundreds of thousands at the summit of the World Trade Organisation in Seattle, where the leaders of global business and government were gathered. This protest, the first of many that would take place across the world, happened in the same year that *Any Given Sunday* was produced. Hollywood celebrities, like actor and director Tim Robbins, and actor and producer Danny Glover, attended the Seattle protests. Moreover, both Glover and Robbins were involved in organising mobilisations of ordinary citizens to Seattle and attended planning workshops months before the protests took place. This engagement by Hollywood celebrities with a mass anti-capitalist rank and file movement was beyond conception when Stone made *Wall Street* in 1987. The context for *Wall Street* was, instead, a period where mass movements were absent and where corporate interests strengthened their position without challenge.

Reflecting on the 1980s, *Business Week* observed in 1992 that the average US executive's salary at the end of the decade was 160 times that of their employees. It was six times greater than the salary of European and Japanese executives. Unemployment during the 1980s had broken the 10 per cent barrier and 15 per cent of the American population lived below the poverty line. Shockingly, Reagan believed it was acceptable, even desirable, for the working people of America to suffer. In 1983 David Stockman, Reagan's budget director, explained to a private business meeting that unemployment was part of Reagan's plan. According to Stockman, wealth creation through tax cuts and savings and loan deregulation was good for America. If such actions subsequently caused unemployment then that was good too. He went further to argue that unemployment was a 'cure, not a problem'. By 1989 the United States was the world's richest country but also had the widest gap in income between the richest and poorest 5 per cent of the population.

Wall Street attempted to attack this situation but blunted its own critique by individualising the social polarisation of the Reagan era in the characters of Bud, Carl and Gekko. Without a mass social movement like that of the late 1960s or the late 1990s to bolster progressive film-makers in the 1980s, their response to Reagan's America was inevitably individual rather than collective.

The liberal Hollywood response to Reagan

Haskell Wexler argues that many 1980s American films were concerned with 'reinforcing the ideological arguments' of the Reagan government. Wexler suggests that many films of the decade are how-to guides: 'how to screw each other, kill each other and rip each other off'. During the 1980s Wexler joined anti-Reagan campaigns protesting for nuclear disarmament and against the president's policies in Latin America. His most high-profile work during this period was as director of photography on a commercial family comedy about an ex-bankrobber pulled into a last job by a desperate father – *Three Fugitives*. Wexler reflects that very few films of the 1980s explored 'questions of humanity' or presented 'human solutions' to social problems. [17] *Three Fugitives* had at least been about a father driven to robbery to feed his daughter and the softening of a tough ex-con when faced with the responsibility of caring for the child. Tony Garnett, the BAFTA-winning television producer and one-time Hollywood director, adds that 'hustlers and sleazebags are attracted to Hollywood by power and money but some of the brightest people in America can also be found there'. Under Reagan, Garnett suggests, the money-focused sleazebags dominated and 'it became the decade of high concept movies with violence and right-wing assumptions' in which the bright people – like Wexler – found Hollywood a 'very difficult place to work'. [18]

A crucial battle took place over the question of wealth accumulation. Ed Meese, the treasury secretary, spoke to the National Press Club in December 1983. Meese took a classic and often re-told story from literature and inverted its message, suggesting that 'Ebenezer Scrooge suffered from bad press in his time'. In Charles Dickens's story of a businessman who forsakes greed for charity, Scrooge is a grotesque caricature willing to exploit every opportunity for financial gain. Nevertheless Meese argued, 'if you really look at the facts, he didn't exploit Bob Cratchit [the lowly employee of Scrooge's who couldn't afford to buy his children Christmas gifts or care for his sickly son]. Bob Cratchit was paid 10 shillings a week, which was a very good wage at the time … Bob, in fact, had good cause to be happy with his situation.' Cratchit struggles to feed his family, is forced to work at

Scrooge's beck and call and is described as well turned-out but dressed in the poorest of clothes. Yet Meese goes on, 'his wife didn't have to work ... He was able to afford the traditional Christmas dinner of roast goose and plum pudding.' Having a sick child in Victorian England where there was no easily accessible healthcare system, and bearing in mind that most employment for women not born into the middle-classes involved hard labour, Meese seems again to have missed the point. Oblivious to this context, Meese confidently concluded, 'let's be fair to Scrooge. He had his faults, but he wasn't unfair to anyone.'[19]

In response to Meese's twisting of the 'facts' of the fictional Scrooge story Hollywood progressives produced films that made individual statements about modern-day American poverty and avarice. *Colors* (1988), directed by and starring Dennis Hopper, is a faux-documentary story of an old policeman and his angry young partner trailing the streets of Los Angeles, trying to stop gang violence and witnessing the extreme poverty that leads to violent territorial battles. Where Reagan argued in 1982 that 'there are a million more working than there were in 1980'[20] – his treasury secretary later corrected the figure to just 100,000 – *Colors* responded with a representation of the desperate poverty inflicted on urban communities in 1980s America. That the poor people in *Colors* are black is recognition of the way Reagan attacked black communities, claiming in one 1984 press conference that the 17 per cent unemployment level in some urban areas was because black people would not look for new jobs. Reagan neglected to mention that the federal fund for employment training that created opportunities to those communities had been cut by 30 per cent in 1983.

A further response to Meese can be found in the inventive comedy hit of 1983, *Trading Places*. Here comic actors Eddie Murphy and Dan Aykroyd play, respectively, a beggar and a rich bachelor. A bet between wealthy businessmen results in the beggar and the bachelor being forced to swap lives. Aykroyd sinks into the mire of poverty and destitution, even being driven to armed robbery and attempted suicide. Murphy quickly adapts to the life of a stockbroker, making smart business decisions but finding that neither his face nor lifestyle fit comfortably with his new status. When the men discover their change in circumstance was caused by two millionaires they decide to work together to expose stock-market cheating and steal the businessmen's millions. On the surface the film is a comedy about chasing money, the overriding message, however, is about the way money corrupts; it corrupts the businessmen into a bet that directly affects people's lives. The poverty that Aykroyd is thrown into by having his financial support removed is a dirty one. The motifs of his life become homelessness, ill-fitting clothes, starvation and a dependence on the charity of a call girl. When Aykroyd approaches the two millionaires for help they reject him, for no other purpose than trying to win their bet. This is an America in which the callousness of the modern-day Scrooge pushes others to destitution. Just to thrust that message home, Aykroyd is pictured unshaven and dressed in a sullied Santa Claus costume at one point – as if to suggest the spirit of Christmas had been ruined by the greed of the businessmen.

There are common threads running through both these films and also through *Wall Street*. Whilst *Colors* is a tough urban drama, *Wall Street* a high-society corruption tale and *Trading Places* a wacky comedy, they all feature a certain kind of hero. In *Colors* Dennis Hopper's mature cop tries keeping the streets clean and, though he may have to get dirty by threatening street kids sometimes, he approaches his work with a certain set of values. He tells his impetuous partner – played by Hollywood radical actor and director Sean Penn – that their role is not to instigate violence but to diffuse it, and throughout the film he manipulates a set of relationships that he has formed to maintain what he calls 'the peace'. This cop is compassionate too, arguing that the citizens of this broken, impoverished Los Angeles community deserve better than welfare cheques and gang warfare. In *Wall Street* there is a similar character in Carl Fox. Carl is loyal to his colleagues at Blue Star Airlines, he is compassionate about their situation and works hard to ensure that his actions do not jeopardise their security. Carl acts in accordance with his values, refusing to jump at the chance to save Blue Star when Gordon Gekko offers to buy the company, for fear that Gekko will act without compassion for the staff. Carl believes his colleagues deserve better and is willing to stand up for that ideal.

Similarly, but with comedic veneer, both Murphy and Aykroyd are men of values in *Trading Places*. Aykroyd cannot stomach the disloyalty of his former millionaire associates and Murphy is appalled when he overhears them talking about their bet. Both men eventually put their personal values – not to be cheated by others, not to manipulate others, to right injustice – above their own position. Murphy could keep the fortune that has been bestowed on him but instead chooses to do the right thing and expose the millionaires' bet. The continuity here is threefold: all the films demonstrate sympathy for poor and working Americans; the films attribute strong personal morals and compassion for others to their heroes; and finally, the actions of these heroes are instrumental in determining the direction of the film. The *Trading*

Places plot turns on Murphy's decision to reject his new-found wealth and right the wrong done to Aykroyd. *Wall Street* concludes with Carl's son, Bud, exposing Gordon Gekko's corruption to the authorities, but in order for this to happen Carl has had to persuade Bud of the importance of values. In *Colors* the presence and action of Hopper's cop prevents an explosion on the Los Angeles streets that his partner, left to his own violent devices, would have certainly provoked.

These special individuals, elevated above those around them by their humanistic values – the very ones that Haskell Wexler appeals for – are a recurring feature of films produced by Hollywood progressives. Compare the heroes of these films to Detective Virgil Tibbs in *In the Heat of the Night,* on which Wexler himself worked. Tibbs is made special by several factors: he's a black man in a white town, a homicide detective among inexperienced policemen, he deduces and observes more quickly than anyone else, he's slim and fit compared with the town's overweight police chief and he's prepared to resist oppression. Tibbs is full of the values of freedom and equality so that, when faced with a plantation-owning racist white man, he does not back away from a line of questioning that implies the racist could be a murderer. When the racist slaps Tibbs he immediately slaps him back, leaving the racist in a state of shock. By the film's conclusion Tibbs has solved a local murder, changed the opinion of the police chief about black people and proven himself to be an intelligent, tough and determined individual. *In the Heat of the Night* was released in 1967, *Trading Places* 1983, *Wall Street* 1987 and *Colors* 1988. Twenty years after Virgil Tibbs had represented a principled, specially talented black man crusading through a world of injustice, these three 1980s films represented a range of modern-day heroes who shared Tibbs's special individualism and held up their values against the avarice and poverty of the Reagan era.

These films are not, as Haskell Wexler demands, representations of collective responses to the social conditions of the Reagan era. In *Wall Street* Carl Fox walks away from a meeting with Gordon Gekko on his own and later Bud goes alone to the FBI to expose Gekko's illegal trading. Such individual action against injustice is very different to the collective protests at the 1968 Democrat Convention that Wexler filmed in *Medium Cool*. However, the individual acts of resistance in *Wall Street* are in keeping with the tradition of *In the Heat of the Night,* where detective Virgil Tibbs has to stand alone against the racism of the local establishment. *Medium Cool*, it can be argued, is an attempt to take the humanistic response to social problems to a higher level. This was something that Wexler witnessed first hand during the period of urban black revolt and anti-Vietnam War protests in which *Medium Cool* was made. No such movements existed in the 1980s and films such as *Wall Street, Trading Places* and *Colors* had to mine their dramas from the rock of Reaganite dominance, with their filmmakers perhaps believing that individual resistance was the only form of action now available to American dissenters.

If the treatment of individual heroes in these films had first been tested in the 1960s, so had Reagan's ideological perspective. In 1964 he had said, 'public servants [will] say … "What greater service we could render if only we had a little more money and a little more power." But the truth is that outside of its legitimate function, government does nothing as well or as economically as the private sector.'[21] This love of free-market economics in the White House was mirrored in Hollywood, where the financiers who took control of the studios in the 1960s and 1970s were busy restructuring the industry to achieve maximum financial exploitation. Overseas the new Hollywood businesses were aggressive. International co-producers, especially Canal in France and Kadakowa in Japan, secured overseas distribution. By registering films with these companies, even if they were still shot in the USA, the corporations were guaranteed tax breaks from European and Japanese governments and could draw in major banks like Barclays and C Itoh to bolster investment. Banks and investors were chained to specific films through pre-production payment deals, effectively turning overseas investors into distribution champions for the corporations. Reagan's 'right-to-work' legislation even allowed the movie corporations to pay 83 per cent lower wages to new recruits.

It was this situation, of apparently unstoppable growth in Reaganite practice inside and outside Hollywood, which inspired the individual value-laden heroes of 1980s progressive Hollywood movies. Simultaneously an even bigger ideological battle was being waged: one that also had its roots in the strategies of Reagan's government and one that saw Hollywood progressives make their biggest challenges to the Reagan administration.

War – studio spectacle and directorial detractors

Over the last 30 years Saul Landau has been one of America's foremost radical documentary makers. Working with Haskell Wexler, he was the last American to interview Chilean President Salvador Allende before the socialist was assassinated in 1973 in a coup reportedly backed by US forces. Today Landau is a cultural commentator for *progresso.com* and a fellow of the Washington-based Institute for Policy Studies. Landau suggests that to acquire an accurate record of 'how US policy … has led to barbarous military acts' in the Reagan era, it is worth reading William Blum's book *Rogue State: A Guide to the World's Only Superpower*. Blum shares Landau's self-proclaimed 'quest to represent the true picture of our country',[22] is a former foreign service officer in the State Department, was in Chile working as a journalist when Landau visited the country, and attempted to make it as screenwriter in Hollywood during the 1980s. Blum breaks down the major game-plays of Reagan's foreign policy into straightforward explanations like these:

- **Afghanistan** (throughout 1980s) – the CIA funded gun smuggling, encouraging heroin export. They recruited Osama Bin Laden to train Islamist volunteers, who forced occupying Russian troops to leave. A civil war then lasted until 1995 when the Taliban, helped by the CIA, took control.
- **Angola** (throughout 1980s) – military and monetary assistance to the chosen side in a civil war where an estimated 500,000 lives were lost.
- **Chad** (1981/2) – the USA persuaded the government to expel Libyan military forces. The next year a military force, trained by the CIA, invaded from Sudan.
- **East Timor** (throughout 1980s) – a people's movement expelled Portuguese colonists (1975). Nine days later Indonesia invaded the country. Reagan supported the occupation, which Amnesty International estimate killed one-third of the population.
- **El Salvador** (throughout 1980s) – 75,000 civilians died in civil war. The US treasury gave $6 billion over 12 years to its chosen side, losing 20 CIA personnel.
- **Grenada** (1983) – US forces conducted a swift invasion of Grenada in October 1983, killing 400 of the population and installing new rulers in the country.

- **Honduras** (throughout 1980s) – 'American diplomats exercise more control over domestic politics in Honduras than in any other country in the hemisphere'.[23]
- **Libya** (throughout 1980s) – US airforce shot down two planes in Libyan airspace and bombed a 'presidential palace', killing 50 people. Reagan associated Libyan leader Qaddafi with terrorist groupings and incidents, without evidence.
- **Nicaragua** (1980s–90s) – Sandinistas ousted dictator Somoza, suffering a military backlash from the Contras. Reagan called the Contras freedom-fighters. Oxfam said the Sandinistas were 'exceptional in … improving the condition of the people'.[24]
- **South Korea** (1980) – US/Korean force suppressed popular protest in Kwangju, 1980, killing 2,000 civilians. Reagan asked Congress to delay publishing a report on human rights when the leader of the operation, Chun Doo Hwan, was a state visitor.
- **South Yemen** (1982) – USA sent military aid to help attack North Yemen and trained paramilitaries to carry out clandestine operations and torture captives.[25]

Reagan's government provided two justifications for each intervention. The first was usually local: Nicaragua – the Contras are freedom-fighters, the Sandinistas are dictators; Libya – Qaddafi supports terrorism; and so on. The second reason, applied in every case, was the threat of Soviet Russia: Qaddafi was supported by Russia; the repressive Taliban were better than a pro-Russian Afghanistan; the Sandinistas' policies were pro-Communist; and so forth. Reagan was the most vehemently anti-Russian president America had seen. 'Let us pray for the salvation of all of those who live in that totalitarian darkness', he argued. 'They are the focus of evil in the modern world' he suggested, calling on all Americans not to 'ignore the facts of history and the aggressive impulses of any evil empire'.[26]

Hollywood corporations provided a visual arsenal of movies with violent all-American protagonists as a backdrop to Reagan's assault on the globe. The *Rambo* trilogy featured a lunatic soldier faced with hordes of non-white enemies and who, somehow, defeats them single-handedly. Although in the first film, *First Blood*, Rambo is portrayed as a victim of foreign torture, Sylvester Stallone's performance in the sequels was testosterone-induced and excessively aggressive. Military superiors, as well as draping him in the American flag, praised him for his outlandish violence. Similarly *Commando*, *Die Hard* and the *Lethal*

Weapon series are ballistic festivals. The first featured a crack unit of the American military led by Arnold Schwarzenegger bringing down a caricatured Latin American dictator. Not once is the right of American soldiers to enter a sovereign country and depose its leader questioned. In *Die Hard* and *Lethal Weapon* maverick cops spray bullets around in solo quests to overturn villains, with foreign accents, who threaten the security of Americans. The Americans in *Die Hard* are, incidentally, corporate executives and their bosses Japanese.

The Empire Strikes Back, *Return of the Jedi* and *Aliens* were films with futuristic settings, featuring a multitude of high-tech weaponry and battles between the forces of good and the massed armies – or horrific creatures – of evil. Parallels with the America–Russia rhetoric of the Reagan administration in the *Star Wars* films include an evil empire, dressed in the same style of uniform that Soviet soldiers often wore on parade and whom the black-clad half-man, half-machine monster Darth Vader controlled. Moreover, these films were set in outer space where Reagan wanted to situate his costly satellite nuclear defence system. This corporate American cinema, with its ideological and metaphorical bolstering of Reagan's foreign policy, was a safe bet for investors. Cinema was the third most active industry in respect of corporate acquisitions, and the second most attractive for foreign buyers during the 1980s.[27]

However, the presence of critically acclaimed directors like Oliver Stone in the Hollywood machine meant that there was justification for cinema chains giving space to films that were more critical of American society. It was over the question of foreign policy that the biggest fracture between progressive Hollywood and the corporate Hollywood system occurred. *Salvador* is a key example of both the power of the anti-Reagan Hollywood message and the limitations of making a hard-nosed anti-government film in the 1980s. The *History of the American Cinema* book series, published by the University of California and supported by the National Endowment for the Humanities – a government fund – wrote of *Salvador* that it 'chronicles the bloody [Salvadoran] civil war [and] condemns the United States for its support of the country's savage and corrupt government'.[28] The film received two Oscar nominations, but was not tested on a wider audience after being held back from general release. Stone, as director and producer, had secured investment for the film through personal guile. Stone describes how the film had several funding sources, most of them giving him small grants, but how Orion, who were initially due to distribute the film, withdrew their support when they realised what he was creating.

In *Salvador* Stone created a chaotic and bloody mix of war-style footage and personal narrative that included scenes where American officials assist in suppressing the country's citizens. The film was eventually given limited distribution by Hemdale, who had a record of success after releasing the successful science-fiction action movie *Terminator*. Hemdale had begun life as a film distributor in Britain and had opened up a new operation in America with *Terminator*, even making enough money to bankroll Stone's final costs in production. Stone was able to find a financier and distributor despite his initial loss of support because of the general politicisation of Hollywood during this period. Mario Velasquez was an envoy to America for the FMLN. The FMLN was a democratic organisation of Salvadorians drawn into a guerrilla war with their dictatorial government. Their struggle for social justice was the main theme of *Salvador*. Velasquez describes how in the mid 1980s he 'could get a meeting with any producer in Hollywood and they would write out checks'[29] to fund the FMLN. Some of those producers may have been at Orion, willing to write a cheque but not to support the release of a film that might tar them with Stone's anti-government brush. British director Tony Garnett summarises this situation, saying, 'many executives – like most other talent – are Democrats and liberals. They never question the market economics of the system they're in but on social issues they are far to the left of the corporations they work for.'[30]

Salvador is a rare example of a 1980s film that directly challenged US policy. *Romero*, on the other hand, was never dropped by its financiers and was distributed by Warner Brothers. Unfortunately, as *Halliwell's Film Guide* puts it, *Romero* 'pussyfoot[s] around its subject' and is 'no help to anybody in finding the true facts'.[31] The film paints an idealistic picture of a priest, Romero, who defends the rights of citizens in Central America against their repressive government. The film focuses almost entirely on Romero himself and does not show the spectator the social conditions that oppress the citizens. Nor does the film touch upon the role of American forces in Latin America. *Romero* is concerned, as Stone himself has claimed to be, with the representation of a hero who is a shining light by which the audience can navigate the film. Around the same time that *Romero* was released a number of films emerged that showed a similar heroic deference for American troops. *Hamburger Hill, Full Metal Jacket, Born on the Fourth of July* and *Good Morning Vietnam* all showed US soldiers as vulnerable men who are often uncomfortable with their role in war, and who have incompetent superiors. These films revive the heroic status of the American GI but set that heroism in a context of misjudgement and lies. In *Full Metal Jacket*, for example, one soldier is driven to suicide and another becomes appalled at the murderous actions of his fellow men in Vietnam.

Science fiction in the 1980s went a step further to link corporations and government in illicit practices and represent the military industrial monolith that Oliver Stone talked about at the start of this chapter: *Bladerunner* has the murderous Tyrell Corporation; *Robocop* shows corporations and police exploiting cops; *Aliens* sees 'the company' send innocent families of construction workers to their death. The 1980s was, therefore, a decade dominated by right-wing pictures but a decade in which these could be released side-by-side with a handful of cinematic critiques of American society.

Observing these contradictory Hollywood products the president decided to go on the offensive against the entire Hollywood system, arguing that 'America had gone astray, had been misled by the hitherto-prevailing liberal culture'.[32] By the end of his second term in office (1984) Reagan's administration had become closely associated with right-wing organisations. These included the Moral Majority, Eagle Forum and New Right coalition. The Moral Majority was founded in 1979 by wealthy conservative Americans and had sought to censor works of political dissent in literature and at the cinema, as well as being vehement anti-abortion lobbyists. The Eagle Forum had helped to stop an equal rights amendment to the Constitution in 1982. The New Right coalition was a gathering of the extreme right wing of the Republican Party and their close allies at the top of American business, designed to influence policy in favour of gun ownership and to work against affirmative action that ensured black people could get work. Writing about attempts by these organisations to censor movies, Charles Lyons suggests that Hollywood 'made a convenient target … because it was perceived by the Right as morally corrupt'.[33] The sense of assault felt by socially conscious talent and producers was immense during the 1980s.

Peter Bart describes how, while he was at Paramount Pictures, he commissioned a movie that was meant to be a story of children forced into military action by the destructive decisions of the American government. The film was to show young boys taking up arms against Russia but quickly regretting ever having done so and living with nightmares of the battle they had seen. Bart lost control of the film to a newly appointed and more senior executive. The film's content was changed, the director replaced and even the new director's material edited to fit with the perspective of the executive. The result of these changes was *Red Dawn* (1984), a cold-war propaganda film in which patriotic, jingoistic children hold off a Soviet invasion. At around the same time Tony Garnett was trying to make his tragic exploration of the consequences of a culture in which guns are presented as the solution to social problems. Garnett describes how the only way to get this film – *Handgun* (1984) – into production was to go through 'EMI, a British company who already knew me and who let me do it because it only cost them $2 million'.[34]

Reflecting on the 1980s, Kate McArdle – a long-serving television producer with ABC turned organiser for the anti-war and anti-George Bush Jr Hollywood coalition, Artists United for a Win Without War – said: 'the left in Hollywood learned that the right is so integrated vertically … they're integrated from their publications to their television, to their student organisations [and] there's a single message that covers multiple issues … and if we don't stand together more than we do now, then we're SUNK'.[35] The great lesson of the 1980s for progressive Hollywood talent was an organisational one. In truth, however, that lesson was learned in the 1990s when trends established by Hollywood's left political activists during the 1980s came to fruition under the presidency of Bill Clinton. In the 1980s any lessons learned were rammed home by defeat.

Challenge of the creative community

A significant consituent of Hollywood's creative community was mobilised against Ronald Reagan in the 1980s. Bob Foxworth (television star), Michael Douglas, Ed Asner and Elizabeth Montgomery (of television comedy *Bewitched*) helped to set up the Committee for Concern, a Hollywood campaign group that involved hundreds of people in meetings, marches and other actions opposing government policy in Central America. Film star Jane Fonda and her politician partner Tom Hayden formed the Network, an unofficial system of communication by which several hundred Hollywood creative personnel could be quickly informed about protests against Reagan and also about specially organised political education events. Rising acting stars of the decade Ron Silver, Susan Sarandon, Alec Baldwin and Christopher

3. Stars take action: Edward James Olmos (*far left*), Lou Diamond Philips (*centre*) and Martin Sheen (*second from right*) turn out to support Central American hunger-striker Cesar Chavez (*Cesar E. Chavez Institute, San Francisco*).

Reeve founded the Creative Coalition, which set out to raise the profile of a diverse range of issues like foreign policy, access of the poor to education and keeping business money out of election campaigns. Celebrity names alone, however, do not tell the story of anti-Reagan activism.

One Hollywood progressive organisation in the 1980s was the Hollywood Women's Political Committee (HWPC). The HWPC was set up by Jane Fonda and producer Paula Weinstein to provide what Lara Bergtold, one of its full-time functionaries, called 'a cause, a more progressive place to be'.[36] The fact that Bergtold is not a celebrity and that the HWPC director, Marge Tabankin – now the head of actress, singer and Democrat supporter Barbra Streisand's philanthropic foundation – was never an actress or filmmaker, suggests that the 1980s saw Hollywood progressives start to find a resonance with activists beyond the creative community. The HWPC was central to the protest, organising open seminars, distributing political bulletins, advertising protests and fund-raising for causes. With the other organisations listed above the HWPC combined in 1984 to mobilise 2,000 creative personnel to protest at US activity in Central America. In the same year Foxworth and Montgomery gave their Benedict Canyon home over to hundreds of celebrities to meet and donate to the leader of the Nicaraguan socialist government – the Sandinistas – Daniel Ortega.[37]

Although a mass movement of American citizens was only evident in one protest of 750,000 people against nuclear weapons production (1984), there was an energy underpinning this activism that television actor Mike Farrell – star of the long-running television version of *M*A*S*H*, an accomplished stage actor and a regular in television movies – typifies. In 1982 Farrell visited Honduras, Guatemala and Nicaragua. In 1983 and 1984 he went to El Salvador and Nicaragua again with human rights delegations, meeting political prisoners. In 1985 Farrell formed a peace delegation to the USSR, returning to El Salvador to give medical aid. In 1986 it was Chile and Paraguay, in 1987 Israel, Egypt, Jordan, Syria and Palestine, in 1988 El Salvador once more, this time making a documentary. This decade of public activism prepared Farrell well for becoming vice-president of the Screen Actors' Guild and a leader in the anti-war movement in 2003. He remains key to Human Rights Watch California, Concern/AMER-ICA (a refugee organisation) and Death Penalty Focus. His willingness to engage with issue-based campaigns, to work in coali-tion, has made this longevity possible. Farrell has achieved what others failed to do – to carry a progressive sensibility over 20 years and into an era of radical activism. Farrell was a key player in building the alliance of Hollywood talent that established Artists United for a Win Without War in 2002. However, most of the 1980s initiatives did not follow Farrell's lead, gradually becoming more focused on specific issues rather than opening up participants to wider general political activity.

The legacy of such an approach can be seen in the Creative Coali-tion, formed in 1988. Since its formation its presidency has changed hands, usually from one Baldwin brother to another, and presently film and television actor Joe Pantoliano has the position. Although the organisation has offices in Los Angeles it is a New York affair, cur-rently involving around 200 people and campaigning and providing education on electoral campaign finance reform, defending the first amendment and public education. Its electronic activities archive for 2003 consisted of film showings, celebrity dinners, a post-Oscars party, a Ray-Ban sponsored award presentation, an arts advocacy event, an audience with actor Ruben Blades and a preview of the presidential election of 2004.[38] What the Creative Coalition achieves is hard to determine, how it mobilises for action is harder to discern and its insistence on its website that the organisation remains 'non-partisan' robs it of a cutting edge.

The Creative Coalition is the successor to an eclectic and somewhat isolated Hollywood liberalism. The multifarious bodies of the anti-Reagan era were collective enterprises, requiring the combined effort of many campaigners. Yet they had a poor emphasis on analysis compared to anti-globalisation collectives, or Artists United for a Win Without War. The latter organisation actually began life through a series of highly theoretical teach-ins, run by university professors. The anti-Reagan ferment cannot be called a movement. It lacked a broad-based network of activists, as well as confidence and consensus about direction. These anti-Reagan groups were not dissimilar in structure to the proto-Communist associations of the 1920s, 1930s and early 1940s Hollywood. However, they did inherit two things from the Communist organisers. Firstly, there is the perception that the movies you make are a significant site of struggle and, secondly, an intense focus on individual personality. The example of Ed Asner's sacking from *Lou Grant* demonstrates this individualism at work in the protests organised by the 1980s activists.

In 1984, when *Lou Grant* was at the height of its global popularity, Ed Asner took responsibility for squaring up to the State Department over El Salvador. It seemed, perhaps, the opportune moment to stand on the steps of the Department's office in Washington and unofficially launch medical aid for the country. The many press agencies that attended the stunt were attracted, at least in part, because it was promoted as 'Ed's Salvador thing'. In reality Asner was one of several people who set up the initiative. When CBS sacked Asner and cancelled his show he had no basis on which to retaliate against the corporation. He was the figurehead of an activist initiative, one in which figureheads were perceived as the most important people, and consequently could not threaten executives with a mass public reaction.

Reflecting on that situation in 2004, Asner described what he had learnt. 'It's like a pebble', he says. 'You provide your own pebble and you roll it down the hill in the hope of attracting more pebbles, in the hope of not having to cave under or being ignored, or be accused of being a screaming radical who doesn't know what he's talking about.' What you really need for success in your campaign, he suggests, is 'an avalanche'. Asner proposes that there was not enough movement in 1980s Hollywood, not enough pebbles on the hill, to create the avalanche necessary to save his job or to really challenge Reagan's policies. In 2004 things are different: 'I think there's a good potential now for starting that avalanche'.[39] However, before that potential could emerge, Hollywood progressives had to recover from the problems they encountered in the 1980s. That recovery would be held up for almost a decade as their organisational weaknesses were exploited in the 1990s, during the presidency of Bill Clinton.

PART TWO:

The Crisis of Hollywood Liberalism

Hollywood liberals in the early 1990s greeted Bill Clinton's presidency with hopeful excitement. Yet by the end his tenure in the White House (1992–2000) many on the Hollywood left believed that Clinton had merely employed progressive rhetoric as a cover for his less than progressive policies. Actor and producer Danny Glover summarised this sentiment when he said that Clinton set out to 'seduce people into believing he is something that he's not, that he's someone who really fights for issues'.[1] A progressive *on screen* image – nurtured by a collection of Hollywood power brokers known as FOBs (friends of Bill) – had helped to mask Clinton's betrayals of the progressive agenda *off screen* and assisted him in demobilising opposition. Clinton was America's midwife for globalisation who failed to address poverty or racial tension, leaving some Hollywood activists and filmmakers disillusioned to the point of passivity and pushing others toward radical anti-globalisation perspectives.

The context for Clinton

In 1996 the president of the United States of America is a handsome man in his forties, uttering memorable lines like 'together can preserve the world for all mankind'. He speaks with a husky Southern twang and makes conversation with whomever he meets. Against a backdrop of immense social crisis his rhetoric draws together urban black America and the impoverished, sweeping aside bureaucrats on Capitol Hill. He speaks with warmth to the diverse nations of the world where grey-clad soldiers heed his call for a unified humanitarian effort. His leadership is essential to liberating the planet from disaster but he leads with a mischievous glint in his eye. This is the bomber-jacket wearing, ex-fighter pilot president played by Bill Pullman in *Independence Day*, the biggest grossing film of 1996. Will Smith's street-wise airman fills in for black America, a stubble-chinned trailer trash father represents the poor and the international community is rendered in a montage of foreign nationals cheering television screens as Pullman does battle with evil. Aside from the nature of the crisis – an alien invasion – the rest of this fantasy could have been a Hollywood liberal's dream of Bill Clinton.

Clinton's 1992 presidential campaign employed the veneer of social equality and humanitarianism that glosses over *Independence Day*'s action adventure, shoot-'em-up, narrative. Clinton attacked Bush Snr for failing to redress the inequality that had begun under Reagan in the 1980s, when employers earned 160 times what their employees did. In 1991, 16 Republican-governed states slashed welfare spending, with a disastrous effect on the poor; in Florida 16 per cent of families sent one person to bed hungry. Survival for the poor in the last years of Republican governance before Clinton's presidency rested on credit, and national consumer debt soared to $775 billion.[2] Where Pullman's president was the figurehead of united resistance to alien invasion, Clinton was symbolic of widespread opposition to Republican rule among the disenfranchised. As with *Independence Day*'s vision of America – where politicians, business leaders, scientists and the unemployed stood shoulder to shoulder – Clinton found a place for all sections of society in his policies. When *Business Week* demanded a 'Universal Health Care System' to relieve pressure on business coffers Clinton quickly made this a central pillar of his platform. Yet, when his wife Hilary shouted 'we want our healthcare system back' at a 1992 election rally she was directly appealing to the poorest sections of American society, for whom healthcare based on private health insurance had been a failure. In this way, Bill Clinton appeared to be like Pullman's president – a man for all America.

Clinton's doctrine of the international community and belief in humanitarian intervention also added to this image. Bush Snr had employed the ideology of foreign threat with which Reagan had previously diverted domestic disquiet, finding new enemies when the spectacular collapse of the Eastern European Soviet bloc ended the Cold War in 1989. Iraqi dictator Saddam Hussein became one such enemy in 1990 when he invaded Kuwait – which was an American ally by coercion, receiving export credits for transporting a third of US oil supplies through its ports. In his speeches Bush justified going to war with Iraq by replacing the Soviet enemy with the 'rogue dictator' who must be brought to heel. A number of films of the period reflect Bush's belief that that 'the US has a new credibility, and what we say goes'.[3] The *Naked Gun* series of films, with their irreverent sequences of one-liners and prat-falls, provides a salient example. *Naked Gun 2½* opens with Frank Drebin beating up Colonel Quaddafi and Saddam Hussein. Drebin is played by Leslie Nielsen, a widely recognisable American star with some 40 years in the movies – a veritable institution in Hollywood comedy, although he began his career as a leading man and action performer. The *Naked Gun* movies are a big-screen version of *Police Squad!*, a spoof of another institution – the long-running *Dragnet* television series. So when an ageing Drebin easily defeats these Arab leaders, *Naked Gun 2½* welds together an acting legend and popular cultural iconography to legitimise the notion that Americans run the world. *Naked Gun 2½* made $86 million at the US box office – the sixth most popular film of 1991 – demonstrating how well-versed the population would have been in this ideology.

Events, however, conspired to undermine the ideology. Having expelled Hussein's troops from Kuwait, with United Nations backing, Bush saw his popularity at around 90 per cent. However, the war exacerbated America's economic crisis. Operation Desert Storm left America with a bill accounting for 56.7 per cent of global rearmament costs. Bush was also squeezed from below: 150,000 people demonstrated against the Iraq war in Washington, although it hardly made the newspapers. NBC and Fox released triumphalist Desert Storm box sets, featuring hours of location news, GI interviews, war diaries and information about the American military's superior technology. Yet Bush's popularity slumped spectacularly to 46 per cent in November 1991. Bush found himself under attack from all sides. Even the *Wall Street Journal* wrote of an 'indisputable shift of wealth and economic leverage away from the United States'.[4] This, perhaps more than anything, opened the door for Clinton's anti-poverty, humanitarian rhetoric. So effective was Clinton at exploiting this situation that political journalist Joe Klein, who observed Clinton's first successful presidential election campaign from inside the campaign bus, thought he was 'witnessing the arrival of a great new leader. Someone who would … leave the world a better place.'[5] In a similar fashion to Klein, Hollywood liberals, whose films give away their tendency to stake political ambitions on 'special individuals', were among the first to be seduced by Clinton.

Clinton, heroism and the liberal Hollywood tradition

Executives, like Dawn Steel (Columbia), Mike Medavoy (TriStar) and Harry Thompson (television producer), first met with Clinton over dinner on a mid-Western ranch in 1987, when Democratic organisers felt he might be the next presidential candidate. With stars like Richard Dreyfuss and Barbra Streisand, both loyal Democratic fundraisers, this

select group discussed how they might promote Clinton in Los Angeles and beyond. He didn't actually stand until 1992 and by then this
Hollywood network had expanded through several similar meetings.
It was Clinton's unique personality that won friends in Hollywood. As
San Francisco-based cultural activist and commentator Norman Solomon put it, 'Clinton seduced a lot of Hollywood … on the basis of his
persona, with a generally liberal and counter-Republican message.'[6]

Clinton effectively exploited four key features of the late twentieth-
century liberal Hollywood psychology, as identified by film theorist
Dana Polan.

1 A belief in the leadership of special individuals, uniquely honourable and charismatic.
2 The perception that special individuals form coalitions of 'buddies', based on loyalty and trust rather than social or political
   position.
3 Nostalgia for a bygone era – possibly an invented one – when
   these individuals and their buddies could get their way.
4 An inability to grapple with the modern neo-liberalist world
   that can lead to seeing heroes and their buddies as fatalistic
   characters.

These features resonate through the decades of post-war Hollywood
with roots in the socially conscious East Coast television and cinema
movement of the 1950s. Take the classic film *Twelve Angry Men*, written
by Reginald Rose, directed by Sidney Lumet and tackling issues such
as racial prejudice and slum existence. Writing for CBS television after
the Second World War, Rose inherited a social concern from New York
stage predecessors and made it work for the small screen. Rose's work
for the Alcoa Hour, Goodyear Television Playhouse and *The Defenders*
shared themes of social status and equality. Lumet had begun directing for CBS, NBC, ABS on Studio One, the Alcoa Hour and *The Best Of
Broadway*. Lumet and Rose shared a desire to show everyman characters squeezed into great actions by social situations. *Twelve Angry Men*
captures this post-war confident liberalism, personified to many people a few years later by the charismatic Democratic President John F.
Kennedy. (Another president who spoke in clear one-liners about justice and equality, much like Clinton.) Moreover, *Twelve Angry Men*
employs a simple, universal situation that could even take place in a
law court today. The confined locale and limited narrative are made to
work through the character development of a collection of everymen,
led to become sort-of buddies by the special individual (Henry Fonda)

who helms the movie. In the end the buddies get justice for a poor slum-dweller – a kind of victory that would have been represented by a universal healthcare system providing equitable health provision across American society. *Twelve Angry Men's* timeless quality contributes to a myth of a golden age of liberal ascendancy. That Lumet and Rose were able to make many more dramas together makes them and their film a model for the latter-day liberal, faced with a more powerful corporate Hollywood.

Henry Fonda's juror is charismatic and honourable, made unique by his white suit and quietly confident manner – if not by virtue of his individually raised hand of dissent. In order to achieve justice Fonda must win minds through deductive brilliance, earning trust as a pal rather than challenging prejudice or political assumption head-on. This is the archetypal liberal perspective on social change; a special individual can win others to justice through sheer personal brilliance. No wonder 1990s liberals were so easily charmed by Clinton, with his soft-spoken Fonda-esque manner. Former chief economic adviser to Clinton, Joseph Stiglitz, described how Clinton made you feel as if you were the only one in the room when he spoke to you.

To recognise that Clinton was indeed manipulating these tendencies of Hollywood liberals witness his solitary walk through corridors and hallways to the opening of the 2000 Democratic convention, as pictured on network television. He was 'like Russell Crowe in *Gladiator*',[7] according to the *Guardian* newspaper – a man apart, much like Fonda in *Twelve Angry Men*. Further evidence of the tendency of special individualism that Clinton manipulated can be found in contemporary films, made by high-profile Hollywood liberals, which raise questions about American democracy. Warren Beatty (a publicly declared liberal and Democrat, with a long association with left-wing causes) made *Bulworth* in 1999 and Oliver Stone (who fiercely challenged Ronald Reagan from a progressive standpoint) made *JFK* in 1991. In these films central protagonists are unique and other characters tend towards archetypes: Senator Bulworth is manically charming but his political aides are mundanely loyal caricatures, whilst *JFK's* Special Investigator Garrison uses his deductive brilliance and vaguely neurotic personality to bind grey-suited allies to him. Narrative development is dependent on the hero's choices within a social context – Bulworth *chooses* to flee from his re-election campaign and Garrison *chooses* to dig into previously hidden evidence about John F. Kennedy's assassination, all of which implies that special individuals shape history. These heroes do things most viewers could not dream of doing – Bulworth takes out a contract on his own life and Garrison reaches insightful conclusions before unearthing evidence. They pursue abstract ideals regardless of the consequences – Bulworth publicly admits to conning African-American voters despite the potential effect on his re-election, and Garrison determines to out the secret service conspiracy behind Kennedy's death despite threats on his life. Bulworth and Garrison are special individuals pursuing the abstract ideal of truth, in the process exposing corruption and deceit in America's democratic system.

4. Bulworth: Warren Beatty's hero bears all the hallmarks of fatalistic 1990s liberalism (*copyright Twentieth Century Fox*).

This 60-year-old liberal tradition overflows with American icono-graphy – flags, courthouses, the White House – and explores dilemmas in American society – economic deprivation, racism, and the strength of democratic systems. There is continuity between *Twelve Angry Men*'s victorious hero and the heroes of *JFK* and *Bulworth* who ulti-mately fail. In the Rose and Lumet model and its 1990s fatalistic counterpart the hero remains special, brilliant – a crusader for what is right and good. In this way liberal Hollywood cinema can perpetuate myths but not the kind Norman Mailer, a time-served American pro-gressive and respected writer, meant when he called *JFK* 'a huge, hideous act in which the gods warred and a god fell'.[8] Far removed from this mysticism, the liberal myth is concerned with the opposition

of abstract idealists to corruption of democracy. These alternate reso-
lutions of liberal films suggests that the 'basic social message', as
Oscar-winning cinematographer Haskell Wexler calls it, of the liberal
American myth was reversed in the late twentieth century. *Twelve
Angry Men* was the fruit of a confident post-war liberalism. Ronald
Reagan's love of the free market, the failed war of Bush Snr and the
ensuing social crisis led perhaps to the fatal liberal hero in *JFK*, who
fights for ideals but cannot overturn the conspiracy of the American
right who are supposed to have organised the killing of John F.
Kennedy. This fatalism is offset by the fantasy in *Independence Day*,
where the wonderfully special president succeeds in uniting America.
Yet, once again the fatalistic hero returns in *Bulworth* in the late 1990s
where a specially gifted, almost crazy, politician appears to undo the
lies of his election only to be murdered by corporate special interests.
What happened in between *JFK* and *Bulworth* was an immense growth
in the power of institutions of global capitalism (such as the World
Trade Organisation) and Clinton's betrayal of a progressive agenda,
which increased the gap between rich and poor whilst simultaneously
undermining liberal influence on systems of power. This analysis
reveals how useful a barometer of American society the traditional liberal movie is.

It also reveals how far removed from the liberal dream Clinton
became. Take *Gladiator*, the blockbuster epic from which Clinton borrowed the solitary hero image for his 2000 conference appearance. This
blockbuster is not a liberal film, although its imagery does create a special hero. The narrative rises and falls as a result of the unique qualities
and actions of hero Maximus: from war in Europe, to gladiator school,
to the Colisseum, to a coup against a deviant emperor. Maximus
appears to fit the liberal mould, being uniquely gifted (as a warrior)
and driven primarily by the abstract ideal of loyalty to Rome. Yet when
Maximus sees off several executioners early in the film he chooses to
ignore the application of Roman justice to himself. The film diverges
from the liberal model when Maximus refuses to accept his execution
– an execution that is in keeping with the imperial structures of the
social system to which he dedicated his life. Liberalism is concerned
with the social situation in which a special individual operates, but
Maximus does something not only unique but also socially inconsist-
ent. The gap between this blockbuster hero and the liberal hero may
seem narrow but the distinction is key. Fundamentally, the de-
socialisation of Maximus, through making it possible for him to act
outside the constraints of his society, prevents his story becoming a

metaphor for anything in the life of the spectator. *The Matrix* trilogy
exhibits the same thin coat of liberal iconography. Its cast gush about
the 'universal themes and ideas' behind the trilogy on a 'making of'
DVD documentary included with the two-disc special edition of
Matrix Revolutions, released in 2004. They define its messianic hero –
Neo – as an 'innocent, he believes in love'. Neo's unique ability to re-
program the Matrix, discovered in the first film (*The Matrix*), establishes his superiority to the collective of warriors led by Morpheus,
who have long been fighting against the machines that run this dysto-
pian future world. It could be argued that the first film is a metaphor
for working life – Neo starts out as an office employee. However, the
second and third films (*Reloaded* and *Revolutions*) dispense with familiar worlds and make Neo's gift of programming valid outside the
Matrix, elevating him to a magician. The films become what critic
Roger Ebert called 'a superhero comic book in which the fate of the
world comes down to a titanic fist-fight between the designated representatives of good and evil'.[9] That Clinton chose an image from a film
like these and not *Twelve Angry Men* – he could have worn a white suit,
for example – suggests that he was concerned with the cartoon symbolism of his presidency more than the substance of his actions.

In *Bulworth* we meet a special individual in a world that speaks to
the spectator's everyday experience through location (downtown LA),
iconography (KFC, racist police) and narrative (the succession of election rallies). Whilst leaving the *Matrix* films can be like waking from a
dream, leaving *Bulworth* is like moving from a particular vision of reality – where special individuals are the main players – back to your own
reality. Herein lies the strength and weakness of the liberal Hollywood
tradition; it is socially rooted but focused on special leaders who are
driven by abstract notions. In the real social world Bill Clinton was not
driven by ideals but by a particular strategy for reckoning with globalisation; or rather, for supporting it. He cut welfare spending, gave tax
breaks to corporations and established trade agreements to carve up
the world for US business. Promised health reform was abandoned,
civil liberties pegged back and race issues were not addressed. In the
long run Clinton undermined his support base in Hollywood and created what the *Washington Post* called a 'political vacuum'.[10] Ed Asner,
a veteran of countless campaigns against American foreign policy in
Central America and star of both television and cinema, started out by
believing in the special individual: 'I regarded Bill Clinton as probably
the most brilliant man to occupy the Oval Office'.[11] Yet by the turn of
the millennium even Joe Klein felt compelled to say that 'if Ronald

Reagan had challenged the pessimism of the post-Vietnam era, liberals hoped that Bill Clinton would challenge the cynicism. In the end, cynicism won – with a major assist from Clinton himself'.[12]

Globalisation and the alternative media exposé of Clinton

Hollywood actors, trained to deliver pithy lines with pathos, can often find the words to summarise a moment in history. Alec Baldwin, whose frightening turn as a casino boss in *The Cooler* (2004) and less than amicable public divorce from Kim Basinger demonstrated he is still a bona fide 'star', also has a long association with centre-left American politics. This leader of campaigns for 'clean elections' (free from corporate lobbyists) argued in 1999, 'Clinton … said, listen, if I can't accomplish what I want to do, let's go and accomplish those things they [big business, the Federal reserve, Republican Congress] want to do'.[13] By the end of his presidency and despite his manipulation of liberal imagery, Clinton had not transformed the lives of the victims of the social crisis caused by Reagan's policies and Bush Snr's war. Haskell Wexler, in his usual direct manner, backed up Baldwin's view by highlighting continuing problems with healthcare: 'now no one has a doctor, and if they do they have to spend a lot of money'.[14] Joe Klein, who had been in awe of Clinton early on in the presidency, now wrote a fictionalised account of a lying politician, dogged by sex scandals, who told the American poor, 'No politician can bring these jobs back … No politician can make it the way it used to be … we're living in a new world now, a world without borders … We've got a world market now.'[15]

Klein's book *Primary Colors* – which originally carried the author name 'anonymous' – quickly became a film, squashing his initial denials that the story was based on the president as John Travolta brought Clinton look-a-like Jack Stanton to the screen. So close was Travolta to the real-life president that the *Sacramento Bee* commented, 'what's truly uncanny is his smile, which is a dead-ringer for the President's'.[16] The film was directed by Mike Nichols, whose *Catch-22* and *Silkwood* examined, respectively, war during the Vietnam conflict and nuclear power at the height of Reagan's arms programme. With *Primary Colors* Nichols again dissects social phenomena, showing Stanton treating globalisation as if it were *Star Trek*'s Borg: 'resistance is futile'. Clinton promoted the third way philosophy of British theorist Anthony Giddens and Prime Minister Tony Blair, a path between free-market liberalism (*à la* Reagan) and active state intervention. Clinton converted Bush's watchdog-of-the-world ideology into 'manager of the world'. No wonder Nichols was so quick to criticise: Clinton was working with the corporate gamblers who'd benefited from Reagan's policies, the same 'office boys' who'd taken over Hollywood business and whose speculation caused recession in 1987 and again in 1991.

Any hopes that Clinton might stand up to this new breed of capitalists were quickly dashed. In 1993 Clinton's economic advisers suggested that to lower the national debt he'd need to keep the Federal Reserve full – ready to bolster banks and brokers in the event of another crisis. He protested, 'you mean to tell me that the success of the program and my re-election hinges on the Federal Reserve and a bunch of fucking bond dealers?'[17] Yet he proceeded to cut federal spending by $140 billion and accepted that, as respected political journalist Bob Woodward put it, 'his fate was passing into the hands of the un-elected Alan Greenspan [head of the Federal Bank] and the bond market'.[18] The national debt was indeed cut by $500 million between 1992 and 2000, but Democratic Treasury Secretary Robert Reich noted how Clinton had been asked by banks and business to 'give up your $50 billion a year investment plan' and had quickly agreed.[19]

In cutting his federal programme Clinton was, by default, operating on the global playing field he claimed he was unable to influence. New capitalists studio owners in Hollywood had global interests in their other businesses and in their expanded media empires. Having said he could not affect the global market, the net result of Clinton's triangulation was assistance in its development. Public consciousness of this would explode into protest in the late 1990s, but filmmakers and artists – perhaps by virtue of their closeness to the Clinton machine – were among the first to recognise how the president bolstered global capitalism.

Danny Schechter, speaking about setting up the alternative media organisation Globalvision in the mid 1990s said 'our company was global before global was cool'.[20] Global Vision challenges the major media corporations over their news reporting and Schechter writes a daily column – the 'News Dissector' – apparently read by Sean Penn and Danny Glover. Schechter is a respected speaker on the university circuit, always finding a receptive audience in California's film training grounds like the University of California Los Angeles (UCLA), but in the Clinton era his documentary series *Human Rights, Human Wrongs*

(1993–6) was ahead of the game in highlighting the social reality under the surface of Clinton's rhetoric and manipulation of images. This half-hour weekly series about international and domestic issues was broadcast on dozens of international television channels and more than 150 US public stations. *Human Rights, Human Wrongs* examined educational attainment failures among America's poorest citizens, looked at atrocities committed against citizens of countries funded by American schemes and exposed deprivation caused by Clinton's corporate allies. In 1997 the show won the Amnesty International Media Spotlight Award and was nominated for Outstanding Social Programming in 1994 at the Oscars of American television, the Emmys.

As the 1990s drew on, the issues raised by individuals like Schechter came to be more generally apparent. In 1995 Clinton signed the North American Free Trade Agreement (NAFTA) between America, Canada and Mexico. The agreement had catastrophic consequences for American workers and for the Mexican economy. The same week that Clinton signed NAFTA, a vote for universal healthcare was lost in Congress. Clinton said in 2002 that 'there was no way the system could digest the healthcare plan'[21] at the same time as NAFTA. Even if Clinton's healthcare plan had gone through it would have been wedded to private health insurance companies. Media personnel with links to Hollywood progressives continued to lead the way in exposing Clinton. Documentary producer Saul Landau is a lifelong friend of Haskell Wexler and director John Sayles. Wexler and Landau travelled to Chile in 1973 to make the only interview with President Salvador Allende by an American outfit. When socialist reformer Allende was shot in an apparently American-backed military coup later that year, Landau and Wexler were well placed to play leading roles in mainstream media propagandising against their own country's actions. Landau has made countless documentaries over the last 30 years, a number of which have been narrated by celebrities like Ed Asner ('They approach me, I say yes of course.'). In the 1990s Landau picked holes in Clinton's third-way project. In his independent radio broadcasts between 1993 and 1998 he highlighted the exploitation of Salvadorian peasants in the production of National Football League merchandise, the ownership of movie corporations by overseas interests and the collusion of Wal-Mart and *Entertainment Now* presenters to sell sweat-shop-produced clothing. Landau accused Clinton of being the 'informal chairman of the global economic village' who acted for business but showed false 'sympathy for those who will suffer'.[22]

Even in Landau's own backyard – at Pacifica Radio, where he recorded his weekly political commentaries during the 1990s – aggressive tactics of the global marketplace could be observed. Pacifica was a network of five stations across the USA originally launched by journalist Lewis Hill as a non-profit network committed to free speech, but a new national committee began ruthlessly overruling decisions by local advisory boards in the late 1990s. Their actions included harassing staff who protested over working conditions, closing Berkeley-based KPFA station when it became less economically viable, banning broadcasts of the *Democracy Now!* show when it carried reports from the United Nations conference on racism in South Africa (2000) and ditching a range of freelance contributors. The national committee was quick to oust the *Democracy Now!* production team and to send private security to enforce their decisions at the New York WBAI (the independent radio network that spans the USA) office where *Democracy Now!* was based. In 1999 an impromptu coalition of commentators like Jim Hightower and Norman Solomon, as well as intellectuals and writers like Noam Chomsky, Mike Davis and Howard Zinn united to protest at the national committee's actions. The American Federation of Television and Radio Artists (AFTRA) said it was 'no longer satisfied that the WBAI studios are a safe and appropriate working environment'. Saul Landau did not join the coalition against the new Pacifica Radio board, and expressed some specific disagreements with the protesters. Meanwhile, his broadcasts continued to highlight examples of globalisation's effects on the media industry, and combined with similar commentary from other alternative media personalities to make a strong general case against globalisation. Despite Landau's personal decision over Pacifica, what Norman Solomon calls the 'defend Pacifica movement'[23] began to draw in a wider network that included Hollywood celebrities. Thus Tim Robbins and Danny Glover added their names to the list of protesters against Pacifica posted on znet.org (the radical anti-globalisation website) in 2000.

Ed Asner's unequivocal statement about globalisation is a prime example of the resonance that people like Landau and Schechter had in Hollywood:

> I used to think how wonderful it would be to be one big global family, then I saw what globalisation was doing to my country … impoverishing your own people … and all this work is exported to other countries. We don't have any checks and balances to see how humane their treatment is … At the same time our own workers are being downgraded and debased. You can preach globalisation for

the world, but when it means the corporations are getting richer but your *people* aren't getting any richer then I think it's a crock of shit.[24]

In the final analysis, Clinton's actions gave him away as the main cause of these problems in America. Every budget of his administration instigated Reaganite tax cuts, draconian law and order policies, privatisation and tens of billions of dollars on military spending. According to *World Policy Journal* the result was that 'in the United States, with its enviable record of economic growth ... the number of working poor, who usually lack health or pension benefits of any kind, is increasing'.[25] As early as 1994, IBM, AT&T (who then owned seven television networks including HBO, producers of critically acclaimed and controversial series like *Sex in the City* and *The Sopranos*) and General Motors had fired 75,000 workers each – whilst chief executive officers got an average 30 per cent income increase.[26] This continuity between Clinton and Republicanism startled Hollywood liberals and fractured the support Clinton had sought to build, creating a political vacuum. Society, like nature, abhors a vacuum and in the late 1990s the emerging movement against global capitalism signalled its intent to take the mantle of protest. It did so on the very terrain where liberalism had been strong in the 1980s – opposition to United States foreign policy. In December 1998 thousands of protesters angered by Clinton's missile attacks on Sudan and Afghanistan were harried by police officers outside the White House as they chanted: 'Killing children's what they teach – that's the crime they should impeach'.[27]

The president's Hollywood friends

In 2001 Toyota negotiated an exclusive deal to dictate when and where their products appeared in Vivendi Universal films.[28] Take *The Fast and the Furious* (2001) and its sequel *2 Fast 2 Furious* (2003). Both featured modified Toyota cars involved in prolonged street races, fast-talking blond blue-eyed undercover cops, extensive chase sequences and the first film had Hollywood's newest all-action star in the lead – Vin Diesel. *The Fast and the Furious* made $134 million worldwide, implying it had a significant global audience and demonstrating how Toyota have been able to associate themselves with popular Vivendi productions. Just how 'cool' *The Fast and the Furious* became for a mass audience is demonstrated further by the selling out of its official Universal poster on the e-bay internet auction site in 48 hours. Vivendi owns 34 television channels in 15 countries including the huge USA Network and the trend-spotting Sundance Channel, which broadcasts films from the popular annual film festival of the same name. They own six film studios, including not only Universal but also PolyGram and Gramercy. They own the Get Music website, Def Jam records and the MCA music label. Hence Toyota sell their cars, televisions, etc. as both products and as television, music and cinematic icons. Vivendi are paid off with theme park redevelopment, the kind of technological support that created extreme stunts in the *Fast and Furious* films and special assistance with film distribution in Asia. The model for Toyota's transaction with Vivendi could well have been Bill Clinton's relationship with similar Hollywood corporations that, by the mid 1990s, were fast becoming what James Schamus has called 'super-trans-national global media empires'.

Schamus – producer, writer and one-time head of the judges' panel for the Spirit Awards for independent film – was the production brains behind the success of director Ang Lee's kung-fu drama hit *Crouching Tiger, Hidden Dragon*. After 25 years as an independent producer, Schamus wrote in 2000 that presentday independents 'owe much of our existence to the growth of ... remarkable companies' [29] like Vivendi. The six biggest of these corporations have a 95 per cent share of the global film exhibition market and have steadily bought out independent producers. Disney bought Miramax in 1993 and owns Buena Vista, the largest distribution company in the world, whilst AOL Time Warner now own Fine Line and New Line. Meanwhile, international news media mogul Rupert Murdoch bought the Fox network, subsequently developing what *Box Office Magazine* called 'speciality arms',[30] like Fox Searchlight Pictures to replace independents. Furthermore, as Schamus implies, small producers became completely dependent on big Hollywood business. Artisan, for example, claims on its website to be the 'leading independent producer and distributor of theatrical, television and home entertainment product' and yet makes all its films for release 'by third-party major studios'. Bill Clinton's perspective on this situation of concentrated corporate power in Hollywood can best be summarised by his statement in a BBC interview in June 2004, the day before his no-holds-barred autobiography was published in the UK. In response to a question about American economic power he answered, 'the reality is that I believe we live in an inter-dependent world'. A world, in other words, where you must work with the power players in society in order to succeed. In Hollywood this approach led Clinton into relationships of mutual reward with the new concentrated corporations.

An overview of the decade reveals that Clinton's strongest supporters in Hollywood were people bound up in the corporate expansion. The Democratic Party could raise $8 million[31] from Hollywood per campaign cycle in the 1990s – which often meant three times a year. Donations had a distinct corporate flavour: executive and producer David Geffen gave average of $200,000 per year; former Disney chief executive and now joint head of DreamWorks Jeffrey Katzenberg averaged $125,000; Steven Spielberg $200,000; vice-president of Universal home entertainment Robert Rubin $80,000; ABC Family network's chief Haim Saban $250,000; DreamWorks made corporate donations averaging $500,000; Disney $1 million; Miramax $600,000; AOL Time Warner $500,000; Seagram, who owned 80 per cent of Universal and were bought out by French giant Vivendi in 2000, gave $250,000; telecom and television giant AT&T $500,000.[32] The organisations that led anti-Reagan protests and mounted hugely successful fundraising activities for Central American guerrilla armies in the 1980s were largely priced out of this relationship. The Hollywood Women's Political Committee – one of the three most prominent of these organisations – raised a total of just $6 million during the whole of the 1990s for the Democrats. This situation gradually developed into resentment and disillusion among Hollywood progressives. Ed Asner, in typically direct fashion, summarised the mood of non-executives in Hollywood towards the end of the Clinton presidency: 'money has become the total kingpin of politics in this country … The media controls candidacies, and money controls candidacies. It's a grossly unfair system.'[33]

One of Clinton's rewards to supportive executives was the 1996 Telecommunications Act. In keeping with his use of progressive rhetoric Clinton sold the act to talent as a way of breaking corporate monopolies in cable television and home entertainment. Instead the act helped AOL Time Warner increase its cable subscription rates by four times over the following year.[34] In 1997 a research and development tax credit, instigated by the 1996 Act, lost the taxpayer $1.7 billion. This financial bolstering helped the media corporations live the globalisation dream. AT&T exploited Latin American broadcasting with the extra money, assisted by the donation of 'first rights' in global media markets by the World Trade Organisation and by Clinton's ability to give personal 'fast-track' approval on trade deals. Further rewards came in the form of unfettered conglomeration. In the 1980s Hollywood companies completed 190 merger/acquisition deals with overseas partners, worth $17.22 billion.[35] By the early 1990s Columbia, MCA, Paramount and Time Warner (soon to merge with AOL) were buying up global theatre chains. These corporations re-read the Supreme Court anti-trust decision of 1948, and Clinton did nothing to stop them exploiting the ruling that a buy-out of theatres had to be of *proven* detriment to competition. Every buy-out from 1983 to 1999 was scrutinised by the Justice Department and every one sanctioned. This further undermined independents like Schamus, with independent productions unable to secure distribution deals rising by 258 per cent. Meanwhile the corporations increased their first-look deals with independent producers by 130 per cent[36] – meaning that media cartels could scupper a small film's chance of being shown by holding off on their decision to distribute it.

The Telecommunications Act also assisted Hollywood companies in challenging the rise of East Asian business successes like Sony. Sony owned American-based Columbia but made 70 per cent of its profit in Eastern Europe and the Third World.[37] To offset this, distribution channels were de-regulated and the development of film commissions that sold cheaper labour and facilities to media corporations encouraged. Florida and North Carolina became new sites of cheap film production. (North Carolina's research triangle helped especially by developing digital technologies that sped up production and lowered costs.) One trend assisted by Clinton's de-regulation in the late 1990s was movement of production to Canada; 61 per cent of 550 film projects in Canada in 2000 were of American origin, employing a large number of actors and crew members. Speaking about making a film for Disney in 2003, Oscar-winning British director Mike Figgis said, 'It's like in music, we used to use the Eastern bloc countries until it became cheaper somewhere else. We went to Canada because Disney saves 10 per cent on the production.'[38]

Gerald Levin, head of AOL Time Warner, expressed the confidence that Clinton's business relationship with Hollywood gave media corporations when he said, 'We are witnessing a deep stirring in the world … Time-Warner welcomes the role it can play in … a new diversity of thought and expression … the world is our audience.'[39] The founding of DreamWorks SKG – with Clinton sponsors Spielberg, Katzenberg and Geffen as its executive heads – was a product of this confidence. This triumvirate were perceived to be typical of many executive Friends Of Bill, as long-time Hollywood liberal activist Stanley Sheinbaum told *The Nation* in April 1999: 'their interest isn't ideological. They just want to be invited to Camp David … to sleep in the White

House.' Perhaps as part of a quest to get into the White House, or per- haps simply as a result of recognising the success of the corporate model in Hollywood, these three power players nevertheless created from scratch the very model of an integrated Hollywood empire.

Before DreamWorks had even been dreamt of, Jeffrey Katzenberg was one of Disney's three most powerful executives. Working with CEO Michael Eisner, Katzenberg led an organisational re-design that increased Disney's value from $2 billion (1984) to around $22 billion (1992).[40] *LA Village Voice* and *Box Office Magazine* journalist and Holly- wood insider Ray Greene observed how Disney's success was the result of a ruthless 'integration of various corporate operations in a cross-pollinating and self-sustaining entertainment conglomerate'.[41] When Greene interviewed Roy E. Disney – nephew of the company's creator and the figurehead throughout the Katzenberg period – it became clear this meant downsizing unprofitable sections like libraries and warehouses of old sets or equipment, and planning future enter- prises to achieve multi-market saturation. So *The Little Mermaid* or *Beauty and the Beast* were not simply animated films, they were total lifestyle packages complete with soundtracks, stage musicals, posters, post cards, dolls, school bags, pens, pencils, writing pads, children's costumes for Halloween, computer games, t-shirts, jeans, baby romper suits, learning materials for young children, spin-off television series and, in the case of the latter film, a particularly annoying non-stop talk- ing kettle voiced by television detective stalwart Angela Lansbury. Organisation of arguably the world's leading animation brand was now structured around the idea of 'synergy' – each department mov- ing in unison to the tune of the latest product, producing a range of commodities that would permeate every aspect of the consumer's life. To ensure this was a successful process, Disney patented all their char- acter images and took out at least eight cases against individuals who used their characters for personal purposes in the early 1990s.

When Katzenberg left Disney after an internal spat in 1995 – Eisner did not promote him to chief operating officer after the death of exec- utive Frank Wells in a shocking 1994 helicopter crash – he went on to co-found DreamWorks. DreamWorks had the perfect trio at its head to replicate the multi-market accumulative ethic Katzenberg had achieved with Disney. David Geffen had a long history in music pro- duction and took care of the music, soundtrack and associated merchandise division. Steven Spielberg was already much more than a director, having produced and directed several films with assorted spin-offs and merchandise with great success at his Universal-based

Amblin Productions. At DreamWorks Spielberg became more or less the creative director, dreaming up concepts for film- and merchandise-based profit making, like the surprisingly violent toys-run-wild narrative of *Small Soldiers* and the big effects, minimal character development of meteorite disaster movie *Deep Impact*. The multi-media strategy that Katzenberg exemplified at Disney was also evident at DreamWorks. So much so, in fact, that for films such as *Small Soldiers* Spielberg and Katzenberg recruited animators directly from Disney, winning their loyalty by arguing that these 'authors' should have absolute rights over their products, entitling them to a percentage payment out of the gross revenue from the film's box-office sales.

The best example of Disney-style strategy at DreamWorks is, however, not to be found in animation. Instead it is perhaps the cross-pollination of *Band of Brothers* (produced for television by Tom Hanks, Katzenberg and Spielberg) and *Saving Private Ryan* (produced by Katzenberg, starring Hanks, directed by Spielberg). Geffen produced the soundtrack, of course, and this, together with countless books, videos, DVDs and other merchandise created a Second World War DreamWorks brand that became so synonymous with that historic event that the entire *Band of Brothers* series was shown over one weekend on a BBC digital channel during the anniversary of the D-Day landings in 2004. DreamWorks was, as Spielberg's lifelong friend George Lucas put it, a way of this trio of FOB's gaining 'control over the means of production'.[42] Further proof of the assistance that Clinton gave to Hollywood corporate interests can be found in the graphic portrayal of a beach-landing during the opening sequence of *Saving Private Ryan*. This exceptionally well-crafted blood-soaked 20 minutes of chaos and death benefited from an exchange of technology, research and manpower between DreamWorks and the Department of Defense. The Technology Reinvestment Project and Advanced Technology Program, initiated by Clinton in the mid 1990s, set out 'to stimulate the creation of an integrated civilian–military industrial base'.[43] Spielberg and Katzenberg led the way in this exchange by visiting military leaders, sharing their digital-imaging technology used to create special effects, bringing military technocrats and researchers onto their sets and into their development labs, sending technicians on secondment to military research centres, attending (or sending substitutes) to conferences where technological knowledge and equipment were shared. As well as helping create the superb opening to *Saving Private Ryan*, these kinds of military–cinema partnerships won research grants for corporations including DreamWorks, Sony, Lucasfilm and AOL Time

Warner. The military were paid back with advances in flight simula-
tors (which can also be found at fairgrounds), submarine sound
detection (also used to enhance music recording technique), Ozone
data monitoring systems (also used in digital imaging) and missile tar-
geting technology (also used in computer games software).

The collaboration rewarded Spielberg with a Distinguished Public
Services Award from the Department of Defense in 1999, something
usually reserved for military personnel who do good works. Such
handsome public rewards for filmmakers were repaid not only by the
sharing of technology and financial donations to the Democrats but
also by the way filmmakers treated the president in their movies. So
profound had this collaboration been that former Columbia and Paramount executives Peter Bart and Peter Guber observed in 2002 how
Spielberg became obsessed with showing off combat photos that the
military had given him.

As with the Vivendi–Toyota deal, Clinton's relationship with Hollywood business had a product placement element. The product in this
case was a Clinton-esque progressive president. *Dave* (1993), for example, contributed to a Joe Public, reformist presidential iconography. In
Dave a Baltimore businessman is asked to impersonate an ailing president. This ordinary guy who speaks in soundbites about the average
Joe becomes popular with everyone in the White House, except a devious vice-president. Kevin Kline brings warmth and honesty to the lead
role, showing emotions such as fear over the effect of budgets on working guys, anger at the vice-president's corruption and a burgeoning
affection for the first lady. By applying the logic of a simple accountant
to the highest office in the land, challenging stuffy politicians with
direct language, Dave becomes a likeable rogue and ultimately ousts
the cheaters from the administration. More intimate scenes show Dave
in Aran sweaters and slacks, like an easy-going father figure. *Time*
called *Dave* 'dear and funny', and that is exactly the impression it gives
of this ordinary guy who winds up running the country. That Dave fin-
ishes the film running for office in Baltimore – as himself this time, not
a phoney president – implies that good guys really can prosper in
politics.

Dave is like the Bill Clinton who spoke at the Labour Party Conference in the UK in 2001, just after leaving office. Here Clinton talked
about how politicians are misunderstood and that he and his great
friend Tony Blair (UK Prime Minister) shared a deep understanding of
what it was like to be the ordinary man or woman in the street. Indeed,
after his presidency was threatened by the Monica Lewinsky scandal –

5. President Clinton's closest friends in Hollywood were well rewarded, but they tended to be successful businessmen, like DreamWorks SKG founder Steven Spielberg (*courtesy of* The Tribune, *India*).

where he was impeached for infidelity with a White House aide – Clinton went on national television to apologise for 'making a mistake'. He was, he said, human after all and just like everyone else he sometimes got things wrong. In *Dave* Kevin Kline shocks his White House bureaucrats by admitting that the government got a policy wrong, vowing to change it and immediately winning the respect of his public. This is how close the social and the cinematic world sometimes got during the Clinton era! What is particularly interesting about the product placement of a Clinton-style president in *Dave* is that the film was not directed by a Hollywood Democrat supporter, but by Ivan Reitman who has a long track-record in comedies including working on *Twins* and *Junior* with Arnold Schwarzenegger. (The former being the story of an odd-couple of brothers separated at birth, the latter of a dad who gets pregnant!) Reitman's relationship with Schwarzenegger continued after Arnold was elected as governor of California in 2003, with Reitman being appointed to Arnold's 'transition team' for ensuring he moved smoothly from Hollywood star to trustworthy politician in the public eye. You might ask why a director with clear sympathies for a Republican movie star like Schwarzenegger would make such a Clinton-influenced film as *Dave*. Product placement of the presidential kind is a transaction between politician and director, just as it was between Toyota and Vivendi. In this way Bill Clinton can be perceived as manipulating his relationship with Hollywood to become what Thomas Doherty, perhaps the leading academic analyst of presidential representation in American film, called 'the televisual president'.[44] However, this mutually beneficial relationship did not exist between Clinton and most progressive filmmakers. Even loyal Democrats like Warren Beatty did not follow Clinton's policy of pursuing interdependency with the corporations dominating Hollywood.

Progressive Hollywood responds – the new anti-corporate thread

The growth of corporate power encouraged an anti-corporate trend among independent-minded filmmakers in the 1990s. Warren Beatty intended that *Bulworth* would have 'an underlying theme that is anti-corporate'. Despite this film featuring a special individual playing out the fatalistic tendencies of late 1990s liberalism, Beatty wanted to convey in subtext a broad contemporary social problem summed up by his belief 'that the greatest danger to democracy is big corporations'.[45] In the film's opening scenes Senator Bulworth is harangued over the telephone by business lobbyists to change his policy. Later he does an underhand deal with an insurance corporation, and in the final sequence of the film an executive steps back into the darkness on a rooftop from where a bullet is fired seconds later. The bullet fells and kills Bulworth, thus associating corporate bosses with murder. These vignettes within the film create a sense that corporations are devious forces, prepared to take whatever action necessary to get their own way. Beatty was not alone in presenting liberal heroes up against mighty corporations. The table below contains an eclectic range of films from a four-year period (1998–2002) defined by narrative, character and aesthetic. Though these films generally feature more successful heroes, they all nevertheless share Beatty's willingness to make corporations the enemy.

Title	Narrative	Character	Aesthetic
Chicken Run (1998)	A group of production line worker hens revolt, find unique new ways to go 'on strike' and escape the grind of production for profit.	Rocky, the cock, voiced by Mel Gibson, is a failed liberal hero, who rises to the occasion – through a personal journey where he has to re-learn some good old-fashioned values like loyalty, honesty and bravery. There's also an extended gang of buddies in the hens.	Combining CGI and smooth plasticine animation, not to mention the pear-drop roundness of most of the characters, creates a wholesome extended family feel to the exploited hen coop – a place where values do belong! The farmers are classic evil-doing grotesques.
A Civil Action (1998)	Formerly money-focused lawyer takes on (and loses) a hopeless multi-plaintiff case against a ruthless and corrupt mega-corporation.	Travolta is a suited, smiling maverick litigation talent brought in from the cold to fight for justice. He becomes obsessed with the fight, determined to make things right, regardless of how out on a limb he has to go. It makes him penniless, sends his loyal team of buddies away but makes him a more 'honest' man.	Like most modern court-room dramas, there's a slickness to the film – smooth continuity keeps the narrative flowing and there's a richness to the colour and mise-en-scène that prevents identification with the impoverished plaintiffs (the victims) and keeps focus on the lawyer's personal journey.

Title	Narrative	Character	Aesthetic
The Truman Show (1998)	Truman is born into a TV soap controlled by a ratings-hungry corporation. Through personal ingenuity he uncovers the lie of his existence and escapes into the (false) horizon.	Truman is a humorous everyman, made identifiable to the spectator as the guy-next-door by the caricatured society around him. Yet his quest for truth, his boredom with the corporation's kid-glove control and the cunning used in his escape mark him out as smarter than average.	Two worlds are presented: a twee, sun-drenched, picket fence, perfectly formed soap set and a darkly lit, windowless, editing suite full of screens and gizmos but without comfort items. It's symbolic of the hope expressed in Truman's innocence against the corporate soulless heart.
The Insider (1999)	Scientist and TV journalist combine to expose the brutal corruption and lies of tobacco companies, despite threats of violence and to their careers.	Two heroes: a larger-than-life crusading journalist and a fearful but ultimately brave family man. Their righteousness is a given and they become loyal buddies, willing to pay the cost of taking on the corporations ... two truly special individuals!	Washed-out colours, hand-held camera in high tension sequences, odd angles that discon-cert but always keep the heroes centre frame – creating a chaotic and chilling modern land-scape, which the heroes struggle to compre-hend but ultimately overcome.
Any Given Sunday (1999)	A time-served football coach clashes with new corporate bosses and through resolve and guile wins out for the team and for himself.	Enigmatic coach – he has the loudest voice and people stop talking when he enters a room. He has to overcome personal doubts about his honour, his judge-ment and his loyalty. Then, in the denoue-ment, reveals he always had a game plan that was not only fair but also clever.	High-octane sports sequences, using dig-ital technology and rapid movement force an instinctive, human identification with the athletes. Big TVs and plush furniture in exec-utive offices combine with a grainy film stock to create the sense of something pure being sullied by profit.

Title	Narrative	Character	Aesthetic
American Beauty (1999)	Middle-class corporate employee and family hit crisis. Adulterous, prejudiced, emotionally damaged but hidden tendencies explode and the apparent normality of the suburb collapses.	Lester jerks off in the shower, chooses to work at a Mr Smiley drive thru (resembling the familiar bright colours and plastic façade of fast food outlets like Burger King and McDonalds), takes drugs and fantasises about teenage girls. It's a mini-rebellion by a maverick at his insurance salesman career (which ended when his corrupt boss laid him off) and his wife's equally mundane life in real estate. Lester exposes the family's suburban lifestyle – dependent on corporate jobs – as a sham of deceit and dissatisfaction. Utterly fatalistic, Lester is killed for his exposé.	Carefully constructed mise-en-scène creates a realistic but also typical middle-class home. The dining-room, in particular, has the right kind of furniture, is the right shape and has the right décor to be any suburban US home. It is also symbolic of the underlying crisis in the characters' lives, with Lester and his wife seemingly a mile apart at opposite ends of the table. Also, the floating bag sequence conveys neatly the abstractions from real-life situations that cause liberals like Lester to believe mini-rebellions make any difference in the first place.
American Psycho (2000)	An allegory for the depravity of corporate power. This executive kills off his rivals and those who get in his way, in a symbolic imagining of how business is done.	An anti-hero who's more than a crazed psycho! Christian Bale gives a disturbing performance, conveying a calculated menace from behind the eyes. Initially the executive seems crazed but the genius of the film is in letting the spectator recognise the logic of his murderous habits, in the context of corporate ascendancy and greed.	Satirical in places and chilling in others, the film hangs on the performance of its lead character. Fortunately the casting places an actor whose turn in a moment from smart businessman to killer is believable despite his slightly caricatured manner. The narrative is structured around the lead's performance forces the viewer to recognise the logic of murdering rivals.

Title	Narrative	Character	Aesthetic
Anti-TRUST (2001)	Gifted young computer programmer gets 'dream' job with NURV, the worlds biggest technology corporation, only to find they are corrupt, murderous and profit driven.	Teen talent Milo somehow sees things are amiss at NURV without having any evidence – Spidey-sense, perhaps? Milo brings down the villain (clearly modelled on Bill Gates) through cunning, guile and special ability. He uses spot-on judgement to decide who he can trust and his programming ability to undermine the corporation.	The shiny NURV office and the home they donate to Milo are too clean-cut and neatly-folded to be true and the smile of Tim Robbins's villain is so rigidly fixed it can't be real. All the sinister stuff takes place at night, so you know that when the lights go out NURV is about to murder, cheat or steal.
John Q (2002)	Working father with poor health insurance lays siege to a hospital to get his dying son treatment.	An honourable but desperate black father is driven to extreme action by cold-hearted insurance firms. His mistaken path is based on loyalty and he manages to sustain his commitment to his son whilst doing the right thing in the end.	Straightforward editing and technique uses the enclosed environment of the hospital and a set of diverse hostages to draw out the issues behind the drama. The scenes with the insurance representatives are shot in a colder, harsher light.
8 Mile (2002)	White trailer-trash rapper is forced to work in a factory and choose between his dreams and a steady, but lowly, job.	Marshal Mathers (Eminem) was made for the role, or perhaps the role was made for him! The hero is amazingly talented as a rapper but hampered by fear of rejection and the belief that, as a working-class kid, he will never amount to anything more than factory fodder. Overcoming obstacles put in his way, he establishes his rap credentials, wins a contest but does not escape the factory.	Grainy, largely set at night and with murky city visuals, *8 Mile* balances threatening noir darkness (the uncertainty that comes from never being able to see far ahead) with an accurate re-creation of life on the poor side of the mile. One of the first films to have extended scenes of family life in a trailer and the first in a long time to show production line workers. It's real poor American lifestyle, in an uncertain world.

The production of such films, that so clearly portray corporate power as detrimental or dangerous for American society, stands in marked contradiction to the emerging shape of Hollywood in the 1990s as typified by the DreamWorks example and as exploited by Bill Clinton. It is reasonable to ask why on earth the executives who gained so much from Clinton's policy of mutually beneficial inter-dependency with corporations would be willing to give a platform to narratives and aesthetics that suggested the ordinary American benefited not one iota from such an exchange. The superficial answer to this question is that executives do not make films and, as the classic example of Orson Welles's *Citizen Kane* demonstrates, the talent who actually produce the film can manipulate their studio bosses if they are smart enough.

With *Citizen Kane* Welles made a film that used a diverse range of fresh cinematic techniques to unfurl a narrative about the rise and fall of a media mogul. The late and highly respected film critic Pauline Kael wrote extensively about how the film was produced and the social situation from which Welles, and his writer Herman Mankiewicz, drew. The fictional lead, Charles Foster Kane – played by Welles – was in Kael's opinion based without doubt on real life tycoon William Randolph Hearst, whom Mankiewicz knew personally. Since Hearst was known for wielding his power to destroy detractors when he felt so inclined, it can be understood why the studio backing *Citizen Kane* – RKO – might have been nervous about a film that referred in less than favourable terms to Hearst's life. Likewise, Welles's use of deep-focus camera work, extreme angles that required cutting holes in sound-stage floors, inventive use of a wide range of lighting, aerial shots that entered buildings through the roof and descended to the ground floor, spinning sets that had to change décor after each revolution (used to indicate time lapse), and the employment of a large ensemble cast of actors recruited from his own theatre company, all concerned RKO about spiralling costs. As Kael reports, Welles simply lied and hid as much of what he was doing from the company as possible, using his reputation and charm to persuade them to let him complete his work where deceit failed. Nevertheless, RKO threatened to close down the shoot on several occasions; threatened, but never took action.

That final point is perhaps most important, suggesting that RKO – one of the five biggest Hollywood studios in the inter-war period – was willing to let Welles continue in the hope that this brash 26-year-old with a huge following among critics and the public would produce something of financial value and critical merit. Indeed, according to the *Sight and Sound* poll of critics and Hollywood talent in the early 2000s, *Citizen Kane* remains the 'greatest film ever made'. Without suggesting that the table above contains films of equal standing, it is still possible to recognise the same studio logic at work behind their production. Despite the re-formation of Hollywood companies into global media giants in the Clinton period, the basic strategy for production – give people with ideas the space to make things we can sell – remained the same as it was when Welles made *Citizen Kane* in 1941. Take for example the founding of so-called independent production companies Spyglass and Revolution at the turn of the millennium. Both were locked into the corporate system, the former headed up by Roger Birnbaum and tied into a deal with the company where he'd been an executive, Fox, the latter headed by ex-Disney executive Joe Roth and bound by a similar contract. The particular space in Hollywood production cycles for an anti-corporate thread, which ran counter to the media businesses' relationship with Clinton, had in fact been opened up in the early 1990s by another 26-year-old who would go on to claim significant critical appraisal.

Steven Soderbergh and the brief independent boom

At 26 Steven Soderbergh was some 30 years younger than Warren Beatty when, in 1989, his first low-budget feature film launched not only his own career but also a thousand other independent movie ships. *Sex, lies, and videotape* (1989) cost $1.2 million to make, had returned $100 million from cinema and video sales by 2002 and paved the way for the production of a number of intelligent small films connected to the social context of the 1990s. Not everything that followed demonstrated Soderbergh's adept deconstruction of the American dream, but the independent film market saw a short-lived expansion, with the Harvey and Bob Weinstein-led company – Miramax – making particular inroads. New York-based Miramax made films cheaply and did not need them to be as successful as major studio productions. On a cost-to-earnings ratio they did good business, earning a return that allowed for future investment. *Sex, lies, and videotape* made $21 for each $1 invested in its first year, whilst *Batman*, a blockbuster movie about the popular comic-book hero produced in the same year, made $5 per $1 of cost.[46]

This brief independent revival lasted until the Clinton era, with its hallmark of corporate expansion in Hollywood, was in full swing. By around 1998 very few independents existed, having been consumed by the major corporations or run into bankruptcy. Even independent stalwart James Schamus speaking in 1999 suggested, half in jest, that pioneering coalitions like the Independent Feature Project should disband. His argument was that Hollywood big business had 'consolidated its political power' by subsuming the production base of the independent movie into their own system. Thus big business had rendered independence nothing more than a set of niche markets based on style, form or content that could be sold to smaller but profitable audiences. Schamus then pointed out, in an article for *Filmmaker Magazine* in 2000, that films that had a connection of some form or other to corporations had dominated the 1999 Independent Spirit Awards. Using Clinton's language, Schamus stated that filmmakers now had to accept that they could never be anything other than 'interdependent' with major media companies and that all that remained independent was their 'mentality'. Crucially, Schamus's analysis suggested that the very success of independent movies in the early 1990s, inspired by the *sex, lies, and videotape* model, had encouraged corporations to chase the independent dollar. Steven Soderbergh, therefore, has a symbolic centrality to both the brief independent boom of the early 1990s and the independent mentality that underpinned the anticorporate thread in the later 1990s.

Sex, lies, and videotape got its first exposure in competition at the Sundance Film Festival. Sundance began life, in its spectacular mountain surroundings, as a project of the Utah Film Commission. Sometime before the end of the 1980s Robert Redford set up his Sundance Film Institute to encourage and promote new talent. Sharing a name and a mission, the two came together in 1989 to become the US film festival with a kind of other-side-of-the-Atlantic-Cannes aspiration, and the highlight of that occasion was Soderbergh's first feature. Just to prove how small the independent scene was at the turn of the decade, *sex, lies, and videotape* was immediately snapped up by the only small-scale distributor at the opening Sundance Festival: Miramax. In the 1980s Miramax had brought overseas hits with critical acclaim to an American audience – like the story of UK political sex intrigue *Scandal*, the quaint and uplifting Italian rites-of-youth tale *Cinema Paradiso* and the dramatic performance by Daniel Day Lewis as a disabled Irish writer in *My Left Foot*. Miramax garnered production credits without actually doing all that much in production and had Oscars to show for their contribution. So, although still a fledgling distributor, they were the most serious independent distributor in America. Miramax's emerging reputation for uncovering cinematic gems undoubtedly gave the talented but unknown Soderbergh the break he needed.

In 1986 Soderbergh had been invited to film a tour by the band Yes. He shot, edited and produced *9012 Live* in his own style, giving it a narrative drive most other music videos failed to attain. The result was a film with all the carefully constructed documentary style of his later Oscar-winning fiction films. The minor recognition he earned for *9012* persuaded Columbia Pictures to part with a little cash for the development of a film concept based loosely around a story about broken relationships, employing a film-within-a-film twist. However, it was a tiny production outfit, no longer in existence, called Point 406, who raised the less than $1 million budget for *sex, lies, and videotape*. This distance from Hollywood corporations meant the film could be made in Soderbergh's own time, on his own terms. As he himself commented in his production notes for his 1999 box-office hit and Oscar winner, *Erin Brockovich*, he never again regained the complete control over a production process that he had in making his first feature. Indeed, even after he had made the film he experienced the flexing of studio muscles. His choice of title didn't please Columbia, whose investment guaranteed them video rights in the USA. They thought that it implied a trashy straight-to-video home audience and reduced sales potential. When Miramax bought the cinema distribution rights at Sundance they ignored Columbia's nervousness and promoted the film diligently to ensure success, not only on a cost-to-earnings ratio but also critically.

A significant minority of the American audience in this time of George Bush Snr seemed to love Soderbergh's take on relationships, society and technology. Part of what drew them to the films was Miramax's deliberate use of the 'independent' tag in marketing. So successful was this in carving the film an audience who wanted something different that Soderbergh got a little carried away. In his witty account of his early years as a filmmaker, *Getting Away With It*, he played to his own independent hype by suggesting he'd cut megastar Harrison Ford out of *sex, lies, and videotape* to keep it out of the mainstream ambit. Critic and writer Jason Wood later exposed this assertion as a myth. Despite this error on Soderbergh's part, *sex, lies, and videotape* transferred to Cannes where it beat Spike Lee's equally inventive and socially charged *Do the Right Thing* to all the awards.

There is another important element to this story. Soderbergh nurtured his success outside the corporate system and as a result he never got caught up in either Clinton's networking with talent or his transactions with executives. Although Soderbergh was by his own admission unable ever again to reach the complete independence from corporations that he attained in making *sex, lies, and videotape*, his initial distance seems to have been a significant factor in the perspective he developed in the late 1990s. Simply put, Soderbergh never became part of the traditional Hollywood liberal milieu that Warren Beatty or Oliver Stone were involved in. He never expressed a desire to meet with Clinton or to sleep in the White House as Stanley Sheinbaum had implied Barbra Streisand or Richard Dreyfuss wished.

On the other hand, Soderbergh's films exhibit a distinctly liberal flavour. *Sex, lies, and videotape* features a special individual, Graham, who makes home movies about sexual activity. The film hinges on non-conformist Graham's clash with the establishment, in the figure of his old college pal John, who is now a lawyer. The narrative hangs around the relationship between Graham and John's wife Ann, and in particular her confessions about sex to John's camera. However, sex can be seen as just a nail on which to hang a much fuller picture of American social phenomena. In the final analysis Graham is the happier, despite his lack of material and social wealth, whilst John's life collapses in on itself. Soderbergh's inventions in narrative and style, made possible by his freedom in producing the film, allow him to demonstrate the way capitalist society fetishises technology. The video camera becomes an artificial mode of communication in the lives of the characters, but it does not assist them in grappling with their inadequate and dissatisfying existence. The subject of the title – the videotape – is simply a shovel to turn over the earth of society. The act of talking truthfully about sex to video further plunges the characters into their own discontent. John's only recourse is to destroy the video equipment, to cover up the reality of his life. The conclusion of the film is that existence, in the post-Reagan Bush Snr era of American society, is dependent on the telling and re-telling of lies. So when Soderbergh says 'sex, lies, and videotape is what the film is about and a lot of what this country revolves around: the selling of sex, the telling of lies and the inundation of video',[47] his statement should be understood as a liberal assertion. *Sex, lies, and videotape* is consistent with the liberal tradition in exploring contemporary social phenomena – the breakdown of family relationships and the media fetish for sex. It is clear that John and Ann are not coping with the challenge of modern society, as neither Senator Bulworth nor investigator Garrison in *JFK* manage to do, but as Henry Fonda's juror in *Twelve Angry Men* did at a time when liberals were much more confident.

Soderbergh can be seen to follow a late twentieth-century model of liberalism but to do so in an original and challenging manner, perhaps made possible by his distance from the existing milieu of Hollywood liberalism. So when Graham develops a gang of buddies they are drawn in by the uniqueness of his persona and of his odd video-making mission. The gang is not formed out of abstract loyalty 'come what may' – as it is with Bulworth's aides – but consists of women Graham interviews about sexual experiences, who are bound to him because they have shared their secrets. John and Ann are Graham's buddies some of the time but do not trust him completely, as Bulworth's aides trust the senator despite his madness and Garrison's team follow his quest even when it becomes dangerous. In *sex, lies, and videotape* trust is threatened if Graham's pals feel he is prying too much or if he exposes darker truths. Whether Graham, played with a slightly unnerving limited range of expression by James Spader, is heroic is also less certain than it is with either *Bulworth* or Garrison in *JFK* but he is certainly the driver of the film's narrative. Moreover, he pursues the abstract ideal of truth in the most direct fashion, conducting an exploration of deeply personal matters that would not be appropriate to the more public playing field occupied by Garrison or Bulworth. Whilst it is clear from both the film text and from Soderbergh's own words that the ideal of truth and the sense of a corrupt modern society are at the centre of *sex, lies, and videotape*, it is also clear that his film is more complex than the others we have compared it to. Perhaps the conclusion here is that Soderbergh is a more sophisticated director.

What is certain is that he quickly became aware of how Hollywood corporations were seizing on his success to forge inter-dependence between themselves and independent producers. Soderbergh recognised this much more quickly than Hollywood liberals like Ed Asner appeared to recognise the real nature of Clinton's relationship with Hollywood. Whilst Asner talks of only beginning to recognise the path of the Clinton presidency in the late 1990s, Soderbergh took just one year of observation to tell the Sundance Festival audience in 1990 he was 'concerned by what *sex, lies, and videotape* might have wrought here … this can become more of a market than a festival'.[48] History was to prove him right, and those who were to feel this effect most sharply were represented by that other American director whom Soderbergh beat to all the awards at Cannes in 1989: Spike Lee. Much like the corporate monopolisation of the independent scene a promising set of African-American directors – of whom Lee was the most prominent – were undermined by Hollywood's media giants in the mid 1990s. As Soderbergh's words unintentionally warned, the market of Hollywood dismantled a half-decade of magnificent work by Hollywood's exciting Black New Wave.

Race and the independent movie

'A whole generation of Young directorial Turks had built on the *sex, lies, and videotape* precedent to create some of the boldest American movies of recent memory', commented *LA Village Voice* journalist Ray Greene in the late 1990s. Soderbergh's cost-to-earnings success at the start of the 1990s had not only encouraged an independent production boom, it had also drawn attention from the major Hollywood production outfits. Soderbergh explained to *Mr Showbiz* magazine that his ability to make a quality movie at minimal cost had been a key factor behind a telephone call he received from divisional head of production Casey Silver at Universal in 1997. This call led to Soderbergh getting the director's chair on the George Clooney vehicle *Out of Sight* (1998), a big studio film with a small budget designed to reap the kind of box-office rewards that independent movies had in the early 1990s. This new space for the independent-minded director in corporate film production would be occupied in the 1990s by anti-corporate films but had initially been cornered by a set of talent young African Americans.

Very soon after Soderbergh beat Spike Lee to the prestigious Palm d'Or prize at Cannes, Hollywood corporations were giving Lee budgets to make films based on his own concepts. Lee had relied upon money from smaller outfits like United International Pictures (UIP) to make his first two features, *She's Gotta Have It* (1986) and *School Daze* (1988). His breakthrough film that Soderbergh beat to the awards, *Do the Right Thing* (1989), though funded by UIP, had extra support from JVC. It also credited Jon Kilik as a 'line producer'. Kilik was already a respected production figure and would become a recurring name associated with films made by talent like Lee and John Sayles but backed with studio money. (Whether Kilik plays this role in order to advocate and support socially minded talent or to assist the corporations in monitoring their franchise is not something we can answer here.) *Do the Right Thing* is at least as concerned with social malaise as Soderbergh's award winner and far more dramatic in its exploration of the tensions under the surface of modern America. The film centres on a street in Brooklyn where most residents are part of a disenfranchised generation of black youth, and where an Italian-American pizzeria becomes the focus of discontent for impoverished, oppressed African Americans. Largely set over the course of one day *Do the Right Thing* concludes with the pizzeria trashed and set alight in an act of frustration at society's problems, taken out on the wrong targets. This tale of urban discontent, focused on the black community, typifies the kind of films that first made headway in the wake of Soderbergh's revival of independent space in Hollywood.

Do the Right Thing was Oscar nominated for its script and earned significant artistic praise from Terence Rafferty in the *New Yorker*. Unlike Soderbergh's economic style of composition, Lee demonstrates a completely fresh urban aesthetic: use of music to almost over- rather than under-score dialogue; long shots that sometimes attach themselves to characters' faces, and at other times swivel alarmingly to reveal previously unseen sections of a location; well-placed use of extreme close ups to heighten actors' performances; establishing shots that enrich the mise-en-scène with a complete but enclosed landscape of a Brooklyn street; quick edits between stills and moving shots in moments of action; a rich colour scheme that creates an intensity of image, enhancing the feel of extreme summer temperatures. Lee creates characters recognisable to citizens of inner-city projects and uses street names like Da Mayor, Radio Raheem or Mookie (the weedy pizza delivery boy that Lee himself plays and who re-appeared in a series of Nike commercials with basketball star Michael Jordan). Lee's dialogue is mined from real experience in urban communities and he gives characters in cliques a subtle language whilst retaining each character's individual quality of speech. Lee's style of filmmaking was uniquely brilliant and his critical success opened the Hollywood establishment's eyes to other black directors who could explore urban and ethnic themes.

Lee himself benefited with *Jungle Fever* (1991) – the story of a black married architect who becomes sexually involved with a white colleague – being made with finance from Universal. *Mo Better Blues* (1990) – featuring Denzel Washington as jazz band leader Bleek whose career is destroyed when he saves his manager from gambling creditors – had funding from JVC Entertainment and Criterion. Both films credited Kilik again, featured elements of the setting and style of *Do the*

Right Thing and both embedded significant African-American icons in their aesthetic. Flavor Flav, the front man of popular rap ensemble Public Enemy, has a cameo in *Do the Right Thing*, and *Jungle Fever* opens with a specially written and performed track by legendary musician Stevie Wonder. For the corporations this was an early foray into the territory of niche marketing that they would later try to bundle all independent filmmakers into. At its zenith a rapid production of films by black directors, based around the African-American experience, earned the auspicious title of the Black New Wave.

Another beneficiary of this period was University of Southern California graduate, a boy from the projects and impressive talent, John Singleton. Partly due to Lee's pioneering success on the East Coast, Singleton never had to work as an independent and received cheques from Columbia-TriStar and New Deal Film to make his West Coast-set first film *Boyz 'N the Hood* (1991). He describes his entry into the film-making world during the ramble that is his DVD commentary for a special release of his second film *Higher Learning* (1995) – based on Singleton's experiences of black students struggling to earn respect on university campuses and concluding with the murderous rampage of a neo-Nazi. The value of this Black New Wave to the corporations was demonstrated when *Boyz 'N the Hood* returned $57.5 million to Columbia from a budget of $6 million.[49] The moving story of two black youths struggling to find their way through a maze of poverty, police oppression, pop culture, gang warfare and violence was again based on Singleton's own experience and, as in *Higher Learning*, culminated in the death of an innocent black teenager. The cinematic style of the film was not nearly as inventive as Lee's, tending to stick to traditional composition, camera angles and score but the narrative was highly engaging, the dialogue direct and subtly revealing of characters' emotions. Singleton also drew out exceptional performances from debutant Cuba Gooding Jr, Laurence Fishburne and Ice Cube – a former rapper with NWA (Niggaz With Attitude). Singleton became the youngest writer to be nominated for an Oscar for best screenplay and was also nominated for best director. *Variety* wrote that *Boyz 'N the Hood* was a 'smartly made dramatic encyclopaedia of problems and ethics in the black community'. It was this brave commitment of the Black New Wave directors to represent in graphic detail the social problems of the urban experience that eventually led Hollywood corporations to abandon them.

Singleton stated just how targeted the films of the Black New Wave were: 'I made *Boyz 'N the Hood* specifically for a young, black audience.

6. The 'Black New Wave': socially conscious African Americans burst onto the cinema scene with popular socially engaged films like John Singleton's *Boyz 'N the Hood* (*copyright Ben Dickenson*).

The same audience that buys rap albums … as hardcore and street as possible.'[50] Initially this niche marketing complemented a short boom in independent production. Miramax, Gramercy, October Films, New Line, Touchstone and United International Pictures found that they could get their smaller budget films into more cinemas as a result of both the *sex, lies, and videotape* success and the studio marketing of directors like Lee and Singleton. The small companies profited from niche marketing at a quicker pace than the studios because they already had a bank of cheap work in production utilising themes, ideas and styles appropriate to a new generation of Americans.

   A number of factors combined to make significant sections of this generation dislocated from the mainstream, blockbuster Hollywood fare. Rodney King and the 1992 LA riots increased awareness of racial injustice and a desire to challenge it. John Singleton's widely publicised words outside the trial of the officers accused of beating King – 'you people don't understand, it's a time bomb' – must have said to this generation that there were directors interested in making films about their concerns. Equally anti-McDonald's, Wal-Mart and Nestlé campaigns, as well as growing negative publicity about globalisation must have made the naked product placement of early 1990s Hollywood stick in the throat of this new generation. Clinton's arrival in Hollywood, so obviously a friend of the corporations, can only have exacerbated the gap between the studios and this section of its audience. That is not to say that Hollywood stopped making money – the previous generation hadn't evaporated overnight – but the corporations became increasingly aware that they were losing touch. After interviewing a selection of corporate heads Ray Greene again commented in the early 1990s: 'a new and supposedly radically different youth audience is said to be emerging, with a different priority system and a fundamentally altered perspective on itself and its place in American life … Variously called "the *Slacker* generation" … "generation X" … or (yecch!) the "Twenty-somethings".'[51]

It is clear that the studios had woken up to what they were missing: a new, young audience. After Soderbergh's immense *sex, lies, and videotape* success independent producers began flooding theatres with their produce, and the studios used the Black New Wave to try and catch up whilst they explored other ways to emulate or take control of the cost-to-earnings success of the independent producers. Historically, young audiences have been key players in box-office success. The young don't have kids, don't have mortgages, are expected go out and have a good time rather than stay in, so they are key targets for the film corporations. The big studios learnt in the 1990s that their financial muscle could buy them a piece of the new generation's pie, without having to work for it. The cynical manner in which the studios went about using the Black New Wave and later began gobbling up the independent companies in the pursuit of profit stood in contrast to the objectives of most of the filmmakers involved. Whilst it would be false to suggest all niche-marketed films had a political edge, for many of the niche-marketed filmmakers the motivation was not financial but social. None were more socially engaged than the frontrunners of the Black New Wave, who felt they had nothing in common with the studios' cynical attempt to catch up the radicalized youth. As Singleton put it, 'that has nothing to do with me. The only thing that qualifies me as being part of the X generation is I'm one of the first generation born after the death of [radical black nationalist] Malcolm X.'[52] Before the studios muscled in, it was apparent that the small producers were making films much more in touch with the full range of issues concerning the new generation.

A glance at a small selection of 1992's independent films – all of which were in the top 25 domestic box-office list for the year – demonstrates the number of contemporary social issues to which the independents related.

1 *The Crying Game* (Channel 4/Miramax) – an American soldier is taken hostage and an IRA operative falls in love with a transvestite. Irish nationalism and sexual freedom are explored in a gentle but emotional story where every individual is made to appear of value to society and oppression of all kinds is challenged.

2 *Love Field* (Orion) – a woman shocked by John F. Kennedy's death travels to his funeral and, breaking all conventions of her community, becomes involved with a black man along the way. Racism and the repression of communities dominated by the evangelical right are both challenged.

3 *Passion Fish* (Achafalaya/Miramax) – an ex-soap star is robbed of her public popularity by disability but, with her new nurse, who has a series of social problems of her own, they find a way to find hope through collective support.

4 *The Mambo Kings* (Alcor Films/Regency Enterprises) – two Cuban brothers flee to the USA in the 1950s where they experience hardship and discrimination but find solace and minor fame through their music. One of the only films of the decade to explore the Cuban immigrant experience and also to launch Latin culture into the mainstream.

5 *The Last of the Mohicans* (Morgan Creek) – British and American imperialism and Native American struggle, told from the Mohican point of view. An action adventure from America's wild past where the hero, although played by a white man, is not a modern American and where oppression of Native Americans is addressed.

The subjects of the four top-grossing movies of 1992 demonstrate that the studios were still running to catch up with the social content of the independent producers and catch the new audience. *Aladdin* was a family cartoon, with a very white Aladdin leading us through a familiar tale, the main attraction being star voices. *Home Alone 2* was an annoying and farcical family action with no social relevance, except as a warning to burglars who go near Macaulay Culkin's house. *Batman Returns* was a disappointing sequel in this now long-running action franchise, with tons of special effects and over-the-top performances. *Lethal Weapon 3* was essentially a re-making of the storyline of the previous two movies of the same name, with the bad guys replaced by newer versions with bigger guns. The Hollywood corporations must have taken note of the disparity between their big successes and the independent producers' work by the time of the Oscars in early 1993. At those Oscars the independents received more nominations than any of the studios did. In fact all the independent films discussed above were Oscar nominated and, despite having shorter releases in less cinemas, had all had made a much greater profit on a cost-to-earnings ratio. It can hardly be a coincidence that in 1993 Hollywood corporations began to buy up the independent producers and distributors. This appears to be a change in tactic away from using the Black New Wave as a niche market counterweight to the independents. Another strand of evidence that suggests the corporations made such a tactical shift is what happened during and after the 1992 Los Angeles riots.

John Singleton's comments, after the four police officers accused of beating Rodney King were acquitted in April 1992, were in effect a prediction of the chaos that erupted in Los Angeles within hours of the verdict. The 2003 police drama *Dark Blue,* for the first time in a Hollywood movie, attempted to portray the pre-riot tensions and actual riot scenes that took place in Los Angeles that April. *Dark Blue* is largely a story about a corrupt police officer uncovering yet more corruption at a senior level in the Los Angeles Police Department (LAPD). Played with the maverick rough-neck bravado that Kurt Russell has employed many times in his career, the film's lead character must choose between betraying bosses who have previously bailed him out, thus getting some real justice, or doing nothing and becoming complicit in far more serious deceit than ever before. After drinking, soul searching and being deserted by his wife, he ultimately chooses to expose his commanding officers. As he undertakes this dangerous task news of the King verdict comes through and South Central LA becomes a war zone. At least that is how the movie makes it seem. Russell drives through streets of tenement blocks and decrepit houses, where gangs of men eye him aggressively. Later a gang menacingly advance at a fast walking pace towards him and he feels the handle of his gun before managing to drive away. Finally, the streets become filled with dust and smoke. Debris from buildings and smashed shops litters every corner, cars are overturned, people are dragged from other vehicles and kicked repeatedly, women run with shopping trolleys full of stolen goods, crowds run with baseball bats down alleyways, older residents appeal for calm, a shop owner begs for his store to be left untouched and some scared citizens hide behind a wall. Russell is lucky to get out alive, driving his car at breakneck speed into crowds in order to escape. A staccato camera movement, a rapid cutting between moments of crisis and a knee-level shot of a rampaging crowd all add to the feeling of chaos, fear and panic.

The accuracy of this dramatisation is hard to ascertain. However, it is clear from non-dramatic sources that – despite riots taking place within a few miles of their exclusive homes – left-leaning Hollywood talent were sympathetic to the urban poor of South Central. George Clooney demonstrated the outlook of socially minded talent when he said, 'for every person looting or torching, there were 500 people cleaning up. Volunteers ... blacks, Latinos, Asians, whites, etc ... a great many people in those damaged neighbourhoods saw that there were a lot of people who honestly care.' Clooney 'didn't like the way the riots were reported', ignoring the multi-racial aspect of the South Central area and always 'focused on the gunfire, burning buildings and looting'.[53] The alienating effect of the LAPD's draconian Operation HAMMER, which had taken place in the months before the riots, or the 'war on marijuana', which seemed to penalise the black community hardest, were not discussed in the news coverage. Nor were they mentioned in *Dark Blue*. The fact that the average income for black families in 1990 was only 55 per cent that of white families was not mentioned either, but pre-riot location shots in *Dark Blue* present a yellow-grey dusty landscape of urban decay and poverty. From this film representation of the deprived social context of the riots it is not hard to believe that four Californian cities had unemployment rates of 12.5 per cent (1992), that the fall out from Bush Snr's Iraq war meant another 150,000 industrial Californian jobs would go that year, or that 30 per cent of Los Angeles office space was empty.[54] The father of 1960s and 1970s African-American low-budget all-action Blaxploitation movies and outspoken filmmaker Melvin van Peebles describes how police action and poverty combined so that the urban poor 'felt powerless' in American society, and the King verdict just 'set them off'.[55] This alienation was shared across racial divides, as it had been in late 1960s social movements. (52 per cent of those arrested during the riots were Latino and 30 per cent were black.)

For a liberal or progressive to 'care' in this context meant to recognise the social context of the riots. Which may explain why Clooney and his Hollywood friends didn't just attend the clean up operations he described earlier, they organised them. Some reflection of this understanding of the causes for the riots is given, in an extremely simplified form, at the conclusion of *Dark Blue*. Kurt Russell's police officer bursts into a ceremony awarding his senior officers and launching yet another police initiative to keep LA's streets clean. Bruised and bloody from the riots, Russell exposes the corruption and, indeed, murder committed by his senior officers. He makes a defiant if somewhat confusing speech about holding the values of protecting the public and being a good citizen paramount. He is then arrested but so too are the senior officers and from the shadows a senior black police officer emerges to protect Russell from those he has exposed. Outside the ceremony these two officers share an exchange of dialogue whilst Los Angeles is in flames behind them, 'it will keep on burning' says the black officer. Although this concluding sequence by no means apologises for the acquittal of the King police officers it does imply that the LAPD has a responsibility for the tensions that led to the riots and that, unless something is done, the riots will be back again. Remember that this film was made 11 years after the riots took place and conveyed a generally liberal message about the necessity of sticking to abstract values to resolve future conflicts. What this represents is the lasting and deep impact that the 1992 riots had on Hollywood liberals. A similar impact was also had on Hollywood's power brokers, though their response was anything but sympathetic to the situation of African Americans.

The corporations allowed their news teams to assert that that the riot was essentially racially motivated. Hollywood corporations now owned the television news stations along with global moguls like Rupert Murdoch, who owned News Corporation, the parent of Fox. Looking back in 2002, screenwriter John Ridley said the executives of these corporations were 'twenty-five middle-aged white multi millionaires ... out of touch ... not just with black people, but with everything'.[56] Nearly every station headlined the day after the riot with George Bush Snr's presidential address: 'What we saw last night and the night before in Los Angeles is not about civil rights. It's not about the great cause of equality ... It's been the brutality of the mob.' A Berkeley media study in 2001 concluded that this fusing of criminality and race had made the words 'young black males' synonymous with the word criminal in *Time* and *Newsweek* reportage during 1992.[57] What corporate Hollywood did was, as Haskell Wexler put it, 'tighten the screws.' This had a knock-on effect that 'reduced the possibility for independent people, particularly independent directors'.[58]

So despite Spike Lee's commercial and critical success, despite John Singleton's Oscar nomination, despite other directors, like Bill Duke and Carl Franklin, starting to emerge the corporations began to close down the Black New Wave. Ray Greene, who three times interviewed Singleton about this developing situation, was qualified to say in 1995, 'the wider movement that Singleton had appeared to epitomise was in full retreat. The riots ... dampen[ed] the enthusiasm for developing controversial and racially-charged subject-matter at studio level'.[59] Initially, black directors found their artistic choices questioned: witness the battle Spike Lee had to produce *Malcolm X*, having funding withdrawn, cutting the film dramatically to convince distributors, fighting to keep the most provocative moments. After that, corporations began to produce race-themed films that borrowed aesthetics from black directors but avoided engagement with their narratives: *Amistad* is a white version of anti-slavery struggle; *Grand Canyon* is a ghetto-through-white-eyes. There was also a slew of inter-racial buddy movies forsaking the ghetto for the middle-classes: *Lethal Weapon*, *Se7en*, *Men in Black*, etc. The essence of the Black New Wave was sidelined as industry bosses became 'more savvy in how to niche market, but more broadly in how to present a superficial version of a radical critique', as Norman Solomon puts it.[60] The 1990s movie audience was 20 per cent black, 50 per cent of ethnic origin, but at the end of the decade black directors made up 2.4 per cent of Directors' Guild membership.[61] So dramatic was this experience that Spike Lee made a film lampooning white executives for *Bamboozle*-ing the public in 1999.

Then Bill Clinton stepped in. He quickly straddled the competing corporate and creative camps. He talked of the need to heal racial divides, to challenge bigots, and associated himself with seminal moments in the struggle for civil rights, like Jackie Robinson's baseball participation. Clinton became the first white man admitted to the Arkansas Black Hall of Fame, and was called America's first 'black' president by author Toni Morrison. In 1997 he even launched a national 'conversation' on race. This activity mirrors the studios that make films with black themes and, like the studios, Clinton also failed to change the situation for black people in America. For example, in 1994 Los Angeles suffered an earthquake, giving Clinton an excuse to 'pump billions of dollars in Southern California'.[62] It appeared that Clinton was helping people affected by disaster. However, in 1995

Clinton supported Congress's proposed $16.3 billion of federal cuts. The 'disaster aid' scheme renovated 1,400 houses in Beverly Hills and completed 'expensive upgrades' on commercial buildings, but low-income housing, health grants and unemployment programmes were scaled down. A late 1990s drive through 'black neighbourhoods' revealed 'a new crop of derelict buildings and empty lots [added] to the large inventory still remaining from the 1965 and 1992 riots',[63] according to social commentator Mike Davis.

Throughout his presidency Clinton made symbolic gestures: the appointment of record numbers of black people to cabinet and judiciary; the nomination (and then withdrawal) of a black candidate for attorney general; the proposal (and then withdrawal) of a 'racial justice' clause to a crime bill; the continuance of 'affirmative action' programmes; the second-term racial initiative, which lifted Clinton's rating among blacks to 67 per cent; and the public quest to prosecute people setting fire to black churches in the South. However, his rhetoric was cover for the horrific situation of America's ethnic communities in the 1990s: welfare changes lowered incomes; between 9 per cent and 28 per cent of workers were paid cash-in-hand; LA's illegal employment accounted for 39 per cent of economic activity and 11 per cent of the population had less than a sixth grade education; the low paid earned 9 per cent less than they had in 1990. Meanwhile Enron, largely California-based, took home $400 million in tax refunds (1996–2000).[64] Clinton justified this contradiction with talk of an urban underclass, subscribing to the New Democrat (or Republocrat) idea of a 'victim mentality' in black communities. This confused people like Clooney, whose quote above exhibits a basic belief in community. As David Kusnet, Clinton's former speechwriter, has said, Clinton used the 'language of everyday experience' and spoke in euphemistic terms about 'community, values, opportunity'.[65] He suckered Hollywood liberals, who thought he was talking about their idea of positive, pro-active community unity. Clinton himself never actually presented a model of what this better community would be like, as Clooney tried to do when he visited post-riot South Central LA in 1992, but the very fact he used the same language contributed to the general seduction of which Hollywood celebrities fell foul. This seduction eventually gave way to a deep sense of betrayal.

Money can't buy you Bill

Ed Asner summarises the sense of betrayal expressed by Hollywood progressives when they reflect on Clinton today:

> Absolutely we were seduced. Absolutely we were held back ... the Democratic council felt they needed to move the centre rightward to achieve power ... I can list innumerable times and cases in his presidency that he failed to act like a progressive and could have; the land-mine treaty, the homosexual subject, the Kyoto treaty, the welfare programme, failed attempts at medical.[66]

This betrayal is undoubtedly heightened by the continued support that many on the Hollywood left showed for Clinton, even at times when his integrity was most called into question. It was people like actor-activists Ed Asner and Alec Baldwin who became involved in anti-impeachment missions to Washington during the Monica Lewinsky scandal at the start of Clinton's second term (1996–2000). Baldwin, with Warren Beatty, spoke on television and in *The Nation* about their disgust that American politics had been reduced to a media circus focused on Clinton's infidelity. Speaking about this situation in his 2004 interview on the BBC, Clinton describes how the 'American people and my close allies' saw the impeachment trial – led by Republican Special Prosecutor Kenneth Starr – as a 'witch hunt' by the American right.

This view is subscribed to by Clinton critics in the alternative media, like Norman Solomon, a 20-year associate of non-governmental organisation Fairness and Accuracy In Reporting (FAIR) and founder of the Institute of Public Accuracy, which consistently challenges the mainstream media and politicians when they tell untruths. Solomon says, 'people felt they had to band together around Clinton for fear of the whole progressive community being under attack'.[67] Kate McArdle, the one-time ABC producer and now chief organiser of Artists United for a Win Without War – the coalition founded to unite Hollywood talent against an American attack on Iraq in 2003 – concurs with Solomon. McArdle goes so far as to argue that 'people like Mike Farrell [founder of Artists United] felt they had to stand up to the right, a lot of people did. That's how you got things like MoveOn.org.'[68] The Move On coalition, founded by actors and Democrat supporters to stop the impeachment and force Congress to get on with helping Clinton run the country, became one of Artists United's greatest supporters. During the 2003 war with Iraq the Move On website was an organising centre and guide to help Artists United supporters mobilise in their thousands to protest. Asner talks with great satisfaction about how Move On, which he was involved in himself during the impeachment, was able to pool enough celebrity resources to make an anti-war television advert featuring high-profile actors, like Martin Sheen. Clinton, of course, survived the impeachment but did not take the wider concerns of those who helped him out more seriously. So Asner's long-running campaign for American CIA agents and troops to leave El Salvador was ignored, for example. It should be little surprise that MoveOn.org now questions the Democratic National Committee's agenda and credibility. By the end of his tenure Clinton found his own people attacking him for taking their support but ignoring their agenda. Treasury Secretary Robert Rubin, for example, assailed his old friend over an issue key to the president's loss of support in Hollywood, arguing that 'at the end of the 1990s, beginning of the 21st century, I think it's fair to say we have more wallet than will. I do not think this country has marshalled its resources to a degree commensurate with the [welfare] problem.'[69]

Clinton's handling of the welfare issue was a crucial turning point. With an average of seven million unemployed and poverty at a peak, welfare reform was, arguably, the crucial social justice issue of the 1990s. In his 1992 election Clinton rallied liberal support by talking of an 'end to welfare as we know it'. According to Robert Reich this should have meant 'guaranteed health care, child care, job training and a paying job'[70] for all people on welfare. By 2000 Clinton had removed 10 million people from welfare and cut the federal bill dramatically – but employment figures had not improved. In New York State, after Clinton's flagship welfare repeal bill was passed in 1996, just 19 per cent of people who were pushed from the welfare-to-work programme were earning as much as $100 per quarter. Whilst in Missouri, the state Clinton called the model for his welfare strategy in 1997, one-third of workfare employees were below the poverty threshold or at risk of serious injury due to health and safety violations by their new employers. Clinton's promises on welfare evaporated into poverty and forced employment in sweat-shop conditions. The welfare repeal exemplified the strategy of the Clinton administration. The *Minneapolis Star Tribune* claimed: 'Eleven million poor families will lose income as a result of the legislation ... 10 percent of all American families ... It simply ends the federal assurance of help to needy families with children ... The excuse made for President Clinton when he signed the legislation was that he had to do it to win re-election.'[71]

That excuse did not pacify the Hollywood left, as their movies testify. In *Erin Brockovich* (1999), directed by that key figure for independent-minded talent – Steven Soderbergh – the lead character Erin spends 20 minutes searching for employment. One montage of phone calls, newspaper searching and cold calling at offices results in her looking forlorn and downbeat with no employment and a baby on her arm. Erin comes back victorious by the end of the film as a legal clerk who brings down a huge corporate employer. An interesting affirmation of the nature of de-humanising work under Clinton's rule is given by the casting of the real life Erin Brockovich in the role of a largely ignored café waitress. In *American Beauty* (1999) the treatment of the employment and poverty issue is more ironic. The film's main character, Lester Burnham, is fired from his open-plan, clinically white, high-rise office as part of a downsizing activity but exposes the inequity of the situation by blackmailing cash out of a corrupt boss. Later, in a moment symbolic of the degrading situation of Clinton's welfare-to-work policy, Lester ends up working behind a fast-food counter having to force a smile whilst he serves his philandering wife and her wealthy lover. The possibility that being thrown on society's scrap heap drives a person crazy is explored in the subtext of *One Hour Photo* (2002). Here Si, the repressed, lonely photograph processor at the local hypermarket, is laid off and becomes obsessed with the deceitful lifestyle of the comfortably-off middle-class family he used to serve. In *8 Mile* rap star Eminem plays nervous street rapper Rabbit whose family live in a trailer park. Rabbit dreams of escaping to a world of fame and fortune but has to face the tough reality of a choice between his mother's limited welfare lifestyle or equally limited and low-income monotonous factory work in one of Detroit's many car plants. The impression of a growing opposition to Clinton's welfare programme was confirmed when he chose to hide from celebrating its achievements, as the *Washington Post* reported:

> To mark the fourth anniversary of the day he signed welfare reform into law, President Clinton had planned to herald the nation's progress in moving millions of people from dependency to jobs by appearing in Atlanta with an employer committed to hiring welfare recipients. But when the anniversary came yesterday, Clinton was conspicuously absent.
>
> The Department of Health and Human Services yesterday posted a news release and fresh set of statistics on its Web site … [which] shows that the number of Americans receiving assistance continued to decline last year … The rolls have decreased by nearly

half since the start of 1996 ... About two-thirds of recipients in 'work activities' actually held paid jobs [and] earned an average of nearly $7,200 a year, $800 more than in 1998 but still $6,000 below the poverty line for a family of three, the typical size of families on welfare.[72]

In Hollywood progressive activists predicted this possibility before the welfare repeal was enacted and, still believing the movie-generated image of a caring and listening president, sought to persuade Clinton not to pass the bill. Liberal activists were never invited to the White House but still sought to win Clinton's personal support. In 1996 the Hollywood Women's Political Committee helped the Democratic National Committee organise a Hollywood gala. The HWPC had been a significant influence on anti-Reagan artists on the West Coast in the 1980s. It had run workshops, seminars, training and education events, as well as being an information centre about activity and initiating various protests against American policies in Latin America, over women's issues – including the right to abortion that Reagan was utterly opposed to – or the moral assault led by Reagan on progressive cultural products. The HWPC's former director – Marge Tabankin – links the organisation to a number of Hollywood personalities who were later drawn to Bill Clinton's rhetoric.

Tabankin, through a long history as a progressive and pro-Democrat activist, has crossed paths with several personalities. In the 1970s Tabankin was head of VISTA, the domestic wing of the Peace Corps originally dreamt up by President John F. Kennedy in the 1960s and which has mobilised 100,000 volunteers over 30 years to do anti-poverty work. In the 1970s both the Peace Corps and VISTA had high-profile support from Jane Fonda. Indeed, Tabankin joined Fonda in visiting Hanoi in a peace mission during the Vietnam War. Tabankin is a director of the Defenders of Wildlife trust, which has been mentioned by environmentalist Ed Begley Jr as an organisation he supports. For the last 15 years Tabankin has joined actors like Ted Danson on the advisory board of the Liberty Hill Foundation, which was founded on the free speech, anti-discrimination and anti-poverty ideas of journalist Upton Sinclair. The foundation supports initiatives that campaign for social and economic justice, giving out America's perhaps most high-profile award for progressive activists – the annual Upton Sinclair Award. The advisory board vote for the winners and recent years have witnessed actor Mike Farrell win for peace campaigning and Tim Robbins and Susan Sarandon win for being associated with more or less every political campaign on the West

Coast. Over the last few years Tabankin has become particularly associated with Barbra Streisand, heading up the outspoken actress's
philanthropic foundation. Philanthropic is a misleading term, for the
foundation publicly and financially supported left-wing Democrat
Ariana Huffington in the elections for California governor in 2003. In
November 2003 Tabankin became synonymous with a gathering of 300
Hollywood notables at the Beverly Hills Hilton to plot an anti-Bush Jr
strategy for the presidential elections of the following year. This meet-
ing drew in Robert Greenwald – co-founder of Artists United for a Win
Without War – creator of hit sitcom *Seinfeld* Larry David, producer
Paula Weinstein and once again Mike Farrell. So deep does Tabankin's
Hollywood connection go that in June 2004 she was interviewed by
Fort Wayne's *Journal Gazette* as an expert in the relationship between
Democrat presidential hopeful John Kerry and media personalities.

With a phonebook over 30 years old of associates in Hollywood and
a credibility earned through her range of activism, Tabankin could in
1996 persuade celebrities to turn out and perform at the HWPC gala
event for Clinton. The HWPC hoped that organising a gala in a high-
class hotel, complete with music, comedy and speeches, might help
them sway Clinton's opinion on welfare. Tabankin and her Hollywood
friends appealed at the gala to Clinton as he was portrayed on screen,
as a special, honourable individual – exposing the individualism that
is a key trait of liberalism. Once the HWPC had set the event up the
Democratic National Committee increased ticket prices to a minimum
$2,500, charging $25,000 for access to a separate function with Clinton
himself. The Democratic Party made $4 million in one night. However,
Clinton went on to sign the welfare bill. An act that, as Marc Cooper
wrote in *The Nation,* caused an immediate crisis among HWPC supporters and among most Hollywood progressives. They simply learnt
that they could not influence Clinton's policy no matter how organised
and supportive they were. As a result Tabankin wound up the HWPC
within the next 18 months.

Primary Colors is a metaphor for the experience of Hollywood liberals and their organisers, like Tabankin, who supported Clinton. The
narrative backbone of the film is Henry Burton, the grandson of a civil
rights activist, who hopes Jack Stanton will fulfil the dreams of the
frustrated urban black poor. Burton is drawn into Stanton's electoral
campaign but when the campaign is successful Burton is not optimistic
that Stanton will address the concerns of black people. The implicit
conclusion drawn by the film is that the electoral victory has become
the be-all and end-all of American politics in the 1990s. Once elected

there is little that Stanton/Clinton can realistically achieve, and all the progressive rhetoric along the way becomes irrelevant. Or to use the words of Kate McArdle, one of Hollywood's most effective activists in recent times: 'ultimately you're driven by something else other than ideology ... I don't know how you can be a politician and stand by your beliefs.'[73] *Primary Colors* is therefore emblematic of the dangerous capitulation of power that was the premise of Clinton's triangulation, and the damaging practice of progressive activists hanging their hopes of change on one man. The progressive agenda in Hollywood was, in fact, far too complex and significant for any individual to deliver.

Crisis of the progressive agenda

The issues that make up a 'progressive' agenda are diverse and encompass many political/social objectives: Mike Farrell talks of an ethical policy in Central America and of ending the death penalty, Warren Beatty wants 'reproductive freedom' and economic justice, Richard Gere demands that the USA intervene to free Tibet, Tim Robbins and Susan Sarandon demand (among other issues) free access to HIV treatment drugs, John Sayles calls for re-assertion of labour rights and for self-determination for East Timor, Danny Glover appeals for corporate regulation and racial justice, Paul Newman calls for an end to nuclear defence, Annette Benning argues for 'Medicare for all', Jeff Bridges wants an increase in initiatives to tackle domestic child poverty, Joe Pantoliano is for increased access to education, Alec Baldwin fights for electoral campaign finance reform, Woody Harrelson wants an end to the war on drugs and the legalisation of cannabis, Ed Begley Jr is a voice for environmental protection ... and so on. Pinning down the progressive or liberal Hollywood agenda is not easy. What is clear is that on a range of issues, each finding a resonance in this matrix of concerns, Bill Clinton – as Alec Baldwin put it – 'didn't step up to the plate'[74] and deliver change during his presidency. His presidency featured countless Republican-like policies: he outlawed gay marriages, reduced the measures required for states to take welfare recipients off the books, recommended stopping teenage parents getting financial help if they left school, supported lowering capital gains tax, continued to support execution, supported removal of financial assistance to immigrants until their status is agreed – something even muscle-bound Austrian-born action star and affirmed Republican Arnold Schwarzenegger backed away from in his Californian election.

As this list indicates, Bill Clinton's actions ran counter to the range of concerns that made up the Hollywood progressive agenda in the 1990s. More than this, Hollywood progressives could measure Clinton's betrayal in the facts and figures of his presidency – as former Clinton ally Joseph Stiglitz testifies. Stiglitz has travelled from establishment policy-maker to what the *Independent* called a 'heretical economist [who has] ruffled the feathers of the global establishment that once fed him'[75] – mirroring the path of Hollywood liberals. Stiglitz, Nobel Prize winner and former chief economist of the World Bank, was recruited by Clinton to chair his Council of Economic Advisers. Stiglitz summarises the 1990s as a period when the world was shaped in America's image – via trade deals and the World Trade Organisation. He describes several years of political life in the West Wing, explaining that, 'of all the mistakes we made ... the worst were caused by a lack of standing by our principles'.[76]

Stiglitz's attack on the failings of the Clinton administration – in his popular book *The Roaring Nineties* – proves that Hollywood disenfranchisement was typical of a wider crisis of American liberalism. Where Stigltiz responds with a 400-page book, Hollywood responds with *Bulworth*, *Primary Colors* and *Wag the Dog*. Stiglitz's analysis of how the liberal crisis was caused identifies the underlying trends of Clintonian policy. First there was unbridled wealth creation: by March 2000 the value of US stocks was $17 trillion, nearly twice the size of the gross domestic product. This created a 'celebrityhood' for 'a handful of superstar' chief executive officers.[77] Second, there was industry de-regulation: telecommunications companies lobbied for cable TV de-regulation worth $5 billion a year and Clinton obliged. CEOs used de-regulation to make sure 'prices and profits would go up ... each household had no choice of cable provider',[78] creating 'a large electronically disenfranchised population'.[79] Thirdly, Stiglitz lambastes the tax cuts bestowed upon the celebrity rich, 'taxed more lightly than those who earned their bread by the sweat of their brow'.[80] Finally, the refusal to tax meant that 'problems in our air traffic control systems, our bridges, and our roads' were ignored whilst 'we under invested in our inner cities ... [leading to] poor schools ... high crime ... which has led America to be a world leader (for a country of our income) in so many dimensions that we should not be proud, such as one of the highest prison populations in the Western world as well as the highest infant mortality rates'.[81]

The venom in Stiglitz's description of Clinton's policy is sympto-
matic of the liberal malaise. Stiglitz describes how his contemporary
progressives were fooled by the liberal rhetoric that shrouded the third
way. Simultaneously he veers between pessimism in the face of globalisation and sceptical optimism encouraged by anti-globalisation
protesters. He also remains fooled by the Clinton image, always speaking highly of Bill the man as opposed to Clinton the politician. It is
important not to dismiss the global dimension of Stiglitz's criticism.
Stiglitz describes how the fall of the Soviet bloc allowed the USA to
dominate global trade. The effect of US-style corporate expansion, cuts
in spending for the poor, de-regulation and privatisation led to, for
example, a 40 per cent reduction in GDP in Russia by 1999 and a 10-
fold increase in poverty. Stiglitz concluded, 'if globalisation was benefiting everybody and making everybody's lives better off, many
seemed not to know it ... we bullied other nations into doing things
our way ... [to] help our businesses ...'.[82]

Take the North American Free Trade Agreement as an example.
This treaty was signed by America, Canada and Mexico in 1995. It was
the result of a process of negotiation, led by Clinton, to forge a set of
trade protocols that could be enacted at the behest of American corporations. A year after being signed just 535 jobs had been created and
12,000 lost. Environmental matters were worsening; in Cuidad Juárez
(an industrial city in Mexico) factories produced 55 million tons of raw
sewage daily.[83] Ninety per cent of Mexicans in *colonais* (slums) had
hepatitis by the age of 35.[84] A Department of Labor ruling found conditions in US-owned factories in Mexico to be atrocious. There is not
room here to explore the full effect of NAFTA or other such treaties.
What is clear from this brief example is that globalisation meant poverty in the pursuit of US profit. Stiglitz – like organisations involved
with the anti-globalisation movement such as ATTAC, Drop the Debt,
Indymedia, National Labor Committee, Sierra Club, the Zapatistas –
points to a round of international governmental discussions in the mid
1990s (called the Uruguay Round) and the inauguration of the World
Trade Organisation as key markers in the development of global institutions of capital, and in the awareness of globalisation at a grass roots
level. Above all things Stiglitz has been forced, by checking off the
scorecard of the Clintonian presidency, into bitter acceptance that his
progressive agenda was failed. Some evidence of this bitterness in Hollywood came when Clinton stood aside for Al Gore and Joe Lieberman
in 2000/1.

Hollywood reacted badly to Lieberman and Gore's initial announcement that they would run for the White House. Gore (via wife Tipper's censorship drive) and Lieberman (via his assault on Clinton's affair with Lewinsky and attacks on movie morality) were less Hollywood-friendly than Clinton. However, both had been present at Hollywood fundraisers and met and worked with executives prior to Clinton's departure from the White House. In 2000, writer Joe Eszterhas, who said 'politics is a movie' with Clinton 'the first rock 'n' roll movie star' and who helped produce Clinton promotional events, suddenly turned on Lieberman. A full-page advert in *Variety* attacked Lieberman for restricting creative freedom. Lieberman and Gore were forced to 'mend fences with the ... entertainment industry' – Al even dragging old room-mate Tommy Lee Jones out to parade with him. Lieberman, counter to previous speeches, found himself proclaiming in September 2000: 'we will nudge you, but never censor'. The Gore/Lieberman situation was a marked departure from the fraternal relations Hollywood liberals held with Clinton.[85] Although Clinton himself arrived in Hollywood in late 2000 to help Gore fundraise, the frosty Gore/Lieberman–Hollywood relationship continued and its very public existence was emblematic of the disillusion with the Democrats that was growing in Hollywood. Equally emblematic were the presidential films of Oliver Stone; a metaphor for progressive Hollywood's view of the White House during the 1990s.

JFK (1991) and *Nixon* (1995) expose Hollywood's changing view of the presidency during the Clinton period, suggesting that disillusion began around the start of the second term. In *JFK* there is a sense of re-capturing American politics' golden moment – the capture being carried out by two especially idealistic and intellectually brilliant men (Kennedy and Special Investigator Garrison) prepared to challenge what Stone had once called the military-industrial machine. The film, like liberalism itself, was nostalgic for a better past but prepared to indulge in the idea that a heroic crusader could turn back the clock and through his own sheer brilliance change the present – read Clinton and his impending election. In *Nixon* Stone has retreated into pessimism and fatalism – the flip side of liberalism's nostalgic idealism. Nixon, whose portrayal is surprisingly sympathetic, is completely bound to the military-industrial complex by virtue of his social position – by virtue of being the president. Where Kennedy/Garrison are somehow 'pure', Nixon is a 'guilty' man. As 'myths' for contemporary America, these two films neatly summarise the transition in sentiment for Clinton among Hollywood liberals. This was a transition that began in

wider American society the day after Clinton forced through an early
NAFTA agreement in Congress in November 1993: the day that Jesse
Jackson, Ralph Nader, union leaders, environmentalists and disgruntled Democrats met to discuss (but not yet act on) their wish to form a
new, more progressive political party.

Ten years later protagonists of left politics in Hollywood claim an
early twenty-first-century burgeoning of progressive ideology. Ed
Asner observes that today 'there are more of us in what we call the
"industry" who are open to ideas and actions that are left-leaning than
in the past'.[86] Haskell Wexler suggests that, 'more people are questioning the status-quo',[87] whilst his friend and documentary maker Saul
Landau picks out a particular indicator of how the openness to left
ideas in Hollywood is reflected more widely in American society. He
argues that, 'the sales of Michael Moore's books prove an audience
now exists'.[88]

Moore's books, *Stupid White Men* and *Dude, Where's My Country?*,[89]
have indeed sold in the hundreds of millions, whilst his film *Bowling
for Columbine* was the most successful documentary at the box office in
25 years. His popularity is due to, not in spite of, his voluntary role as
the undisputed megaphone of dissent in the USA. Popularity does not
equal universal agreement but it does suggest that Moore is a credible
source of reference. Particularly useful is his definition of the type of
American who might be drawn to the new, never actually formed,
party discussed above. These Americans would be 'liberated, free
thinking … abhor guns … strongly believe in equal rights for women
… take personal responsibility [to] cut down on pollution and waste …
live together and don't get married … members of the liberal party, or
worse, independents'.[90]

The terms 'progressive', 'liberal' and 'radical' will always be dis-
puted. Using an impressive array of statistics Moore paints a picture of
a broad socially progressive, left majority in contemporary America. In
the gap between the mid 1990s crisis of liberalism and the physical
manifestation of this progressive constituency (at the 2003 anti-war
protests) there was the anti-globalisation movement, with its heightened consciousness of domestic and global politics. A similar arc of
political development took place among progressives in Hollywood,
moving from traditional idealistic liberalism, through crisis, through
anti-capitalism (understood in Hollywood as anti-corporatism), to
connection with a broader American left.

However, even this useful formula can be misleading – political re-
alignment in Hollywood has not happened all at once. Traditional lib-

erals (Alec Baldwin), post-crisis liberals (Robert Greenwald) and broad left activists (Tim Robbins) co-exist. So when Ed Asner calls for 'progressives to be proud of taking the label', he is talking about a broad left-wing consensus fused into being from the crisis of liberalism and development of anti-globalisation. That fusing has not always been a smooth or comfortable process. For some key individuals, like Warren Beatty for example, it has been a rocky road leading to depressing and fatalistic outcomes; a road upon which he has nevertheless erected signposts which have helped future Hollywood progressives find a clearer path than his own – perhaps the brightest of these signs was *Bulworth*.

Old heroes – Warren Beatty

Senator Jay Billington Bulworth (CA), played by Warren Beatty in *Bulworth*, is a charming politician working to the Clinton model. Bulworth deals with insurance corporations, courts affection from Hollywood, gambles on the stock market and hires underworld characters to do 'weekend research projects'. Days before re-election, in his darkened office with a storm raging outside, Bulworth is confronted by a montage of campaign soundbites: 'fight to abolish unnecessary affirmative action', 'welfare systems out of control', 'I like people who live by the rules and work hard'. The soundbites represent the Clinton policy programme of 1996, and so awful is it that Bulworth is driven to tears and even to authorise a hit on his own life. From this opening, the film's surreal narrative, symbolic aesthetics and witty comedy expose what film theorist Dana Polan has called the 'confusions [created by] the unavoidable conditions not only of a man and his cinema but of a whole way of conceiving politics and change at the end of the twentieth century'.[91]

The confusions are represented in *Bulworth* as a cross between epiphany and emotional breakdown, caused by realisation that the politics he supports are damaging the agenda he once dreamed of. The storm outside the office window is a metaphor for the one inside Bulworth's, and indeed Beatty's, heart. Beatty's ambition for the film was to expose what was really going on in his old pal Clinton's America: 'the underbelly of this country isn't being heard. They don't have the means of being heard, and the disparity of wealth does not decrease, it increases. My beliefs – even though I am a pampered, rich, Hollywood cultural plutocrat – my leanings are to articulate something on behalf of those people.'[92]

This 'underbelly' is indeed apparent in *Bulworth*, represented starkly in Beatty's stylistic and narrative choices. Disaffected South Central citizens pack out a gospel church and demand the money Clinton promised for inner-city re-generation after the 1992 riots. In an urban landscape of deep-cast shadows, where it always seems to be the thick of night, children are assaulted/racially abused by police, an extended family squeeze around the dinner table and gangster L.D. calls in loans while recruiting youths to crime because 'there ain't no jobs'. This darkness is complemented by a sense of chaos: hand-held camera; the same homeless philosopher on every corner; random narrative (like sudden stop-offs to buy fried chicken); multitudinous subplots (insurance executive, philandering wife, hit-woman, etc). This is the modern world that outmoded Hollywood liberalism struggled to cope with in the 1990s, generating nostalgia for a past era when Henry Fonda could gradually win justice and 'suggesting [Bulworth] is living in situations that surpass him, that are beyond his control'.[93]

Senator Bulworth is a metaphor for the Hollywood liberal. Beatty has said, 'I'll always be a Democrat'.[94] A personal friend of Clinton in the 1980s, Beatty remained a FOB throughout the 1990s. When Beatty created *Bonnie and Clyde* in the late 1960s he showed how a driven liberal could make an impact. He was a shining example of individual success as producer, star and co-writer. So significant a symbol of liberal endeavour was Beatty that he opened a Hollywood fundraiser for Clinton in 1991. By 1999 Beatty had become symbolic of the new mood of Hollywood liberals, saying: 'I don't see enormous passion from the creative community for the Democratic Party'.[95] If there is any doubt that Senator Bulworth is symbolic of the Hollywood liberal then his visit to wealthy Hollywood capitalists gives proof. In the Beverly Hills mansion – complete with security gates, valet parking, a fountain and exclusive artwork – Bulworth, now in full rebellious flow, lambastes the poor quality of franchise-focused Hollywood. This scene creates a sense of immediacy, of sudden comprehension of corporate power. The sensation of the scene is reactive; created by jumpy camera work and quick editing. The spectator is 'in the moment' of Senator Bulworth's crisis. Beatty and other Hollywood liberals, who were suckered by the abstract ideals in Clinton's rhetoric before they checked the practice of his governance, experienced that same crisis.

In *Bulworth* Beatty creates a charismatic liberal who has become fatalistic, saying 'these days no chance of getting anything changed'.

As Bulworth's would-be assassin – Nina – explains, the restructuring of the American economy (globalisation) has outmoded old styles of leadership. This fatalism is generalised in Bulworth's gang of buddies, who are inept without his guidance. The buddies' connection to Bulworth is not political – one describes how his commitment is based on personal loyalty. When Bulworth runs out on the election campaign the buddies become desperate, but when they find him in a bizarre mental state they still shove him in front of television cameras and audiences. The undeniable implication is that Bulworth's buddies cannot succeed or survive without him. Moreover, the use of iconography and symbolism in *Bulworth* strongly suggest its meanings are meant to apply outside the fiction. The American flag, for example, appears at crucial moments and at one point Bulworth is silhouetted against it as if his diatribe against corporate power casts a shadow over the whole nation. This fatalism is played out in the final sequence of the film. By then Senator Bulworth has rapped on national television, in sunglasses and shorts, against the American political system's marriage with globalisation:

> … they speak for the rich 20 per cent when they be pretending they defending the meek …
> … the Democratic party's got some shit to pay …
> … Corporations got the networks and they get to say who gets to talk …
> … We got Americans who can't get their family a meal,
> Ask a black fella who's been downsized if he's gettin a deal,
> Or a white guy working into a grave,
> You ain't gotta be black to live like a slave,
> Rich people have always stayed on top.

Bulworth has publicly denounced the insurance corporations for getting cheap labour in Mexico, for paying US workers the same as they pay peasants in Peru. He goes so far as to say 'Bill's just getting all weepy' and doing nothing to solve the situation. Finally, his maverick breakdown over, Bulworth puts his suit back on and walks off with Nina, who is now to be a more truthful lover than his adulterous wife. The spectator is fooled into believing you can stand up for principles and be a politician, until a shot fells Bulworth, a shot from the dark rooftop where an insurance executive stood just moments before. *Bulworth* ends with the corporations literally killing off their opposition and the conclusion is that there is nothing the old liberals like Beatty can do.

The narrative of the film focuses on Bulworth's journey, avoiding digression into the workings of the politician's team. In *Wag the Dog* a special aide to the president recruits a movie producer to manufacture a war on television. The focus of this film is systemic rather than individual. Collective meetings of officials are held in the White House/ Pentagon, several protagonists are drawn into the charade of 'producing' the war, soldiers are recruited to lie, musicians are drawn in to write pretend old songs, and all the while the special aide has command of a cacophony of governmental resources and people. The whole film is about process: process of television production, process of government cover-up, process of 'democracy'. The comparison with *Bulworth's* narrative focus on the individual is stark, although the theme of infidelity is present in both films, as it was in Clinton's presidency. *Bulworth*, unlike *Wag the Dog*, is constructed from the traditional liberal perspective and is therefore both individualistic and fatalistic. Clinton the special individual failed his buddies, was not honourable or trustworthy and did not turn back the clock to deliver justice as if it were the apparent golden age of liberalism. Clinton did grapple with the neo-liberal, modern world and succumbed to it, or worse, willingly promoted it. Bulworth's inability to change, to adapt, to make a difference in the face of globalisation, is, therefore, much more a parallel for the traditional liberal in Hollywood than it is for Clinton. Senator Bulworth is what liberals would have liked Clinton to be, and what they felt themselves to have become, a failed liberal hero.

Using Polan's analysis, Bulworth's crisis and the crisis of Hollywood liberalism post-Clinton stem from the same logic. Both start from the individual politician as a charismatic vehicle for change (Bulworth and Clinton). The HWPC, for example, hoped to be one of Clinton's buddies. Both find the charismatic politician fatally flawed (Clinton's welfare bill, Bulworth's insurance company deals). It can be suggested that liberalism misreads its own history. These 1980s activists also focused on an individual in their opposition to Reagan, but they challenged him through collective action. The demise of liberalism in the late 1990s saw Beatty, so emblematic of the liberal crisis, wrestle dramatically with individual and collective responses to social situations. Two examples give ample evidence. The first is Warren Beatty's refusal to support a protest at Elia Kazan's award of an Oscar in 1999. Beatty avoided confrontation with those who stuck to the principle of not recognising someone who had given names to the McCarthy-led House Un-American Activities Committee hearings in the 1950s. Beatty entered the Oscars through the back door and stood

to clap the man he later described as his 'old friend' – thus putting personal loyalty to an old buddy ahead of collective action and principle.
The second example is from 2001, when Beatty co-launched with his
wife Annette Benning the Progressive Majority organisation with its
agenda of free education, healthcare and economic justice. This was a
clear attempt to 'hone down what being progressive means' in a time
when 'the Democratic party is so confused' about how to win real
change.[96] The attendance of several familiar celebrity faces and a
number of Democratic senators and other notables ensured that this
was Beatty's last serious attempt to interject into politics. By then, however, the tide of anti-globalisation and the re-constituted left, identified
by Michael Moore, had already stolen the 'majority'. In Hollywood
new filmmakers were taking Beatty's progressive mantle with the
father of the independent revival in the early 1990s, Steven Soderbergh, at their head.

New heroes – re-inventing the liberal tradition

Actor and heart-throb George Clooney has begun to move into production in the last half decade. He has done so in partnership, via the
Section 8 production company, with his friend and confidant Steven
Soderbergh. Between them they have made explicit a decision to pursue a certain kind of film project that has nothing to do with
blockbuster, corporate Hollywood profit making. Soderbergh suggests
that 'George's [and my] thing is, "I don't need any more money; what
I want is a legacy of movies I can look back on and feel good about"'.[97]
If Warren Beatty's political principles were easily overridden by his
personal, individual motivation when applauding friend Elia Kazan's
Oscar award in 1999, then the same personal approach to making films
about political subjects can be extracted from Soderbergh's comments.
Soderbergh's sentiment echoes the artistic, auteurist rationale
espoused by the late 1960s New Hollywood generation from which
Warren Beatty emerged. Films are personal products of directors and
their allies, and in this sense when Soderbergh talks about 'sneaking
something under the [Hollywood] wire' he means he is producing *his*
film, to *his* rules and that he must do so with cunning so that *his* vision
is not corrupted by the corporate system. This turns the filmmaker into
the hero of his own narrative – a special individual who refuses, as
Soderbergh puts it, to produce 'dumb movies that make a lot of

money'.[98] Much like Beatty, then, the directors who took over his mantle in Hollywood were liberal individualists, something reflected in
both the auteurist status given to their films and the treatment of the
central characters within their work.

For example, much was made of the fact that *American Beauty*'s
director – Sam Mendes – was British, implying the film had an objec-
tive view of American life. Actor Kevin Spacey, who was the lead in
the film, told an ABC journalist on the red carpet outside the Oscars in
2000 that Mendes had 'brought over with him [from the UK] a unique
vision and talent'. The implication is that only Mendes could have
made this film. *American Beauty* has the credit: 'A Sam Mendes Film',
which has a somewhat different flavour to a 'directed by' credit. The
former suggests that the whole package, almost from mechanical production of the film stock to projection in the cinema, was planned and
delivered by Mendes. This auteurist status is highly flattering, especially considering this was Mendes's first Hollywood film and that he
had only a track record in London theatre beforehand. Mendes's credibility as an individual talent was further bolstered after the release of
Road to Perdition (2002), about which David Denby wrote in the *New
Yorker* 'a solemnly beautiful art concept' and Jonathan Ross in the *Daily
Mirror* 'a consummate work of movie-making art'. By now Mendes
had made two films exploring the shape of American society and the
place of values and ideals within it, the first set in a repressed and
deceitful present-day suburbia and the second in a dark pre-war world
run by mobsters and their paid-off state officials.

Both films feature families in which husbands and wives lie to each
other to maintain the pretence of happiness. Both films see these families torn apart by the pressures of an American society run by corrupt
hoodlums or businesses. In both films parents and their children
attempt to re-connect, there are uncomfortable silences or confronta-
tions at the dinner table and both fathers (Kevin Spacey in *American
Beauty* and Tom Hanks in *Road to Perdition*) take paths outside the conventional parental role in an attempt to undo the pressures placed
upon their familial relationships by the outside world. Money – lack of
or corruption concerning – is a major element of both films. In *American
Beauty* lead character Lester is laid off from work, which begins his
journey of personal discovery and regression to adolescent behaviour.
In *Road to Perdition* Mike Sullivan is a debt collector whose son inad-
vertently witnesses a crime, a moment that sets Mike off on a mission
to either kill his bosses or to escape from the lifestyle of avaricious murder he's become accustomed to. Underlying the character journeys of

the central protagonists in both films is an abstract liberal value that Warren Beatty adhered to in his filmmaking and which led him to ignore his principles and support Elia Kazan. That value is loyalty, and it is loyalty to family – especially to children – that makes both Lester and Mike sympathetic characters. Lester could betray his daughter by sleeping with her schoolmate but does not. Mike could hand over his son to the gangland boss John Rooney – played by veteran of anti-nuclear arms protests Paul Newman – but does not, choosing to risk his own life ahead of his child's. Repeating the fatalistic tendencies that underline *Bulworth*, both fathers' adherence to liberal ideals in Mendes's films result in their murder in the final act – just as Bulworth's pursuit of truth results in his murder.

What this demonstrates is that, far from being utterly unique visions as Kevin Spacey implies, Mendes's films are a continuation of the liberal tradition that began with heroes confidently pursuing their ideals in the post-Second World War era and that finished up with heroes being punished for their idealism in the late twentieth century. This analysis does not degrade the artistic merit that some journalists perceive Mendes to have earned by making these films; it simply puts into perspective the question of the new liberal director as an auteur with a special individual artistic vision. So when Steven Soderbergh suggests that each film he makes expresses a 'side to my personality',[99] his comment must be understood in the context of his historical situation, in the context of his place in the liberal Hollywood tradition. In fact Soderbergh himself undermines the view that he and Mendes are unique directorial visionaries.

When talking about his film that studies the drug culture in American society and the government's contradictory attempts to tackle the drug issue – *Traffic* (2000) – Soderbergh reveals that he recognises his work can be part of an ongoing political discourse: 'If we've done our job properly everybody will be pissed off … It would be great if everybody came away thinking we took the other side's point of view.'[100] This quote is fascinating because unlike Spacey's remarks about Mendes, Soderbergh is attempting to marry an individualistic approach – taking a controversial position within the film – with a role as a reflector of society's problems. Soderbergh wants to make the film a personal statement that says that he is an individual and doesn't bend to this or that lobby. Like Beatty, he expresses his liberalism through a personal individualism. Yet at the same time, like Mendes's work, his film is related to real social issues and he has a 'job' to do in representing those on screen. The implicit contradiction in

Soderbergh's quote is that he cannot divorce his individual position from the social position of his work. In other words, Soderbergh's perception of the individual's relationship with society is more sophisticated than Beatty's was. A reflection of this is found in the heroes of Soderbergh's films, who are undoubtedly talented individuals but whose idealism is metered by the social situation that they grapple with. Unlike Senator Bulworth, Soderbergh's heroes must pursue their ideals on a pragmatic and realistic basis.

When Soderbergh and Clooney describe what feeling good about a movie means, they talk of making films that are about something. Indeed, even in their biggest joint box-office success, *Ocean's 11*, Soderbergh and Clooney made references to the corruption of present-day Las Vegas. Furthermore, Soderbergh's Oscar winners in the 1990s – *Erin Brockovich* and *Traffic* – were set in contemporary locations and explored social issues (corporate corruption, drug abuse), utilising a faux-documentary style that gives them a veneer of authenticity. Soderbergh – emblematic of the new liberal generation – has no interest in all the action, all special effects and confused themes of *Matrix*-style comic books and every interest in creating a legacy of socially relevant movies much as traditional liberals have done, but with significant differences. Warren Beatty's films were largely individual acts – witness the personal fight with Jack Warner over *Bonnie and Clyde* or use of 'I' when describing *Bulworth*.[101] Indeed, Beatty is famed for his ability to create space for a film in corporate production schedules with the power of persuasion alone. Whilst Beatty denies his reputation in public, many producers avoid him because he is notoriously good at finding a way to get his own ideas on the screen. In the case of *Bulworth* Beatty waited until Fox executive Barry Diller left the company, then quickly called Diller's replacement reminding him to schedule a date for shooting the film. Diller had never signed any paperwork and had held a single conversation about *Bulworth* with Beatty. Yet, as *Variety* editor Peter Bart suggested in his book *Shoot Out* – written with Mandalay executive Peter Guber – Beatty's speed of thought and action ensured the film got made right under the nose of Fox's parent company News Corporation. News Corporation's CEO Rupert Murdoch was, according to Bart and Guber, highly displeased that such an anti-corporate film was released and blamed Diller.

Soderbergh's filmmaking conversely is collaborative, as the lighting director on *Erin Brockovich* explains: 'his real signature is that he brings out the best in all his collaborators'.[102] Soderbergh describes the enjoyment of working with actors and writers, his wonder at the diversity of jobs on a film set and his feeling of being involved in a social enterprise. George Clooney likewise is famed for his collaborative, even democratic, approach on set. Wolfgang Peterson, who directed the Clooney action vehicle about a fatal commercial fishing expedition – *The Perfect Storm* (1999) – describes how Clooney is the only person he's worked with to know every crew member by their first name, and to have set up basketball tournaments involving actors and kitchen staff on equal terms. Having taken the role of doctor Doug Ross in the Steven Spielberg produced, Warner Television-owned drama *ER* in the late 1990s, Clooney refused to go to work unless Warner did away with two-tier dining arrangements on their Burbank lot. Clooney was successful, creating an environment where television and movie stars would eat next to grips and runners for the first time in the history of the company. Yet, at the same time, Clooney aggressively pursues individual success.

He hassled both *ER* producer John Wells to give him the Ross part and *Three Kings* (1999) director David O. Russell to let him play Major Archie Gates in the Iraq war heist movie. Clooney, by his own admission, then came to the point of butting heads with Russell on set because he didn't like his physical directorial approach. According to Clooney, Russell shouted 'you want to hit me – hit me, you pussy!' and the actor obliged, later writing a stern letter to the film's producers that forced a change in Russell's style. That's not to suggest that Clooney is a brute. Peterson describes him as a 'really friendly guy' who bought the entire crew and all local people hanging around the set of *The Perfect Storm* regular meals and drinks. However, Clooney nurtures the collaborative set at least in part to help develop his own ambitions. His fraternity with colleagues on *The Perfect Storm* – which features Clooney as the captain of a rag-tag, blue-collar crew who sail to their death in some massive special effects – allowed Clooney to recruit his own co-star, Mark Wahlberg, and change sections of the script. Clooney has married collaborative working with individual tenacity because, in his own words, he doesn't want to ask in years to come 'what's my legacy?'[103] He wants to be remembered as a real talent in his own right. Soderbergh and Clooney's sense of a creative individual who is dependent on complex social relationships is a development from the traditional liberal perspective, where the director was a special man making history. This mentality is reflected in Soderbergh's films.

Conversely, *Erin Brockovich* is part of history, not its architect. Erin differs from predecessors in *Bulworth* or *JFK* in two respects: first, she is less romantic and idealistic; second, she does things most spectators could do if they had the resolve. Erin does not believe in abstract values like love or truth: she rejects her potential lover because she is cynical about his intentions. Even when she does accept the biker-next-door into her family, a barbed, short speech makes certain he is prepared to work around the practicalities of her single-parenthood. In this way Erin's choices evaporate romanticism, in stark contrast to Bulworth's decision to follow his heart and pursue a woman outside his social circle who has just tried to kill him. Erin is a real person, whose choices are directed by her social context. This less abstract hero is consistent with the changing shape of progressive Hollywood in the late 1990s: Clinton's presidency had tainted belief in the purity of special individuals (it is worth noting that neither Clooney nor Soderbergh chose to be Friends of Bill); and the effects of globalisation re-established poverty as an unavoidable feature of everyday life.

However, this insistence on making the hero unromantic and her actions in keeping with everyday reality does not prevent Soderbergh incorporating other traditional liberal hallmarks. Erin forms a gang of buddies based on loyalty to her cause and trust in her resolve, which draws in lawyer Ed Masry, his staff and the town of Hinckley. Her place in the narrative and mise-en-scène make Erin stand out. Her clothing (garish at the start, more homely later) is often brighter than other characters, her dialogue wittier ('I don't need some lady in bad shoes to tell me what I should do'), and her intelligence changes situations (exposing the corporate lawyers by making them think they're drinking toxic water). These aspects mark Erin out as a liberal hero, but again a modified one. Erin's special individual traits are ones most spectators could develop. Her clothing and wit are refined everyday qualities and Julia Roberts's performance imbues her with one other defining feature – resolve.

The final piece of Soderbergh's heroic jigsaw is society. What he does that Beatty does not is to remind the spectator consistently that society is a player in the narrative. Courts, lawyers, childminders, etc. influence Erin's quest, and she wouldn't even end up working at Masry's law firm if she had not been dealing with the justice system herself. What Soderbergh does, which follows Beatty's lead, is to ensure Erin's personal choices navigate the narrative for the spectator. So we see Erin's decision to take on the corporation polluting Hinckley, rather than the decision of the actual victims in the town. In this way society's influence is asserted but an individual dominates our interpretation of that society. Soderbergh simultaneously breaks with and continues the liberal aesthetic, justifying the need for the definition 'new liberal'.

AntiTRUST and *Any Given Sunday* prove that Soderbergh is not the only exponent of a new liberal model. In *AntiTRUST*, hero Milo uses technical expertise to expose a corrupt software company (NURV). Milo's narrative journey is concerned with a particularly Clintonian conundrum – can you trust those who say they're on your side? In particular, Milo's fiancée claims to be loyal but betrays him, and his boss at NURV oozes enthusiasm but is a profit-hungry autocrat. As it is those closest that betray him, Milo's belief in the abstract ideal of loyalty becomes irrelevant and, as with Erin, personal resolve determines Milo's heroism. Also, there is an apparently authentic social set up in *AntiTRUST*. Milo starts off working in a suburban garage; we see him as a student; we see the whole structure of NURV, the boss, departmental heads, security, cleaner; there are recognisable police officers and government officials; there are rival businesses. This is a real world complete with a seedy violent underbelly. Moreover, Milo is often dressed in neutral clothing, wears clunky glasses and is fairly typical of the other programmers employed by NURV. The only thing that makes him stand out is a code he invented when a student. The implication is that if we had the same university training, we too might end up like Milo.

Any Given Sunday's Tony d'Amato is confronted with leaders who may not be trustworthy – new shareholders who take control of the American football team he has long and successfully coached. The new owners have a commercial sensibility and Tony has to decide how to respond to enforced changes. The film is explicit in representing social relations between Tony, bosses, sponsors, lawyers and the athletes: arguments over the direction of the club and day-to-day decisions are depicted; Tony ruminates on his new lack of control; players discuss who is really in charge; players' lifestyles are contrasted with the exorbitance of the owners'; paid legal hacks cancel what Tony has moments earlier organised. One narrative strand is an argument over the decision to play an injured player at immense physical risk – an argument the board wins. Tony has a reputation as a great tactician and coach but he has real emotions that are laid bare in the less overplayed moments of Al Pacino's performance. Tony does not take outlandish action and even walks away from battles that an idealist would take on. He plays a waiting game so he can leave the club on his own terms. It is determination, not abstract idealism, which makes him heroic.

Any Given Sunday is an Oliver Stone film – he even appears in it as a TV commentator – and, like *JFK*, it focuses largely on personal relationships, the football team echoing Garrison's gang of buddies. However, Tony's gang is built on the legacy of his success, not on the abstract ideal of loyalty, so when his bosses degrade him some of his gang desert. This demonstrates that Stone, always quick to adopt new trends, had perceived and implemented the new liberal perspective by the late 1990s. This is further evidenced by the fact that *Any Given Sunday* is essentially an anti-corporate film; Tony is nostalgic for a time when football was played for enjoyment, not to pay shareholders; he holds up the idea of fan-owned clubs as a way forward. An even more significant marker is that Tony – like Milo and Erin – wins against the corporations. Where Bulworth or Garrison were abstract heroes, obsessed with failed ideals and beaten by corporate interests, Tony, Milo and Erin are everyday people with determination that corporations cannot break. As characters they represent a general anti-globalisation trend in Hollywood, which during the transition from the twentieth to the twenty-first century pitted anti-corporate heroes against the corporatisation of society. This is the new liberal aesthetic that we can observe at work in present day Hollywood.

The new liberal aesthetic – the individual in society

Globalisation is in essence an inequitable relationship between the haves and the have-nots, between rich and poor – the corporate owner and the working masses. For example, the pitiful wages paid in American-owned factories in Mexico, or welfare-to-work programmes that sent urban workers in the USA to make profits for corporations at minimal expense. As Bill Clinton's midwifery of globalisation was a key generator of the 1990s liberal crisis in Hollywood, the significance of social class to the emergence of new-liberal and more radical anti-globalisation filmmakers cannot be dismissed. Why the word 'class' itself has been little used by old liberals or re-invented liberals is explained by Ed Asner when he talks of the residual fear in Hollywood of being accused of 'being a commie'.[104] The use of the word 'class', associated with the work of Karl Marx, might well lead to such an accusation. Nevertheless, when Warren Beatty talks of the 'underbelly' of America and has Senator Bulworth rap about the unity of white and black people as 'slaves' to poverty wages, this is a clear indication of the significance of a class analysis to his late 1990s anti-corporate mentality.

This mentality was taken forward by the late 1990s generation of Hollywood progressives. So when new-liberal Curtis Hanson situates Eminem in a trailer park in *8 Mile*, it is a clear statement about the sympathies of the director and the roots of the central character: in a working-class home. Likewise it is clear exposition of class when Tim Robbins juxtaposes striking steel-workers to a fascist fraternal steel baron in his historical almost-true story of a banned Federal Theatre Project play in the 1930s, *Cradle Will Rock*. In either case it is clear that the anti-corporatism growing in late 1990s Hollywood was paralleled with the kind of on-screen compassion for people squeezed by the pressures of a class-based society that George Clooney had demanded from the American mass media after the 1992 LA riots.

Social critiques in the 1980s had tended to use middle-class subjects as a route into political discourse. The journalists at the centre of Oliver Stone's attack on American foreign policy in Central America, *Salvador*, were not born into poverty and war but *chose* to leave their luxury hotel and dinners with ambassadors to talk to guerrilla soldiers. Likewise, in Stone's *Wall Street* the central figure is Bud whose working-class background – symbolised by his blue-collar dad – is a mere memory that haunts his high-pressure, high-rolling market trader existence. Then in the early 1990s the socially conscious Black New Wave sought to invent aesthetic and thematic methods of presenting urban poverty to a mass audience. *Do the Right Thing* and *Boyz 'N the Hood* showed the city block, its dress, music, drugs, struggle for money and social tensions. After the 1992 LA riots, movie corporations sidelined such visions of lower-class life, so filmmakers frustrated by Bill Clinton's betrayals in the mid 1990s produced political satires like *Wag the Dog* or *Primary Colors*. However, it can be observed that globalisation and the widespread consciousness of its foreign and domestic effects, generated by the anti-capitalist movement, saw the return of protagonists socially rooted in a complete social matrix in late 1990s Hollywood film.

American Beauty's narrative, for example, answers every question about protagonist Lester's existence: we see where he works (his exchange with his boss explains what his work entails); we see him in different settings with his wife (letting us know the nature of their relationship); we see his children's school (showing his inadequacies in a wider social circle); we see him masturbate (an insight into privacy and intimacy in his world); we see the interior of neighbours' houses (exploring subtle differences between Lester and his community); Lester uses every part of his house (all aspects of his home life are represented). The social whole is so important in *American Beauty* that the film opens with a lengthy aerial shot moving over Lester's suburb. Furthermore every new locale is greeted with a mid-distance establishing shot, ensuring the spectator has an overview of the social set-up. At the same time Lester is often given more space in the frame than other characters, and in some sequences (notably his visit to the school) the lighting of other characters is dimmed. The total effect of such decisions is to generate a social whole and to make Lester stand out within it.

Something is happening here similar to what Marxist theorist George Luckas suggests takes place in nineteenth-century novels. He argues that here heroes are typical individuals in a contradictory historical context: 'the individual life, caught up in and responsive to such forces, demonstrate[s] how the particular is always mediated by the whole'.[105] The 'whole' was a web of social relationships constructed by the novel's author, and the 'particular' referred to the actions of the protagonist. Though this theory seems particularly relevant to those who agree with the idea of the film director as auteur, it can nevertheless be applied to many late 1990s socially conscious films. Lester's rebellion in *American Beauty* would be less affecting if the fiction of the film was not familiar – what investment do we have with Lester's journey if we cannot recognise his social world? If we can accept that the new liberal film is creating a recognisable social whole, then what is it that mediates between the whole and the protagonist?

Steven Soderbergh's *Erin Brockovich* demonstrates how social class defines the relationship of the individual to the society represented in new liberal film. A swift sequence early in the film jump cuts through an array of shots of Erin in different clothing, in different rooms of her apartment, at different times of day, with her child and without. In each shot another symbolic image is employed: Erin circles adverts in a newspaper, she calls an agency, she is rejected, she looks on forlornly. In less than a minute, through montage, the film references the experience of fruitless job searches familiar to any person at the wrong end of society. The narrative of the film carries Erin to court, to a childminder, into arguing with (then enjoying the company of) her neighbour, to eventual employment, to the homes of clients; in short, to every important locale that contributes to her story and to her social status. Following on from the job search sequence, we are left in no doubt that Erin travels her journey with the baggage of being poor, unemployed and part of the working class. A series of stylistic choices also help to situate Erin in the working class.

She drives a battered car down streets with smart, shiny automobiles in the background. Erin's clothes are plastic not leather, high heels not Prada shoes, bright red lipstick, dyed hair and long nails: street wear and not office etiquette. None of this is allowed to demean Erin. It accentuates her difference from the middle-class world of the law firm where she finds employment. Later Erin wears more appropriate clothes for legal meetings. Yet she is still distinguished from those around her in some way – a bright yellow cardigan, for example, worn when she meets citizens of Hinckley, who are dressed more mundanely. Using these tools of setting, clothing, narrative and editing, Erin is made to appear both connected to a social whole and, in a less obvious manner, a special or 'particular' part of it.

This demonstrates how the liberal individualism of the Soderbergh generation had moved on from Warren Beatty's fatalism. Senator Bulworth was a charismatic man apart from society, crashing on the rocks of a neo-liberalist reality. Erin is part of society and both aesthetically and dramatically displays the special qualities needed to avoid the rocks. After the down-in-the-mouth, dimly lit moment at the end of the failed job search, Erin becomes pushy, direct, determined and clear-headed. Changed from casual clothes to a tawdry dress, she marches into the office of a law firm and demands a job. Her appearance – garish by comparison to the clothing of others in the office and to the dowdy brown walls – ensures she stands out like a sore thumb in the mise-en-scène. This visual set-up, imbued with class connotations, is a perfect platform for Erin to demonstrate that her specialism is steel and passion. Where traditional liberals exalted loyalty, trust and honour, re-invented liberals presented diligence and drive. Erin becomes the determined individual we'd all like to be and replaces the abstract charismatic hero who was so insanely foundering in *Bulworth*.

Erin Brockovich uses other tools to generate a complete social set-up. As Soderbergh puts it, 'I wanted to come up with a style that wasn't too theatrical. I wanted it not to be glossy, not to feel prepared. I wanted situations to feel like they were caught rather than staged.'[106] In the meeting scene between Erin, her boss and law firm head Ed Masry and a corrupt corporation, the swinging camera movement indicates reaction to dialogue as opposed to staging. The use of a hand-held camera in other places and the viewpoint narrative structure of certain scenes – such as when the camera follows over Erin's shoulder

during a covert fact-finding mission – adds to an impression of immediacy and authenticity. This was helped by the decision to shoot for
four months in the actual town in the story – 'I push for using the actual
locations unless there is a compelling reason not to'[107] – and the mix of
'indoor light, outdoor light, cool light and warm light ... so that it
would look as though we had just walked into these locations'.[108] In
other words, the film was an attempt to reconstruct the experience of
Erin's quest for justice. Soderbergh had experience with hand-held
cameras and lots of location shooting in his breakthrough *sex, lies, and
videotape*. Moreover, Soderbergh counts among his influences European neo-realists who often asked actors to improvise scenes and shot
them as the action unfolded, giving a sense of immediacy and a certain
kinetic energy.

He could have taken a contemporary lead from British director Ken
Loach, who made a moving social realist film about the 1930s military
battle with Franco's fascist army in Spain, titled *Land and Freedom*
(1996). In *Land and Freedom* there is a scene involving people from the
International Brigades of the anti-Franco militia and local peasants in
a small agricultural centre. They debate what should happen to the
land and whether or not the peasants should collectivise their farms.
The dialogue lasts an incredible 14 minutes, with only two or three
cameras used to shoot it. The scene has some eight or nine characters
speaking from all corners of an average-sized room. Camera movement follows the haphazard pattern of the dialogue, stopping from
time to time to focus on one or other speakers, or on a reaction from
another character. This jumping around gives the scene a tenacity and
drive that Loach has regularly managed to generate in meeting scenes
in his other work. A researcher on the film has described how much of
the debate was taken up with arguments between local residents in the
rural town where Loach was shooting and that these residents had
been involved in, or had lost family during, the war with Franco. The
poetic line 'if you kill the cow of this revolution, you kill the calf of our
future' made by one peasant in the scene receives a round of applause.
The applause came from the crew filming, not from the others in the
improvised scene, such was the impression that the speaker – a veteran
of the anti-Franco battles – made.[109] This spontaneity and immediacy is
what Soderbergh attempts to replicate in moments of *Erin Brockovich*.
The director of photography on the film, Ed Lachman, suggests that
Soderbergh consciously set out to 'shoot a major motion picture with
an independent approach'.[110]

This need to re-create a social reality, complete with representations of social strata, is present in other Soderbergh films, such as *Traffic* and *Full Frontal*. These are not documentaries; the production team cannot make what *Screen* journal calls a 'literal representation' of their subject[111] because their project takes place years after the real events they are concerned with, or because their subject is fictional. However, these films re-create disjointed camera work and natural light often associated with television documentaries, described by John Corner in *Screen* in the following fashion: '… nonfictional television is not particularly interested in offering itself as an aesthetic experience … with promoting an appreciative sense of its creative crafting with the audience. Strength of content … is seen to be enough.'[112] Oscar-winning director Mike Figgis confirms that the films mentioned above are concerned with the staged re-creation of the complete social situation where an event occurs: 'you can illuminate certain important things for the public in documentary style … re-create a recent political situation. Filmmaking is not restrictive. It's a creative coverage of events.'[113]

These faux-documentary attempts show how the re-constituted Hollywood liberal broke from the abstractions of the charismatic hero in favour of protagonists with class relationships. The affectation of documentary style, representing authenticity, supplants abstraction with the artifice of reality. A sequence in *Traffic* when the drugs tsar drives downtown to find his daughter is doubly referential to the spectator's experience of class; we see the working-class blocks, run-down homes and poverty-stricken citizens but as a passenger in the politician's car, the camera swinging from side-to-side in panicked survey of the area. This real downtown scene and viewpoint photography create both references to the spectator's experience and an emotional engagement. The style drags the spectator into the action. This camerawork, much of it done by Soderbergh himself, is repeated throughout the film. It is also repeated in *Full Frontal* but here the fly-on-the-wall style is counter-productive, each scenario leaving you with more unanswered questions. In particular the relationship between a dominatrix and her interviewees becomes caricature, making the spectator an uncomfortable in-the-room observer of a woman without a distinct personality. Her later emotional breakdown is not only unsympathetic but incomprehensible. *Full Frontal*, unlike *Traffic*, demonstrates a pitfall of the faux point-and-shoot style of some new liberal films. As we have previously noted, re-invented liberals retain the special individualism of their old liberal predecessors, and documentary style serves them best when it draws the spectator into a false sense of witnessing the real, socially stratified world of the protagonist. In *Full Frontal* the artifice of documentary style becomes more important than the subject of the film, so the locations and costume become average, almost neutral, and social situation is less significant than character. Consequently, most of the time we have no idea what part of society we are in. The spectator–audience relationship is lost, because the mediation of class society is lost.

Mike Figgis's *Timecode* employs a similar narrative structure to *Full Frontal* (Hollywoodites in emotional and inter-personal turmoil) but more successfully. *Timecode* has simple but better-constructed referential locations such as a Hollywood mansion, a production office, a limousine and a screening room. The attention paid to character in production (Figgis work-shopped with the actors, in rehearsal, to establish 'where every character came from'[114]) and on screen – with each character having at least 10 minutes of personal exposition – establishes their social status and class position. We know who is a company boss, who is a struggling actress, etc., and the costumes (provided by the actors but in keeping with their characters) are appropriate. The film's split-screen, multi-story artifice provides not only amplification of the documentary style but also a way for the spectator to manage the story. In this way, being able to choose which scene to watch (and on the 2004 DVD release which one to listen to) allows the spectator to engage yet more with the protagonists and become more involved in the action.

In the case of *Timecode* the use of faux-documentary is highly effective at establishing the social situation of the narrative and in binding the spectator to a range of special protagonists. The result is an example of how the new liberal aesthetic can develop through experimentation but retain its core qualities. The relationship between the individual and society is rendered, as it is with many of Soderbergh's films. Nevertheless the hero remains a special person, with special qualities. Where Bulworth may be someone no spectator could become, these heroes – set in a world we can recognise and understand – might be people who spectators could aspire to be. Though, on the other hand, to emulate Erin Brockovich, Lester Burnham or any of the characters in *Timecode* would require the viewer to have immense personal courage and determination. Looking back on the origins of the liberal tradition in *Twelve Angry Men,* the same could be said of Henry Fonda's juror who needed the fortitude to stand up against a room of bigots and cowards and fight for justice. By the late 1990s, then, it could be argued that the liberal tradition had re-established itself with more socially connected, less abstractly motivated heroes who were sometimes (as with Erin) successful and other times (as with Lester) destroyed by the social system they inhabited.

In all cases one thing remains a constant factor – these characters act primarily as individuals and not as part of collectives engaged in struggle to change society. In this sense, the shadow of Clinton hung over the Hollywood liberal still. Whilst the shape of the liberal film had advanced in a number of respects, some liberals had sunk into a depressing fatalism. Their films reflected their continued belief in abstract idealism and special individualism but concluded that such great men and women would be crushed by a globalised capitalist society. Other liberals had begun to represent more successful special individuals, whose connection to a complex social whole made them determined fighters who could win successes against the corporate world through sheer resolve. The task of developing the progressive Hollywood movie to a new level, where heroes were part of a collective resistance to globalised capitalism, would fall to yet another set of Hollywood personalities. These people would be infected by the spirit of a global anti-capitalist movement at the end of the twentieth century, would become centrally involved in a movement against war in the early twenty-first century and would begin to form a new authentic Hollywood left.

PART THREE
The Next Generation

The late 1990s and early 2000s saw the emergence of a dramatic new movement, launched into the global political arena by anti-World Trade Organisation protests in Seattle in November 1999. Hollywood personnel including Tim Robbins, Susan Sarandon and Danny Glover, disenchanted with the Clinton presidency, attended peaceful activities organised by a range of protest groups. By the evening of 30 November those protests had turned into running battles in the Seattle streets, as activists confronted or ran away from riot police.

Months before the Seattle eruption, Los Angeles Democratic consultant Bill Carrick argued in *The Nation* that 'the Clinton presidency has had a great moderating effect ... The ideological heat of the eighties evaporated overnight', but far from cooling down, many in Hollywood were being set alight by the new political mood. Books challenging the negative effects of globalisation, damning governments for their participation in it and praising grass roots activism – such as Naomi Klein's *No Logo* or Michael Moore's *Stupid White Men* – became bestsellers.[1] Websites (indymedia, commondreams, znet, etc.) and activist organisations (Mexican Zapatistas, Jubilee 2000, Earth First, World Social Forum, ATTAC, etc.) attracted hundreds of thousands of supporters.

As the twenty-first century unfolded, a new progressive activism developed in Hollywood. Carrick should have read the issue of *The Nation* in which he was quoted. On the very same page journalist Marc Cooper wrote, 'there is an authentic Hollywood left that functions beyond the parameters of narrow electoral politics'.[2] This is Hollywood's next generation of progressives, who were to become a thorn in the side of Republican George Bush Jr's administration. By 2003 Hollywood activists could rightly claim to be a central component of global opposition to Bush's war with Iraq.

'Ooooo! We hate Bush and we hate Bush ...

... We hate Bush and we hate Bush. We are the George Bush haters.' So rang the chant from tens of thousands of protesters squeezed into Shaftesbury Avenue in central London, 15 February 2003. This was a small section of a march of anti-Iraq war protesters estimated by its organisers – the Stop the War Coalition of peace activists and the Muslim Association of Britain – to have involved two million people. That makes it the biggest protest in British history. The area around Shaftesbury Avenue, called 'theatre land' for its proliferation of stage plays and musical venues, was a bottleneck where two immense multiethnic human snakes merged. At the end of the marchers' route was Hyde Park where a heaving crowd obscured every blade of grass in an immense field, listening to a succession of speeches. From America former United Nations weapons inspector Scott Ritter flew in, as did Reverend Jesse Jackson. Jackson – a veteran of black America's struggle for civil rights – connected this huge British show of force with Hollywood's progressive element by bringing to the microphone actor Tim Robbins to repeatedly chant, 'No war! Give peace a chance!'

Kate McArdle, an ABC television producer of 18 years, has been key organiser of a coalition of Hollywood progressives against George Bush Jr's foreign policy. She describes Artists United for a Win Without War as opposition to the 'move of government to the extreme right'. Its most active members – including *Chicago Hope* hospital drama lead Hector Elizondo, veteran peace campaigner and star of 1970s television hit *M*A*S*H* Mike Farrell and television producer Robert Greenwald – were, in McArdle's words, 'totally inspired' by the London protest. She goes on, 'the American right now runs our country … and we wanted to be part of standing up to that. Those guys in England were doing it and we wanted some of that for ourselves.'[3] Cinematographer and radical campaigner Haskell Wexler suggested in 2004 that Hollywood anti-government sentiment was growing stronger by the day, 'yes definitely there are more people today challenging what is going on with this … extreme right-wing … government'.[4]

In London, 15 February 2003 represented the rolling over into antiwar action of a movement that had begun in Seattle in November 1999. Then American trade unionists, environmentalists, anarchists and countless other groups had joined in protest outside the World Trade Organisation summit. Seattle marked the start of a new movement against the devastating effects of globalisation on ordinary citizens. This movement had begun under the presidency of Bill Clinton but now, in the era of George W. Bush, it had become a global movement against war, against what the star of both big and small screens, Martin Sheen, called 'the military and economic imperatives of the imperialists in our government'.[5]

A small example of such imperatives at work came a year before the Iraq war. In May 2002 *Variety* reported that corporate producer Jerry Bruckheimer was to make a documentary following American troops in Afghanistan, as they pursued Al Qaeda terrorists presumed responsible for attacks – and thousands of deaths – at the New York World Trade Center in September 2001. The television channel VH1 was also to make a reality programme based on the diaries of American soldiers. These programmes were to be funded by the Bush government, personally signed off by Secretary of Defense Donald Rumsfeld. When Sheen damns the combination of military and economic interests that he perceives to have led Bush's America to war with Iraq, he could just as well be talking about this partnership between corporations and government. Corporate giant Viacom, for example, own VH1.

Viacom is a global media empire that in the 1990s bought Paramount Pictures, one of the original five big Hollywood studios set up in the 1920s. Viacom made $23,228 million in profit in 2001 and owns the second largest American national television station, CBS, as well as the UPN network of stations that reaches 96 per cent of US households. Viacom controls over 40 local US television stations, the global MTV music television network, eight children's channels, the Showtime entertainment network, the Comedy Central light entertainment channel, global book publishers Simon and Schuster, half of United Cinemas International and all of video rental store Blockbuster.[6] Simon Redstone sits in the top chair, with 68 per cent of Viacom's shares, and was a contributor to George Bush Jr's election campaign fund in 2000.[7] Actor and one-time anti-Reagan activist Ed Asner summarises the ideological edge to this kind of corporate set-up: 'the Republican right are vicious, they manipulate the media to their advantage because they control it'.[8] Aside from colluding with the government to make their VH1 reality programme about soldiers, Viacom released two films in summer 2002 – via Paramount – that appeared to support the Bush administration's argument that starting a war with Iraq would be an act of self-defence. The argument that Bush felt he 'had little choice with Hussein' was unpicked by political journalist Bob Woodward, writing in the *Washington Post* in October 2002. The choice Bush had made over Iraq was to 'take care of threats early', as national security adviser Condoleezza Rice told Woodward.[9]

The Sum of All Fears is a film that acts on just that pre-emptive premise. An adaptation of a Tom Clancy espionage thriller, it portrays the American secret service response to a terrorist attack in Baltimore by swarthy foreign nationals with bad accents. After explosions and horrific deaths, American agent Jack Ryan – played with little panache by Ben Affleck – pursues the gung-ho solution of personally going to war with the Russians responsible for the attack. In dimly lit, knock-about action scenes glorifying Ryan's bravado, corrupt foreign leaders are murdered or brought to submission. Finally, senior military officials congratulate Ryan for securing America's safety. Similarly, the Mel Gibson star vehicle *We Were Soldiers* – also a book adaptation, this time from a first-hand military account by Lt General Hal Moore – told a particular version of events in the first major battle of the Vietnam War. The film is a collection of panoramic shots of foreign landscapes, where a dirt- and blood-spattered Gibson stands astride battlefields, fights with untold bravery at close quarters and shepherds boyish soldiers into battle to become real men. The soldiers are outnumbered and many die in painful moments, whilst Gibson's gravel-voiced Hal Moore produces cod philosophy and patriotic vitriol. Moreover, the enemy are rendered as a swarming mass of dirty green-grey uniforms.

The Vietnamese are given no dialogue, no close ups, no moments to humanise them. The American soldiers are reluctant heroes who talk about their families back home and their fear of dying. The American flag beams for several seconds in a shimmer of red, white and blue from a camp flagpole in the setting Asian sun. The enemy are darker skinned than the American boys, shot largely in the distance and the effect is a juxtaposition of sensitive but tough and clean American men against an amorphous never-ending foreign threat. This is America against the world, or as *Halliwell's Film Guide* says, both these films are 'advance propaganda for the next World War'.[10]

This was the context that confronted Hollywood progressives in the era of George Bush: powerful media conglomerates, integrated economically and ideologically. 'Working in this media is like Daniel in the lions' den, don't go there as a progressive unless you are prepared to be defamed', Ed Asner commented. Kate McArdle adds, 'it's open season on stars with a progressive agenda, they get invited onto talk shows because they are anti the Iraq war and have to be very well-prepared and strong to withstand the onslaught'.[11] Martin Sheen, as lead actor on a major network television show – playing Democrat President Jed Bartlett in White House drama *The West Wing*, produced by NBC, which is in turn owned by conglomerate AOL Time Warner – had good cause to see the Rumsfeld–VH1 collusion as being on his professional doorstep. Indeed, the government and media partnership came very close to home on 23 January 2002 when NBC showed the documentary *The Bush White House: Inside the Real West Wing* directly before *The West Wing* drama went on air.

Creator and main writer on *The West Wing* Aaron Sorkin attacked NBC executives in a *New Yorker* interview for making a 'valentine to Bush' that was 'pretending he showed unspeakable courage' in invading Afghanistan after the 9/11 attacks on the World Trade Center.[12] Sorkin was a respected New York stage-writer who had been used by long-time liberal Warren Beatty, but not credited, for last-minute script editing on his anti-corporate *Bulworth*. The role of the writer in modern corporate American movies is significantly downgraded from where it was in the time of *Twelve Angry Men* or *Citizen Kane* that we have used, respectively, as examples of liberalism on screen and methods of making a film beyond studio control. In the 1940s and 1950s writers like Reginald Rose, who penned *Twelve Angry Men*, cut their teeth in the single television drama format that afforded them control over the treatment of their material, treated directors as jobbing craftsmen not auteurs and allowed writers to develop strong narratives that could be transferred wholesale to cinema. Today the writer is rarely responsible for the final story or characterisations in a film. Scripts are bought and sold through agents and for 'development' by corporations but it is the script and its ideas that are bought, not the writer's talent. Writers are paid less than one-quarter of a producer's fee, they sign contracts that allow actors and directors to change their dialogue and directions on set and it is regular practice for a producer or director to recruit another writer to 'polish' the script and remove the original writer's style. In this way power over the artistic content of the product is transferred to directors primarily, as they do the work of composing the film, and producers, or actors who can wield influence by refusing to comply with a director's ideas. In the *Bulworth* example it is therefore hard to see how much influence Sorkin exerted and his lack of a credit does not necessarily mean he did not add great content to Beatty's film.

Sorkin, like Reginald Rose, was a New York stage-writer of some renown before entering Hollywood. He had the rare distinction of seeing his play about military corruption, *A Few Good Men* (1992), translated almost intact from stage to screen. Yet his first full writing credit only came with *The American President* (1995) that repeated the presidential iconography of the Clinton era – a cool president, who talked in soundbites and was an ordinary guy. In the Bush era, Sorkin became frustrated with the way that corporate Hollywood limited his say in the creative movie process and dreamt up *The West Wing* for television, making himself executive producer to maintain as much control as possible, and despite writing a drama about the White House he became entrenched in an anti-government view. He apologised if he had caused offence when he said *NBC News* anchorman Tom Brokaw was soft on Bush, but reiterated his political criticisms of *The Bush White House* to the Associated Press in March 2002. This moment of challenge was a sign of things to come from Hollywood's progressive community. Subsequent episodes of *The West Wing* explored how an intelligent, principled president would tackle business lobbyists. Sorkin wrote, and Sheen performed, scenes in which Jed Bartlett consciously rejected the Bush approach to policy. Some of Sorkin's writing on *The West Wing* was award winning, not only at television's Oscars – the Emmys – but also at the Humanitas awards.

The Humanitas Prizes, totalling $130,000, are given out annually by an awards committee headed by Father Ellwood Keiser to writers whose work, as the Humanitas website proclaims, 'communicates those values which most enrich the human person'. Sorkin's award was $15,000 for a single episode of *The West Wing* entitled 'Take This Sabbath Day'. Father Keiser explains that a Humanitas award was given to Sorkin because the episode discussed the validity of the death penalty, something in which George Bush Jr is a self-proclaimed believer. Keiser says the episode was a 'compelling dramatisation of the age-old truths, that we are not only morally accountable for what we do, but also for what we fail to do, that vengeance is no way to manage human affairs ... no way to solve society's problems'.[13] The courage not to kill, not to use the force of the state machinery against a fellow human being, was the subject of 'Take This Sabbath Day'. This was a markedly different kind of courage to that which Sorkin accused NBC producers of attributing to George Bush for his foreign policy, or that could be witnessed in Viacom's war-themed films of 2002.

Sorkin's Humanitas award – the fund for which is annually replenished by Hollywood donors – is evidence that the Bush regime and its corporate allies did not have hegemony over American society. Asner, Sheen, McArdle, Sorkin and Wexler could create spaces for anti-Bush ideas and win recognition for doing so. Inspired by events like the immense London protests against Bush's 2003 Iraq War, these Hollywood personalities challenged their president with their own anti-war protests. When they began to do so they built upon four years of development of the anti-globalisation movement that had first emerged in the late 1990s, when President Clinton was still quietly nursing globalisation into American life. The roots of Sorkin's challenge to Bush and a series of massive American anti-war protests in 2002 and 2003, can be

found in the movement against the atrocities of capitalism that Hollywood personalities like Tim Robbins were among the first to support.

The new movement –
Seattle and *Cradle Will Rock*

Cradle Will Rock is writer and director Tim Robbins's 'almost true' story
– as the opening credits read – of the demise of the left-leaning and
highly inventive Federal Theater project of 1930s America. Alterna-
tively, *Cradle Will Rock* is the dramatisation of writer and musician
Mark Blitzstein's struggle to overcome government repression, including the deployment of troops, in order to get his play about steel
workers – *The Cradle Will Rock* – performed in New York. Robbins has
a long association with theatre, founding The Actors Gang troupe and
playhouse in Los Angeles (1981) where he remains part-time artistic
director. In 2004 Robbins created an Actors Gang play about the pro-
Republican bias of American journalists in the 2003 Iraq war – *Embedded* – so popular that it had to extend its New York run by several
months. Remove this theatre linkage and *Cradle Will Rock* could be a
dramatic account of one Italian American's defiant stand against fas-
cists in his own family. Robbins, in fact, told an anti-war rally in New
York's Central Park (2002) that America's leaders had dangerous 'fun-
damentalist' tendencies that verged on fascism. Then again *Cradle Will
Rock* could be the re-telling of the battle that radical Latin painter Diego
Rivera had with business mogul Nelson Rockefeller, over the content
of a mural the artist was contracted to paint. Robbins told the audience
at the Cannes premiere of *Cradle Will Rock* (1999) that he was concerned
about the line between making 'art [paid for by corporations] and
prostitution'.[14]

Greater than the sum of its parts, *Cradle Will Rock* is a combination
of all these strands in a complex tapestry. The fabric from which Robbins weaves this cloth, however, is not historical but is the
contemporary anti-globalisation movement, the birth of which he personally witnessed when he joined in four days of protest in Seattle in
November 1999. On day one, eyewitness Peter Bohmer describes 'a
huge program at a local Methodist church where Vandana Shiva, Con-
gresswomen Maxine Waters, AFL-CIO President John Sweeney and
many religious leaders called for a cancellation of the debt of the
poorer countries of the world'.[15] On day two (30 November) human

rights activists sneaked into the Paramount Theater – owned by Viacom – and addressed World Trade Organisation delegates. A human chain of 15,000 was then formed around the conference centre. The next day representatives of America's largest trade union – the Teamsters – set up loud speakers, letting protesters take turns to invent slogans. A Native American led a chant that translated as 'the rain is washing away corporate greed'.[16] Then eyewitness Josh Milner, a miner, watched as 50–80,000 people representing the 'AFL-CIO, Sierra Club, students, indigenous people, small farmers, radical feminists, vegans, human rights … etc, etc' marched by.[17] A coalition of third world groups – the People's Assembly – despite having its protest permit withdrawn by the Seattle authorities, was welcomed into the march. On the fourth day steel workers and students spontaneously sang and danced together at a road junction.[18]

Kevin Danaher, a member of the forum that planned the Seattle events, wrote later that protesters turned the World Trade Organisation summit into 'the greatest failure of elite trade diplomacy since the end of World War Two. Even in 1982, when the Reagan administration tried to force through a new round of negotiations for trade liberalization, there was at least a declaration and future work agenda at the end of the conference. Not in Seattle. The Clinton team [said] the talks ended in total collapse.'[19] The WTO conference, where leaders of the world's most powerful businesses and countless heads of state met to sign trade deals, had been shut down completely on its second day. The protest was also a direct challenge to President Clinton, who appealed for protesters to go home on day one but saw his words completely ignored. *Cradle Will Rock* relates directly to the Seattle experience through metaphors for modern-day globalisation, as when American businessmen and the Italian government exchange bags of cash for political favours. The film explores the polarisation of ordinary Americans and corporate interests that Seattle represented.

Steel bosses are shown discussing how to lay off workers with the minimum of fuss. Capitalists Nelson Rockefeller and William Randolph Hearst are pictured in dark, wide, almost ominous suits. American politicians appear as weak men who fraternise with millionaires at parties – at one point they are even clown-like, wearing ludicrous sixteenth-century costumes for a masked ball. They make decisions that punish people in welfare lines and seek to undermine the progressives who run the Federal Theatre with accusations of Communist sympathies. *Cradle Will Rock*, stripped of historical regalia, could be the latter years of Bill Clinton's presidency when the anti-globalisation movement began to emerge, or it could be a prediction of the scale and intensity of social polarisation that would be felt under George Bush Jr.

In *Cradle Will Rock* coalitions of protests develop against unemployment and for workers' rights. A scene in Central Park – where Robbins made his anti-Bush speech in 2002 – involves protesters battling with police. This is exactly what happened at Seattle as protesters were forcibly removed from their human ring around the conference. Tear gas was used and the UK BBC newsreader on the 6 o'clock evening bulletin (31 November) sat for fifteen minutes in front of an image of a riot police officer, dressed in biker boots, black leather and a tinted helmet, surrounded by billowing smoke. *Cradle Will Rock* shows police and protesters fighting, as well as high-spirited citizens marching to an illegal showing of Mark Blitzstein's play.

Robbins presents resistance to corporate power and government repression as an exciting thing – as the citizens march, musicians play their instruments and there is a festival atmosphere. Typical of the new generation of Hollywood activists – including his partner and life-long women's rights activist Susan Sarandon, human rights campaigner Danny Glover, peace activist Martin Sheen and self-proclaimed anti-capitalist Sean Penn – Robbins's representation of social change is far from fatalistic. The *Cradle Will Rock* citizens' march is uplifting and demonstrates how this turn-of-the-century generation of Hollywood progressives celebrated grass roots collective activity. Above all else, the shared interest of everyone who is not either politician or businessman is asserted.

The Federal Theater actors, who are directed by young, brash, actor and director Orson Welles, wear overalls and plain suits – even their costumes in *The Cradle Will Rock* are workers' uniforms. This costume-generated class typicality is reinforced in the march to the illegal play showing, where the actors slip in among workers along the street and disappear, so that only the positioning of the frame picks any particular individual out. The spectator sees this scene as if they too were joining the march, a little like the documentary style identified earlier in Steven Soderbergh's late 1990s films, but with the smooth slick quality of 35mm film. Only one shot is from above the marching crowd, the others are at head height. It can be argued that Robbins's experience in protest inspired this moment, as if he transposed the movement of a protester joining a Seattle march onto this filmic event.

The aesthetic described here is, however, a departure from the independent-minded anti-corporate work of late 1990s directors like Soderbergh. It has never been recorded that Soderbergh joined a

7. Historical parallels: Tim Robbins's *Cradle Will Rock* puts the audience into the moment of protest at injustice, mirroring Robbins's own experience in anti-capitalist protest (*copyright Touchstone Pictures*).

protest and this may well explain the major meeting scene in *Erin Brockovich*, where the townspeople appear as a mob. In keeping with this film's narrative of one determined woman's legal assault on a corporation, the townspeople are shot out of focus for much of the time, and when they leave the meeting the effect is to make them appear as a multicoloured amorphous moving backdrop to Erin's facial expressions. In *Cradle Will Rock*, as in black director Spike Lee's best film for half a decade – *Bamboozled* (1999), his satire about a television show aimed at black audiences – the richness of composition means that, if you pause the shot, you can see almost every face in a crowd. There is no record of Lee attending Seattle but he did attend protests over the death in police custody of black youth Ammadou Diallo in New York in the mid 1990s, alongside Susan Sarandon. In 2003 Lee was a regular at anti Iraq-war rallies and told the German Silver Bear awards ceremony of his disgust at the policies of George Bush.

As well as making members of crowds intelligible and using a camera height that makes the spectator feel part of that crowd, Lee and Robbins also have their characters directly address the spectator. In *Bamboozled* frustrated African-American television producer Pierre Delacroix talks to the audience about the meaning of satire, setting up his ultimately unsuccessful strategy for exposing racism in the media. Delacroix's speech is both a political definition of what satire means and an outline of his intention 'do something' about the treatment of black people on television. When actor Damon Wayans explains in the documentary for the 2002 DVD release that he based Delacroix's mannerisms on Spike Lee, it confirms the suspicion that the words 'do something' are both the character's dialogue and the director's demand on the spectator. In a sense, Seattle's multi-ethnic makeup was a response to that demand. A similar, if more subdued demand is made in *Cradle Will Rock* when vaudeville ventriloquist Tommy Crickshaw addresses the camera as part of his comic stage act. Having given the names of Federal Theater directors to government officials seeking out Communists, Crickshaw finds himself out of a job, isolated and so admits to the spectator his own hidden Communist sympathies, saying that solidarity and unity are the path we should all take. This is not a casual slip in style on the director's part but a clear attempt to treat the spectator as a sophisticated social being, capable of thinking their way through a film. These direct address moments are placed at key junctures in the films – the opening in *Bamboozled* and as the military block the entrance to Blitzstein's play in *Cradle Will Rock* – thus forcing the viewer to consider how they are engaging with the action. Such a method prevents characters on the screen becoming distant, unreal, special individual heroes.

Such techniques show that Robbins and Lee treat the viewer as being part of a shared experience. In *Cradle Will Rock* multiple narratives spend equal time with a number of characters, with families sharing meagre meals, with impoverished young women as they sing for money, with the unemployed in the queue for a job and with actors taking time off to dance romantically. One narrative is left incomplete, as a brief colourful episode gives way to a different, equally interesting, story. Following the eyewitness accounts above, the protests in Seattle had the same sense of various strands coming together to make a whole. Robbins could render this in a film written and commissioned – by Joe Roth at Disney – before Seattle took place because he was involved in preparations for the protests.

When Sarandon and Robbins helped organise New York contingents to join the demonstration they were creating one strand of the Seattle experience. Danny Glover created another by speaking at public meetings during the events. Sean Penn added another when he swung his weight behind the protests, saying 'there's an enormous amount of room for an activism … it's starting to come … Nothing like

Seattle happened in 20 years. It is a very hopeful thing.'[20] So hopeful was this weaving of diverse strands in protest that the balance of electoral allegiance in Hollywood changed. Within a year of Seattle, Medea Benjamin stood for the Senate as a Green Party candidate in California. In the words of her campaign organiser Michael Eisenscher, Benjamin 'was one of the architects of the massive Seattle protests against the WTO, World Bank and IMF'.[21] Benjamin, a resident of the California city of San Francisco, had been the West Coast weaver-in-chief for the Seattle protests.

Eisenscher described how, as a result, Benjamin was able to then weave a broad base of electoral support with: 'endorsements from 25 current and former elected officials, from more than 30 union officials ... from eleven social justice and social action organizations, and more than 100 distinguished public figures, including ... Noam Chomsky and Angela Davis, Barbara Ehrenreich and Michael Lerner, Ed Begley Jr, Woody Harrelson, and Bonnie Raitt, Manning Marable and Norman Solomon, Alice Walker'.[22] Further weaving, on a bigger scale, took place in 2000 when Ralph Nader stood as a radical presidential candidate, having immediate support from Tim Robbins, Danny Glover, Bill Murray (who played Tommy Crickshaw in *Cradle Will Rock*), Susan Sarandon, Ed Begley Jr and Woody Harrelson. Robbins even dedicated his speech, on receipt of the prestigious Liberty Hill Foundation's Upton Sinclair Award for political activism, to Nader. Robbins spoke about 'the ideals, frustrations, and aspirations of a diverse community of people ranging from pseudo-Anarchists to liberal and radical political activists to disenfranchised ex-Democrats and ex-Republicans who are now choosing to stand left of Left'. The open-access radical network of discussion websites, indymedia.com, described a Nader campaign event in 2000 as a further materialisation of this anticapitalist milieu:

> ... Green Party, Public Citizen, Democracy Rising, The Portland Alliance, Cascadia Forest Alliance, The Utilities Reform Project, Industrial Workers of the World, The Portland Coalition Against Weapons in Space, Redirect, Sierra Club, The Sustainable Forestry Project, the Native Forest Council, Bark, Earth Day 2001, the Women's Union Resource Center, the Bicycle Transit Authority, Car Sharing, OSPIRG, Independent Media Center, Animal Liberation, and others ... celebrity Danny Glover acted as Master of Ceremonies.[23]

That Danny Glover was not just present but played host demonstrates how central Hollywood progressives had become to this new form of collaborative activism by 2001. As *Cradle Will Rock*, the Seattle experience and the rise of alternative electoral alliances proves, Hollywood's twenty-first-century generation of progressives were keen to take the most active role they could in organising and supporting an anti-capitalist movement. The arrival of George Bush Jr in office in 2000 created an immediate and obvious target for this activity.

Globalisation and George Bush Jr

In the Home Box Office television production *Six Feet Under*, Season Two (2002), there is a scene in which devious corporate executive Missy confronts the co-proprietors of a small independent Los Angeles funeral parlour – Nate and David Fisher. She tries to persuade them to sell up to her corporate funeral giant – Kroehner. The Fishers spent most of Series One resisting every corporate trick in the book to stay independent and maintain their father's high standards of customer care. They have withstood their false accusation of arson, attacks on their property, the stealing of their customers, offers of phoney 'partnership' deals and Kroehner's paying-off of suppliers to try and undermine the Fishers' service. Now Missy is sitting in a chair in their home telling them they should take her big money offer. Nate replies that they are not rejecting the offer because they don't want her money, rather they 'despise everything you stand for. Corporate profits over care. Greed over people. We hate everything you represent.' Stunned Missy can, initially at least, only muster 'Oh, I see'.

The show's creator, executive producer and writer of the episode in question is Alan Ball, who also wrote the screenplay for *American Beauty*. *American Beauty*, produced under the last days of Clinton's presidency in 1999, told of a family suffering the consequences of compliance with corporations. It was the story of Lester Burnham's individual quest to re-find himself through regression to adolescence, after his corporate employer fires him. The Series Two episode of *Six Feet Under* presents a picture of sharper polarisation in American society. Ball now saw the response of ordinary Americans to capitalism as being both more collective – Nate and David later rally a host of independent traders against Kroehner – and also more confrontational than Lester's private indulgences in drug taking and fantasies of having sex with teenagers. By 2002 Ball was involved with the early shoots of an anti-Iraq-war movement in the USA and was becoming associated with radical intellectuals like MIT professor Noam Chomsky, by signing the Not In Our Name statement against war and imperialism that Chomsky launched. The *Six Feet Under* example above summarises progressive Hollywood's emerging verdict on life under Bush Jr – 'everything' Bush's America stood for should be opposed.

Recent popular books that condemn globalisation, support grass roots campaigns and propose a reformation of society lend themselves to the same conclusion. *No Logo* is an analysis of corporate branding by Naomi Klein, which became an international bestseller and was called 'angry, funny and elegant' by *Publishers' Weekly. Globalisation and its Discontents*, a diatribe against American manipulation of global trade by Joseph Stiglitz,[24] sold in the hundreds of thousands and was critically acclaimed on both sides of the Atlantic, with the *New York Review of Books* calling it 'the most forceful argument that has yet been made against the IMF [International Monetary Fund] and its policies'. *Stupid White Men, Dude, Where's My Country?* and *Downsize This*[25] are Michael Moore's attacks on politicians who have 'whored themselves to big business',[26] which have resulted in hundreds of millions of book sales. Moore's documentary features, *Bowling for Columbine* (about weapons, war and social alienation) and *Fahrenheit 9/11* (a stinging attack on the pursuit of political power that is perceived to have motivated George Bush Jr's government to go to war with Iraq), have established him as arguably the world's leading documentary maker. In 2004 he became the first documentary maker to win the Cannes Palm D'Or award since 1952. These books and documentaries tally with the anti-government political consciousness exhibited in *Six Feet Under*, suggesting the subtext for the Fishers' attack on corporate greed is globalisation.

Joseph Stiglitz describes how globalisation means the establishment of global institutions like the World Trade Organisation and the deals done within those places. Such deals include the General Agreement on Trade in Services (GATS) that demands governments sell their public services to corporate interests. First signed in 1994 after international government negotiations in Uruguay, then reviewed in 2000, GATS is a global trade deal over water supplies, healthcare, public health, education, public transport, postal communications, broadcasting, tourism and finance. GATS, when signed by a government, ties them irreversibly to offering contracts for services to corporations and offering subsidies to help companies get started. Considering that most national economies in the twenty-first century are two-thirds dependent on these kinds of industries, GATS, as the

European Commission says on its website, is 'first and foremost an agreement for the benefit of business'.

Radical actor and director Sean Penn told the *Guardian* (2001) that such globalisation deals were merely a continuation of capitalism's age-old worker–boss division, and that Bush Jr was complicit in that exploitation. Penn's linkage of Bush to globalisation and the tactics used by its corporate leaders is remarkably accurate. For example, Bush was a co-owner of the Texas Rangers baseball team and in 1998 made $15 million from a $600,000 investment, after manipulating a deal with the Texas government to ensure that prime state property was made available for the club's development. This is the kind of strategy that deceased cultural theorist Pierre Bourdieu said under-lined globalisation, 'neo-liberalism [the opening up of all markets to business] and the retreat of the state'.[27]

President Bush, Paul Krugman of the *New York Times* argues, is the figurehead in the 'rise of an unaccountable American right',[28] who seek to liberate corporations from accountability. Krugman has investi-gated the economic strategy behind the Bush government, discovering that the Heritage Foundation – a Republican think tank with close ties to the Bush Snr household – believes wholeheartedly in governments helping business make profits. If milking the corporate cow was what the Fisher brothers were opposed to then they could have been talking directly to George Bush Jr in their funeral parlour. Bush Jr was a direc-tor of Harken Energy at the time that his father was elected president in 1988, shortly after which Harken was offered exclusive rights – by the government – to drill for oil off the coast of Bahrain. In 1990 Bush Jr jumped ship, sold his Harken stock, making more than $300,000 profit. Harken then went bust, having already received both advance payment for stock and federal subsidy. *US News and World Report* said 'there is substantial evidence to suggest Bush knew Harken was in dire straits'[29] but told no one. The escape by shareholders with profits intact before a company collapses, laying off employees and leaving custom-ers without access to their goods, was the same story that anti-Iraq war protesters Mike Farrell and Robert Greenwald told as, respectively, actor and producer on *The Crooked E* (2002).

This television film, made by Greenwald's own production com-pany and starring Farrell as corporate boss Kenneth Lay, was about the situation that occurred when the Enron Energy Corporation imploded in 2002. 'Enron was big issue for Mike and Robert', explains Artists United organiser Kate McArdle, 'energy is a big issue for all of us'. In September 2002 the California Public Utilities Commission concluded

8. Martin Sheen declares his support for Artists United for a Win Without War: founders of this heavily publicised coalition were producer Robert Greenwald and Mike Farrell, who simultaneously challenged President Bush on the nation's television screens (*courtesy of Kate McArdle*).

that the main energy corporations in the USA withheld supplies between May 2000 and May 2001, thus causing blackouts on the West Coast. Enron were profiting from shortages by asking for multi-million dollar government subsidies to clear supposed power choke-points and put the supply back on. In 2001 they admitted to doing 'wash' deals with other companies, where no energy was exchanged but the appearance of trade pushed prices up. This manipulation had been made easier by an energy bill passed by Bush in 2001, which removed restrictions, allowing Enron hike its prices by 3,700 per cent. Enron subsequently went bust. Just before it did, Kenneth Lay sold his share option and made a huge profit, much like Bush had done at Harken.

The resonance of the energy crisis in Hollywood seems to have been akin to that of the 1992 Los Angeles riots. Both took place on the doorstep of Hollywood celebrities, both directly affected the urban poor – one an expression of their anger at injustice, the other an injustice done to them by corporations – and both were dramatic public events. The major difference was the direct connection between the energy corporations and the Bush regime. For example, Enron's partners in the defrauding of the public, Williams Corp., had a board member called Thomas Cruikshank. He held the same job and worked in the same office as vice-president Dick Cheney at oil giant Halliburton. Another of Enron's corrupt allies, AES, had Richard Darman as a board member, who worked with Cheney in George Bush Snr's administration in the late 1980s and early 1990s. Enron also held the status of being number one donor to the Republican Party. These intrigues were all explored in Greenwald and Farrell's film, as if in itself their TV movie was an indictment of the Bush White House.

Bush Jr, *The Crooked E* seemed to imply, was a member of the same corporate club as Enron boss Ken Lay. *Six Feet Under* carries on this argument, using its season-long main character plots and episodic subplots to expose Bush's assaults on ordinary Americans: a gay couple move in together and a gay Christian is shunned by the Church – Bush quashed plans to legalise gay marriage and his Faith Based Initiative exempted churches from anti-discrimination law; a death-row inmate is cremated – as Texas Governor Bush sent a record 152 people to the gas chamber, and his Justice Ministry tried to force Puerto Rico to adopt the death penalty; an elderly woman dies due to lack of healthcare and her husband dies by her coffin – Bush cut Medicare (state health insurance) subsidies to doctors by 5.4 per cent and stopped advice services telling the elderly how to get prescription discounts; Claire Fisher, the artistic youngest member of the family, makes the difficult decision to have an abortion – Bush has removed all funding from organisations who might give abortion counselling abroad, also cutting AIDS prevention services by the International Planned Parenthood Foundation and the Family Guidance Association.

Another issue explored is the environment, as when Nate Fisher visits his old girlfriend – later his wife – Lisa in Seattle and she turns out to be an environmentalist. Bush suspended the New Source Review that required factories to install anti-pollution equipment when they expanded. Bush also withdrew from the 1997 Kyoto Treaty on harmful emissions in 2001, denying America's responsibility for half the world's CO_2 gas pollution. Bush appointed Gale A. Norton to run the Interior

Department that takes care of most the USA's water supplies and its public green land sites. Norton was a former energy industry lobbyist, opposed to emissions controls on corporations. The Interior Department has since given the go-ahead to corporate coal-bed methane drilling amounting to more than 50,000 gas wells on public land in Wyoming, Colorado and Montana. The department has paid several million in state subsidies to begin the drilling programmes. The department also exempted the military's 25 million acres of land from any environmental laws. It's hardly surprising that Hollywood's leading environmental spokesperson, Ed Begley Jr, said he was 'worried' by the prospects for environment protection under Bush.[30] No coincidence either, perhaps, that Begley appeared in *Six Feet Under*'s first two seasons as Hiram, the nature-loving, electric car driving lover of Ruth Fisher. Begley confirms that the car in the show is in fact his own and that he used the opportunity to promote the use of clean fuels to a mass audience.

Aggregated, these elements of the *Six Feet Under* narrative seem to be a direct attack on the basic policy of the Bush administration, which has involved cutting taxes for corporations (2001 and 2003) and a 'jobless recovery' in the economy involving no federal investment in services for the poor. Whilst *Six Feet Under* picks out desperate moments in the lives of Los Angeles's oppressed and destitute, the Heritage Foundation argues against all welfare and believes that Medicare should be done away with entirely. The Bush strategy seems to be the establishment of an American national state of corporate governance, a strategy of several national states, in fact, working together under the banner of the World Trade Organisation, the G8 (where heads of governments in the world's richest nations do deals), the World Bank (which finances deals made at places like the WTO), and the International Monetary Fund (which gives poor nations money in return for policies that benefit corporations). A certain set of national policies result from this deal-making: privatisation of state concerns, deregulation, trade liberalisation, corporate tax cuts, keeping inflation low (even if that causes unemployment), restrictions on labour organisation, reduced public expenditure, shrinking of government, expansion of international markets.[31]

Such a strategy was brutally apparent in 2003 when George Bush Jr invaded Iraq with American troops and left behind a US-led interim administration that organised privatisation of hospitals and schools, the opening up of Iraq's oil markets and the establishment of re-building contracts for American industrial corporation Halliburton. So much had corporations profited that by 2002 General Motors' sales returns were higher than Denmark's gross domestic product, Wal-Mart's than Poland's and Exxon Mobil's than South Africa's.[32] It is possible, therefore, to read the references in *Six Feet Under* as a resumé of the progressive agenda in the Bush era. The issues that underpin this agenda are many, but essentially, as Nate Fisher tells the Kroehner representative, it was the entire social project of corporate profit making – with its close associations to George Bush's presidency – which had become the new target of Hollywood progressives.

Local and global

Michael Albert – founder of znet.org and Zmag, which act as ongoing symposiums of left ideology and strategy with regular updates from intellectuals and journalists – sees the sentiment behind the Fishers' words as a challenge to the entire social system of the modern world. He calls it 'anti-capitalism', a movement in which the smallest activity has the dynamic of a raindrop, creating ripples that expand outwards across the entire muddy puddle of corporate capitalist society. A story of Philadelphia school students campaigning for state-run education, as told by Alissa Quart, is a good example of this dynamic at work.

Quart was a teenager in Britain, but studied at Brown University and the Columbia School of Journalism, she lives in New York, has written for the *New York Times, The Nation* and *Salon*, and feels qualified to write about the situation of contemporary American youth. Her book, *Branded: The Buying and Selling of Teenagers*[33] was called the 'substantive follow up to Naomi Klein's *No Logo*' by *Publishers' Weekly* and won the WH Smith book award for business writing. In February 2002 Quart looked on as fifty school students met at the offices of the Philadelphia Student Union, 'a local non-profit group devoted to school reform and youth activism'. Quart explained how this local campaign against the handing over of the city's schools to a private company had ramifications for wider corporate society.

Eric Braxton, an organiser for the Student Union asked, '"Why are the schools being privatised" … "Edison [the company trying to take ownership of the schools] is like Channel One", says Max Goodman, seventeen … "and the Gap [global clothing giant] has money into Edison, so maybe one day they'll say, this lesson is brought to you by the Gap"'. In this organising meeting, teenagers were joining the dots of corporate association. Edison Schools is a privately owned New York-

based company running nearly 200 American schools, with a reputation for under-investment and for paying major dividends to
shareholders, in particular to its chief executive Chris Whittle. Whittle
also founded Channel One, a broadcaster of television programmes
exclusively for schools. Channel One does not make a single programme without advertising revenue from products like Coca-Cola, it
even places these products in its educational programmes. Therefore,
by opposing Edison in Philadelphia these school students learnt about
and challenged a network of corporate power; a network in which the
American media business was complicit. Quart observed that 'these
students have joined up with the larger anti-corporate movement' and
'have managed to considerably diminish Edison's role in their future'.
Eric Braxton adds 'they are aware of the whole initiative of corporate
America to make money off low-income people, and they are angry
that they are getting the short end of the stick'.[34]

In George Bush Jr's America, public education seemed to be a low
priority. In 2002 Congress passed Bush's ironically titled No Child Left
Behind Act. By the end of 2003 nearly all of America's 50 states were
cutting budgets, sacking teachers, ending teacher-training schemes,
increasing class sizes and scrapping after-school programmes. Ele-
mentary school teachers were judged to be spending $521 of their own
money on classroom resources by the *New York Times*. In February 2003
Bush then proposed a $700 billion cut for corporate taxes. Conse-
quently the poorest Americans saw vital education programmes –
dropout prevention and 'gifted & talented' for underachievers – end
completely. Fifty million dollars were cut from the Even Start Family
Literacy Project that gave vital assistance to the urban poor, the disadvantaged and the ethnic populations of inner cities. By 2004 Bush was
even cutting back on the original proposals of No Child Left Behind,
amounting to a further loss of $6 billion to state education. Simultane-
ously new regulations were forced on schools demanding that they
make 'adequate yearly progress' in tests for children. Without the
resources to meet the new attainment levels, 8,000 schools, most of
them in run-down areas and more in urban Los Angeles and New York
than anywhere else, were publicly shamed as 'failing'. Municipal education authorities were then free under No Child Left Behind to look
for alternative methods of meeting targets, such as privatisation.
Despite its name the Bush education policy was an assault on school
provision in America's poorest communities.

This was the Bush method of governance in respect of all services.
Run them down financially, cut federal investment and then offer the

alternative of private ownership from which corporations like Edison could profit. In 2001 Bush tried to set up a scheme of vouchers whereby a dividend was paid to the families of children who moved from state schools to private ones. The system was voted down by Congress but re-introduced in 2001 in pilot areas like Cleveland. None of the pilots increased the numbers of poor students in private schools. The Bush education policy mirrors the strategies of the International Monetary Fund and World Bank, who loan poor economies money on the condition that they privatise their state industries and open markets up to business. The table below summarises a number of such global manoeuvres and their effects. The table is divided into two sections, one looking at two regions where globalisation has taken effect, the other looking at two issues over which globalisation strategies have exerted influence.[35]

Region	*Latin America*	*Middle East*
Cause of Globalisation	IMF & World Bank loans to Latin American countries in the 1980s forced the privatisation of state assets and opening up of capital/property markets. Two treaties irreversibly removed any remaining barriers to foreign corporations: the North American Free Trade Agreement (1994), and Free Trade Area of the Americas (2001).	The IMF and oil industry have intervened directly in all Middle East countries. From Egypt (in the 1970s) cutting state subsidies for basic goods and allowing Western oil companies in, to Algeria (1988) and Jordan (1988 & 1994) cutting subsidies, letting in oil corporations and privatising key services – all to meet IMF loan criteria.
Effect	**Mexico:** free education scrapped, forcing 14-month student strike (1999–2000). **Bolivia:** (1998) US corporation bought water industry in Cochabamba, hiked prices and prevented citizens collecting rainwater. **Argentina:** (2000–2) strikes erupted as unemployment and prices soared. The government defaulted on $141 billion debts, restricted public access to savings and the Peso was devalued by two-thirds. **Colombia:** USA gave $1.3 billion of *military* support to the country but no food aid.	**Gaza:** privatised water supplies in Palestinian territories three times as expensive as they were before. **Iran:** utilities sold to multinationals, prices rose and access denied in some areas. **Yemen:** IMF loans (1998) built a pipeline to export oil and cut social spending by 50 per cent. **Turkey:** 17 'restructuring' deals in 20 years and forced privatisation of Turk Telecom and Turk Airlines (2000).

Issue	Environment	Labour
Cause of Globalisation	WTO Agreement on Agriculture (1997), IMF/World Bank loans, and Global Agreement on Tariffs and Trade (2001) force maize/crop production and energy industries to be liberalised. Short-term profit can be made from fossil fuels and big corporations who make harmful incinerators have an open path into third-world countries.	WTO, NAFTA force set-up of de-regulated 'export processing zones' (EPZs) accessible to multi-national business. Free Trade Zones, largely in third world, have banned workers' associa-tion under trade agreements. WTO states only a voluntary code of conduct can be applied to corporations.
Effects	**Independent food producers:** 30,000 disappearing a year in USA. **Local maize producers:** over 500,000 Philippine and Mexi-can producers are going bankrupt. **Air pollution:** 3 million people suffer from this globally and NAFTA is estimated to increase truck emissions by seven times before 2005. **GM foods:** WTO prevents gov-ernments stopping imports or production. **Waste:** WTO rules override agreements to reduce emis-sions, toxic waste, etc.	**EPZs:** Mexico, Philippines, China, Bangladesh and India have created a short-term, sweatshop employment econ-omy with poor wages, health conditions and safety. **Trans-nationals:** 'investments' in EPZs have expanded to a com-bined wealth bigger than the world's 100 poorest countries. **Disney:** exploited the situation in Haiti, where workers making $11 t-shirts are paid 4 cents, and regularly complain of res-piratory illness and maltreatment or sexual harassment.

One slogan used in the planning of the Seattle protests of November 1999 was 'think global, act local',[36] and resistance to this global assault on ordinary citizens was often localised. The Philadelphia students in Quart's example exemplify this mentality. Just months before the meeting Quart described at the Student Union office, 2,500 high-school students walked out of class and blocked the main arteries through central Philadelphia. This was a political campaign against the deci-sion of local authorities to give control of education to a corporation but it was a campaign locked into global economics and the Philadel-phia teenagers were fully aware of that connection. Alternative media expert of 20 years, head of the Institute of Public Accuracy, and a San Francisco-based organiser of the November 1999 Seattle protests, Nor-man Solomon, describes how such a local-into-global approach became the new activist orthodoxy during the first few months of 1999. In the run-up to the anti-WTO protests in Seattle, Solomon describes the sensation of growing resistance to globalisation: 'we knew something big was coming. In many places people were meeting, planning, running activist schools. Znet's media institute ran a week-long intellectual and tactical school. It was a painstaking process of education about society, about globalisation and about how we connect each small issue into a bigger stream'.[37] Solomon, who had run daily broadcasts from the Seattle streets for a dozen national radio networks, perceived that Seattle was founded on a process of social education organised by grass roots networks. The language of the Philadelphia school students, who protested against privatisation of education three years after Seattle, validates Solomon's observation. The dynamic of the 1999 protests, of local independent campaigns educating their participants about society and contributing to a more generalised antisystem struggle, had percolated through American society. Indeed, such a dynamic was being repeated right across the world in response to the effects of globalisation summarised in the table above.

In Mexico the Zapatista Liberation Army occupied the town of Chiapas in opposition to the announcement of NAFTA. Led by Sub-Commandante Marcos, who wore a mask and said he was a citizen of every country where globalisation took effect, the Zapatistas organised a mass march to Mexico City (2001) chanting their slogan 'Ya Basta!' meaning 'enough'. In the capital thousands came onto the streets to greet them, cheering their expression of resistance. For over a year Chiapas became a rural commune, where land was farmed collectively and produce shared without charge. In the same year as Marcos led his march, Bolivian farmers, trade unions and community groups organised local committees to mobilise hundreds of thousands of activists. They closed down an area of 400 square miles and saw 17 of their number killed by the military, but managed to reverse water privatisation.

Local resistance in the Middle East had been up and running since 1994, when Egyptian workers occupied plants where the IMF was forcing job cuts. Only military force ended the protest. In Turkey, in 2000, tens of thousands of people protested when the IMF wanted privatisation of public utilities. Their banners read 'IMF out – this country is ours!'. Then in 2002 both in Palestine and Cairo, intellectuals, journalists, trade unionists and artists met to release declarations of resistance to globalisation's effects. Local action over the environment in 2000 saw the Alliance for Sustainable Jobs and Environment – a collaboration of the Earth Island Institute, Friends of the Earth and United Steel Workers – stop corporate giant Maxam cutting down redwood forests in California. In the early 2000s French farmer José Bové was imprisoned for attacking a McDonald's restaurant in opposition to its global take-over of food markets. An anti agri-business collective, Confederation Paysanne, sprang to life and secured his release by mobilising 60,000 protesters outside the prison. Over labour issues the Students Against Sweatshops network – founded 1998 – recruited 400,000 members and set up 150 local chapters in Canada and America. These initiatives forced the purchasing of goods for many universities exclusively from plants with a high standard of employee conditions. A joint student and employee occupation at Harvard University (2001) even secured pay rises and better conditions for domestic staff.

The Harvard students and staff were committed to local activity that impacted on their daily lives, and to local activity that would impact on wider social situations. The underlying concept here is every locality and person is tied into a web of global politics and economics. The problems in your backyard are the product of the same social system that privatises rainwater in Bolivia or makes farmers bankrupt in Mexico. What the Harvard students epitomise is the activist conclusion that follows from such a concept: that every action you take to tackle a problem in your backyard will shake, to some extent, the global web of society. Every local tremor of resistance to injustice has a global aftershock.

One film that demonstrates this dynamic in action was made by the government-run Australian Film Finance Corporation (AFFC) in 2001. Australia had begun to wake up to the local–global concept the previous year. On 11 September 2000 a coalition modelled on the Seattle experience, called the S11 Alliance, organised a 20,000 strong protest at the World Economic Forum summit in Melbourne. A huge number of school students joined the protests, as did three trade union federations. Eyewitness Sean Healy described how protesters filled 'city streets with noise, colour and people' and how 'organisers led loud chants of "fair trade, not free trade"'. So when the AFFC came together with the New South Wales Film and Television Office and Gannon Films to commission *The Man Who Sued God* – a film featuring a collective of ordinary citizens taking on major corporations – it was a sign that the anti-capitalist aesthetic of people like Tim Robbins had also found expression half-way round the world.

Starring Scottish comedian Billy Connolly, who has attracted arena-sized audiences in Australia since the 1970s, *The Man Who Sued God* was a story about one man, a freak storm and his fishing boat. Connolly plays the lead character – disaffected lawyer Steve Myers – who has moved to a quaint coastal town to take up fishing and escape the city. After the storm destroys his boat and injures his leg, Myers finds that his insurance will not replace his vessel due to an 'act of God' clause that exempts the corporation who hold his policy from covering the cost of weather damage. Bitter, angry and a more than a little maverick in his approach, Myers tries a number of ways to get his fishing business back on track. He tries to borrow money for a new boat and fails. He travels to the city and appeals to the sympathy of an executive at his insurance company, again he fails. Then Myers decides to take the insurance corporation to court but quickly realises he has no grounds for a case. Finally, he takes the bizarre action of suing the heads of the major churches, either to hold them liable for his loss or to challenge the existence of God and therefore open up the insurance corporations to multitudinous back-dated claims.

What begins as a series of pleasant panoramas of coastal scenes, and a capable performance of a half-mad fisherman by Connolly, soon becomes a battle between Myers and the Australian establishment. The heads of the insurance corporations meet in secret and plot how to undermine Myers's case, fearing that he may set a dangerous precedent for other claimants who feel hard done by. The publicity and legal advisers who assist the corporate executives, meeting in marble and glass locations, also meet senior priests from all the churches in austere religious back rooms. Myers's personal injustice is revealed as tied up with wider corporate and social interests.

When Myers challenges one corporate executive face-to-face he is manhandled by security guards and thrown onto the street. As happened in Seattle, this confrontation of ordinary person and the muscle of law enforcement attracts media attention. So when Myers begins his case thousands of other people with similar grievances come forward. Myers opens an office to train and organise his fellow anti-corporate insurance claimants, an action that suggests that Myers recognises his individual situation is part of the wider web of social issues. When Myers loses his case on a technicality a gaggle of priests and businessmen rejoice, suggesting that philosophical and economic leaders are united in trampling on the little guy. Despite losing, by tackling a personal issue, the hero of the film has exposed the broad social context of his own problem. He has demonstrated that his backyard, the church, corporations and countless other ordinary citizens are connected. The humour and snappy tempo of scenes in the campaign office also suggest that the coming together of ordinary citizens in action is an exciting, positive experience.

To include this film in a discussion about contemporary Hollywood is important. *The Man Who Sued God* was distributed by Disney's Buena Vista – the largest cinema and home-video distribution chain in the world – for home video rental, and by Icon Entertainment International. Icon, a portfolio of four companies wholly owned by actor and star Mel Gibson, has an exclusive deal with Twentieth Century Fox to arrange finance and distribution of its films. In 2004 it released Mel Gibson's controversial box-office smash about Jesus, *The Passion of the Christ*.

Progressive Hollywood stalwart Ed Asner called *The Passion* 'a filthy and dangerous movie that is essentially right-wing anti-Semitic propaganda'.[38] Along with Asner, the American Jewish Anti-Defamation League accused Gibson's film of being anti-Semitic. The film is a eulogistic re-telling of the story that constitutes the last moments of Jesus Christ's life, portraying Jewish people – to whom Jesus was supposed to be a king – as devious and murderous. Asner talks with some glee about the way Gibson described the response to his film, and to his pro-Iraq war position, when he was interviewed on the popular Jay Leno talk show. Gibson talked about feeling he might have to leave America to escape lunatic radicals who were taking over the political discourse. The presence of *The Man Who Sued God* – an essentially anti-capitalist film – on the same roster as *The Passion of The Christ* is an indication that even the sections of Hollywood most detested by progressives are not immune from the anti-capitalist spirit. Gibson's annoyance at the prominence of progressive attacks on him was a further sign of just how far the local activity of a global resistance to capitalism had penetrated mainstream culture.

Anti-capitalism in the mainstream

In the summer of 2001 Sean Penn was in Europe at the Edinburgh Film Festival. His task there was supposedly to promote his new film *The Pledge*, described by the *Guardian* as 'a compelling drama, part psychological thriller, part parable, part tragedy'.[39] Clearly this reviewer saw the merits of Penn's script and direction, in a film starring Jack Nicholson as Jerry Black, a retired cop falling apart at the seams as he tries to fulfil a promise to a mother to catch the rapist and murderer of her daughter. *The Pledge* is a metaphor for the demise of liberalism in the Clinton era. Here is a policeman who cannot live up to the abstract idealistic values that others place upon him. He is not a heroic special individual in the fashion I have identified to be part of the Hollywood liberal tradition, but is a failure, unable to deliver the desires and wishes of the citizens who are supposed to respect him. Black could even be a metaphor for Clinton's failure to deliver a progressive agenda. His breakdown could be speculation on the internal moral crisis that such a failure might cause. Penn's film seems to reflect the experience of Hollywood progressives who hoped Clinton would be their man but found him to be a greater friend to corporations. In an interview Penn went on to expresses a scathing anger at the way George Bush Jr had moved the country forward since the end of the Clinton era. With *Guardian* film editor Andrew Pulver, Penn talked of an America culture increasingly 'infected' by the destructive ideology of the 'kings of the so-called economic and military world'.[40]

Penn describes the fruits of this infection by referring to directors like Michael Bay, who had that summer released the blockbuster Second World War epic *Pearl Harbor*, as people 'raping society' who should be 'sent running screaming with rectal cancer'. Watching *Pearl Harbor* might well leave directors and actors with ambition to create art feeling somewhat violated. Though trailers for the film featured a montage of explosions and airplane cockpit views of Kamikaze flights into buildings, the film itself is a slow – almost turgid – and formulaic love story. A heavy, overused score and some very simplistic dialogue do not assist a narrative that has the kind of limited dramatic tension that occurs when you know the outcome of a story. Neither writer nor director finds a way of putting events in a fresh perspective or throwing the spectator into unexpected emotional territory. The result is that a decent performance from Ben Affleck, in the lead male role of a young man in the military, is spread thinly over a generally poor product. Rather than simply act as a film critic, Penn went on to identify the connection between the advance of profit-driven globalisation and Hollywood when he said, 'the definition of a good film now is one that makes the bank happy – not one that shines a light on people's lives'. Sitting alongside his wife and actress Robin Wright Penn, Sean barracked those he saw as complicit with the profit ethics running contemporary Hollywood and those in business or government who 'don't care about what is going on around them or the effect they are having'. Penn then presented Pulver with an alternative to the culture of globalisation. 'There is a lot of stuff going on right now around the world. In Seattle and in Italy ... people are putting themselves on the line. People who care about something bigger than themselves.' Although this is the only reference Pulver allows to slip into his article, it is clear that Penn is talking about events that took place days before this interview in Genoa, Italy. When Robin offers the idea that a revolution needs to take place in America and in Europe, a revolution that starts in people's own homes, she invokes the local-into-global sprit of anti-capitalism.

Over four days 300,000 protesters gathered outside the G8 summit of the world's eight most powerful nations – including America and Britain – in the medium-sized port city of Genoa. A series of small protests akin to free public festivals were organised by pacifist groups on the first day, whilst highly organised direct action protesters closed down the city centre, withstanding a heavy battering from carabinieri (riot police) that even *The Times* called 'excessive'. The main protest came on the third day, when groups from across Europe were led by Italian trade union confederations in a whole day of marching around the conference centre, which the police had ringed with huge steel fences and titled ominously 'the red zone'. That protest was televised across Europe, taking over the front pages of the *Guardian*, the *Independent, The Times* and the *Daily Telegraph* in the UK. On the day in between the small and the large protests Italian student Carlo Guiliani had been shot between the eyes by a police officer and became a martyr for activists, who carried aloft his picture from there on, shouting 'assassini' (murderers) at any police they saw. Such a high-profile weekend of action inspired Penn to tell Pulver how he had 'shamefully not done enough' in support of this mass movement.

By verbally assaulting his money-making Hollywood contemporaries, Penn was trying to mainstream the idea that movies should reflect, as *The Pledge* did, the reality of twenty-first-century life. Penn may well have supported the kind of politicised movie-making that grew out of the Genoa protest itself. *Sight and Sound* magazine described how '35 Italian directors gathered to make a documentary about the G8 summit and the protest movement that surrounded it. Ageing radicals took to the streets with digital video cameras, some, like Gillo Pontecorvo ... director of *The Battle of Algiers* (1966) ... overcoming age and illness to do so.' Pontecorvo echoed Penn's sentiments when he argued 'It is our duty to roll up our sleeves and work with others on such an important occasion, when the quality of life in the future is being decided'.[41] The attempt of these directors to form a collective and make a film that represented the new global movement at work is perhaps the clearest indication thus far of how anti-globalisation got under the skin of film-making talent around the world.

When Tim Robbins and Susan Sarandon use the phrase 'anti-capitalist' at an anti Iraq-war rally in New York in December 2002, it illustrates how the language of anti-system protest has become common currency in Hollywood. It has found its way into the news media. Less than an hour after planes flew into the World Trade Center, in September 2001, an anchor for Sky News (owned by media mogul Rupert Murdoch) asked correspondents from CBS if they thought anti-capitalists were behind the attacks. They were not, but this moment demonstrates how anti-capitalism nudged its way into the mainstream media. Penn's interview with Pulver can only have assisted this process. How the Genoa Social Forum must have smiled on reading his words. This broad collaborative body was the main organising centre for the anti-G8 protests and involved the Network Against G8, the anti-racist Association for Open Cities, Ya Basta! (an anarchist movement named after the Mexican Zapatistas), cultural association ARCI, trade union groups COBAS, CUB, SLAI-COBAS, French economic pressure group ATTAC, Catholic peaceniks The Lilliput Network, Drop the Debt, the World Wildlife Foundation, the Green Party, and many others.

The wide-ranging concerns of these bodies gives some indication of the depth and scope of issues that made up the anti-capitalist movement which so inspired Penn's comments. What gives anti-capitalism its status as a global movement is the capacity of these diverse strands to come together in high profile events. A snapshot, taken between 2000 and 2001 provides ample evidence.

April 2000 – 30,000 march outside the IMF/World Bank meeting (Washington DC) and attend debates, fairs and small protests. Despite talk of violence by the chief of police, conflict is minimal. One thousand three hundred arrests work in favour of anti-capitalists: Bolivian World Bank consultant Leon Galindo, held for 23 hours by mistake, became convinced that 'poverty and oppression go hand in hand'.[42] June – anti-capitalism arrives in Europe, as 'Seattle on the Tarn' became the nickname of remote French town Millau. Sixty thousand people take part in two days of debate and protest. July/August – anti-capitalism interferes with American electoral politics. Twenty thousand protested at presidential nomination conferences (Philadelphia, Los Angeles) constituting the biggest such protests in American history. Anti-corporate Ralph Nader goes on to earn 2.5 million votes.

September – 20,000 people from across Europe protest at a World Bank/IMF meeting (Prague). This first protest in a former Communist country draws thousands of locals dissatisfied with both Soviet and free market rule. November – first international event initiated by trade union confederations draws 100,000 to Nice to protest against 'privatisation and corporate un-democracy'[43] at the European Union summit. January 2001 – anti-capitalism flexes intellectual muscles at the inaugural World Social Forum in Porto Allegre, where academics, non-governmental organisations, trade unions, grass roots groups and other affiliates present solid anti-system arguments. April – 80,000 students and trade unionists besiege the Summit of the Americas (where NAFTA had previously been drawn up) during three days of protest in Quebec City. Trade union officials join direct action activists in the most militant protests. It is these mass gatherings that make anti-capitalism a significant enough force to impact on mainstream 'infected' cultures in the way that Penn aspires.

The narrative development of *American Splendor* (2004), an adaptation of an underground comic book featuring hospital clerk Harvey Pekar, is one example of the way that anti-capitalist sentiment began to permeate movies in the new millennium. The film was an award winner at Cannes and the Edinburgh Festival, and received four-star reviews in *Empire*, the *New York Times*, the *Guardian* and *LA Village Voice*. The film centres on Harvey's mundane life but when his comic books find a mass audience he becomes a regular guest on *The Late Show* with David Letterman. Harvey's poverty is not removed by his fame but when he challenges Letterman to pay him better for his appearances and to treat him as a writer, not a comedy guest, he meets opposition. It is made clear that he will never earn money or respect from the NBC network, then owned by corporate giant General Electric. The corporation wants to keep him and his comic books' success in that corner of culture marked 'cult'. Harvey's personal struggle shifts into a battle with a global corporation but this does not seem exceptional. It is just another episode in an episodic narrative, ranking alongside Harvey's battle with cancer in terms of screen time.

Not all social movements develop cultural references in the mainstream. A global audience would be unlikely to recall the 1990 riot of 200,000 people in London's Trafalgar Square against the Conservative government's proposal to change local taxation, for example, simply from a banner that said 'No Poll Tax'. On the other hand, the New Hollywood generation of the late 1960s were politicised by mass movements against the Vietnam War, student protest, radical black

nationalism and strikes of millions of people in Europe. This generation of rebellion made an indelible mark on culture. Witness the crowd
scene in a corporate film like *Forrest Gump* (1994) where a few banners
and some veterans quickly symbolise anti-war protests. Considering
that *Forrest Gump*, a multi-Oscar winner, is essentially the story of one
intellectually challenged man who travels blithely through some horrific life events without ever changing his right-of-centre social outlook
– indeed he receives with pride a medal for bravery in the Vietnam
War, represents his country at table tennis and is only at the anti-war
protest by mistake – it is quite an achievement of the anti-Vietnam War
protesters that they get a reference at all in the film.

The *American Splendor* example is typical of the manner in which the
ideology of anti-capitalism has translated into similar cultural reference points. The conclusion here is that a movement needs to be of
significant impact for it to infect mass culture in the way that Sean
Penn suggests. Moreover, it needs to have a significant enough resonance within the Hollywood creative community for its ideology to
sneak into films like *American Splendor*. This resonance can be witnessed in the new shape of progressive ideology and activism in early
twenty-first-century Hollywood.

Progressive ideology and activism in Hollywood

At the start of George Bush Jr's war with Iraq (March 2003), Tim Robbins and Susan Sarandon were due to attend a 15th anniversary
celebration of the release of a film they both starred in – *Bull Durham*
(1988). It would have been a romantic occasion for them, having met
and fallen in love on the set of the film. The Baseball Hall of Fame
organised the event, recognising the value of the film's story to their
promotion of one of North America's major sporting highlights, the
Baseball World Series. In *Bull Durham*, Nuke (Robbins) learns to
'breathe through his eyelids' and become a top-class baseball pitcher.
The film is a love-affair with the game, pausing occasionally to show
Nuke's progression from a small-town team to major league baseball,
and his battle for the affections of a sultry local English teacher (Sarandon) with an experienced professional ball player (Kevin Costner).
Both Sarandon and Robbins – who looks particularly baby faced
throughout – present interesting characters in their performance and

writer-director Ron Shelton was Oscar nominated for best original screenplay. They would have enjoyed attending the Hall of Fame event if the Hall of Fame hadn't pulled the plug at the last minute.

The Hall of Fame withdrew the film and banned the stars from the gala event because of their outspoken anti-war position. In a move that implied either great anger or great confidence, or both, Robbins published correspondence between the Hall of Fame and himself in *The Nation* and *New York Times*. Baseball Hall of Fame president Dale Petrosky wrote, 'We believe your very public criticism of President Bush at this important – and sensitive – time in our nation's history helps undermine the U.S. position, which ultimately could put our troops in even more danger. As an institution, we stand behind our President and our troops.'[44] Robbins replied:

> I reject your suggestion that one must be silent in times of war. To suggest that my criticism of the president puts the troops in danger is absurd … You are using what power you have to infringe upon my rights to free speech and by taking this action hope to intimidate the millions of others that disagree with our president. In doing so, you expose yourself as a … bully … you dishonour … the men and women who have fought wars to keep this nation a place where one can freely express their opinion without fear of reprisal or punishment.[45]

This was an eloquent and very public piece of activism that tallies with the general shape of Hollywood's new left by the early 2000s. In the 1980s Ed Asner's defiant gesture against American foreign policy in El Salvador – launching a medical fund for the country's people suffering US-funded repression from a dictatorial regime – saw Asner sacked from the popular television show *Lou Grant* and the show was eventually axed. Emblematic of the strength of Hollywood activism in the early 2000s, Tim Robbins experienced no such comeback. Instead he embarrassed Petrosky into a public apology and was applauded for his stance on the radical news website commondreams.org, who gave out the Baseball Hall of Fame contact details so other activists could lodge a complaint. Then in 2004, less than a year later, Robbins found himself the model Hollywood darling, kissing his son on his way to accept a Best Supporting Actor Oscar for his role as child abuse victim and murderer Dave Boyle in the Clint Eastwood-directed urban drama *Mystic River*.

Mystic River is set in a blue-collar Boston community situated next to the River Charles, hence the title. The Boston Society of Film Critics so liked the representation of characters from their city that they gave

Mystic River their Best Ensemble Cast Award at the end of 2003. The film also won the Outstanding Performance by a Motion Picture Cast award from the Screen Actors' Guild in 2004. This cast not only included Tim Robbins but also another of Hollywood's outspoken dissenters – Sean Penn. Penn too received an Oscar for the film, for Best Actor, in recognition of a nuanced, emotionally charged portrayal of Jimmy Markum, ex-career criminal and father of a murdered teenager. Between them, Penn and Robbins scooped 18 awards from film critics, associations and film festivals across North America. It seems that being outspoken, even waging a war of words with an institution of such standing as the Baseball Hall of Fame, did nothing to undermine the popularity of these two progressives. If anything, it helped give added value to the meaning of *Mystic River*'s narrative about vengeance and bloodshed.

On the issue of vengeance Robbins spoke with clarity in 2002. Expressing fears about a war with Iraq, which was then just a possibility, Robbins referred back to his experience of the 9/11 attacks on the New York World Trade Center in 2001 by planes hijacked by terrorists. Robbins and Sarandon live with their children in Westchester, a middle-class suburb of New York City. Shocked by the news that planes had flown into the huge glass twin towers of the Center, Robbins drove for 36 straight hours from Los Angeles – where he was working – to help with the rescue operation. He said, 'the attacks of September 11 made me very angry … I was incredibly moved by the generosity and humanity that arose … all over the country … Still I was angry. Why New York?' Looking back with a year's hindsight he realised he had made a mistake by not immediately speaking out as President Bush Jr went 'after Al Qaeda [who were presumed responsible for the attack] with massive bombing in Afghanistan'. He had stayed silent despite feeling the military action was wrong because he 'understood the motivation'.[46] Despite focusing on the investigation into the death of Jimmy Markum's 19-year-old daughter and appearing to be a crime drama, it is the motivation for revenge – which Tim Robbins understands but rejects – that *Mystic River* explores.

The film explores the childhood experience of Jimmy and Dave Boyle, showing Dave's kidnap and abuse by paedophiles posing as police officers. When the film returns to the present day, perhaps its most dramatic and emotional scene occurs as Jimmy is held back by real police officers, screaming 'they've got my daughter in there'. Eastwood directs the scene with economy but does not rush it. It lasts over five minutes, cutting between Jimmy at the police incident tape, to officers investigating the crime scene, back to Jimmy sneaking into the scene and finally to Jimmy and the officers colliding. As one officer shouts 'take it easy, he's the father', the frame is filled with blue uniforms that highlight Jimmy's reddened face as the camera moves into the sky to watch him from above. This build up gives us time to experience Jimmy's panic, his frustration at not being told who the police have found and so we are sympathetic when his pain bursts forth in a primeval cry.

Eastwood creates an environment that could be almost any urban community, using a 30-second sequence of aerial shots of streets, children's parks and the city block to establish a neighbourhood of family homes. When we see inside the houses there are confined box rooms, cracked paint on the porch, dining tables wedged into kitchens and a clever use of soft light that makes the homes seem slightly dim. The whole feeling is of ordinariness, of being a normal, everyday American community. Eastwood also sets up conventions from the crime story – the film is an adaptation of a novel by crime writer Dennis Lehane – such as the forensic murder investigation, the good cop–bad cop question routine, Jimmy the ex-con trying to make good and the criminal gang he goes back to when he seeks revenge. The police, led by Jimmy's boyhood friend Sean Devine, conduct a slow, deductive evidence collecting but Jimmy wants quicker results.

Jimmy becomes convinced that Dave killed his child. Without substantial evidence he concludes, 'I know he was taken in by the cops this morning. I know he saw Katie the night she was murdered. Didn't tell me about it until after the cops questioned him. And I know he's got a hand that looks like it's been punching a fucking wall. Is there anything else I should know?' Motivated by the kind of vengeance that Tim Robbins criticises, Jimmy kills Dave. The arbitrators of justice in the police force, still carrying out their investigation, are made redundant by brute force. Jimmy has the opportunity to let them do their job, as they match bullets from the crime scene to a gun that is not Dave's. Yet, much like George Bush Jr, who went to war with Iraq in 2003, ignoring the United Nations weapons inspectors who were still collecting evidence and the United Nations Security Council still hammering out a peaceful solution to the Iraq situation in 2003, Jimmy makes the unilateral decision to kill. Having killed Dave, Jimmy then discovers that he was not, after all, the murderer of his child. His wife reassures him that he is the 'king of the neighbourhood' and his mistake matters not because his motivation was 'good'. Not quite convinced Jimmy steps outside his door to join an Independence Day parade, replete with an abundance of American flags. He is the conqueror – as George Bush would be in Iraq – but his victory is hollow as all he has done is rob Dave's child of his father so that everyone loses out. In this way *Mystic River* is an extension of Robbins's argument about vengeance.

Mystic River demonstrates how the progressive perspective of people like Robbins and Penn was asserting itself through metaphor, with style and verve, in Hollywood products during the early 2000s. Whether or not Clint Eastwood intended the film to convey quite this message is not certain, the former mayor of a small Western American town has never admitted such, but it is worth noting that the film was in production and rehearsal in late 2002, during the build-up to the war in Iraq and as Robbins was about to take on the Baseball Hall of Fame. When the film grossed over $90 million at the US box office[47] and began to win awards, it not only carried the progressive message farther afield but also had the reciprocal effect of helping promote its stars' progressive opinions. The *San Francisco Chronicle* ran an article by Sean Penn in January 2004, after he visited post-war Iraq, saying, 'many Iraqis I speak to tell me there is no freedom in occupation, nor trust in unilateral intervention'. As *Mystic River* is concerned with children and crime so Penn talks about children: 'For the children of Baghdad ... the utter lawlessness of the streets are a constant and real threat'.[48] This outing in the mainstream press for a Hollywood progressive was something that had become increasingly common, as minor victories in situations such as the Baseball Hall of Fame incident increased their confidence and made them spokespeople for a wider constituency.

When launching his press attack on Dale Petrosky, Robbins exposed his previous links with Republican politicians. Petrosky had been press secretary to Ronald Reagan between 1985 and 1987 and Robbins suggested he was a friend of George Bush Jr. 'I had been unaware that baseball was a Republican sport', Robbins quipped, 'I wish you had, in your letter, saved me the rhetoric and talked honestly about your ties to the Bush and Reagan administrations'. These references to the Republican Party turned Robbins's dispute with Petrosky into a political battle with the Bush Republican administration. Impressed by his interjection into the world of the news media, the National Press Club invited Robbins to their annual dinner. There he used his speech to attack the war, to expose American nationalists who had made death threats against his family and to become the first person to publicly demand that the US press report the truth of what was happening in Iraq. This was a dramatic gesture that, remarkably, won tremendous applause from the audience. *Mystic River*, the Baseball Hall of Fame situation and the Press Club dinner are just the tip of a large iceberg of progressive Hollywood activism and ideological battle that has grown significantly in recent years.

Aside from giving their support to radical presidential candidate Ralph Nader, Tim Robbins and his partner Susan Sarandon have been involved in numerous activities. Sarandon is the public head of MADRE – an international women's organisation.[49] The two of them were jointly presented with the Upton Sinclair Award by the Liberty Hill Foundation, which has a list of 100 Hollywood sponsors and

9. One of Hollywood's most outspoken actors, Danny Glover, rouses protesters against the Iraq war in spring 2003 (*courtesy of Bob Polizeros*).

claims to fight for 'economic justice ... [and] class-based politics'.[50] African-American actor and producer Danny Glover, unlike Robbins, did not fall prey to anger and sentiments of revenge after the World Trade Center attacks. He spoke at Princeton University in November 2001 as war began with Afghanistan, saying America 'was to blame for bombing and terror around the world'.[51] Glover has won awards from the National Association for the Advancement of Coloured People (NAACP), the TransAfrica Forum and Amnesty International for his tireless campaigning for civil rights at home and abroad.[52] A visit to the Act Now to Stop War and End Racism campaign group website, answer.org, will bring up pictures of a highly animated Glover leading demonstrations for peace in Los Angeles and San Francisco, where he went to university and earned a formidable reputation as a stage actor with the American Conservatory company. Glover seems to typify the grass roots spirit of protesters in the anti-capitalist movement when he says local community activists are 'on the front line trying to make things better'.[53]

Another man proud of his activist credentials is Martin Sheen, whose protests against immigration laws have seen him arrested 60 times at border checkpoints, for helping immigrants cross into America. Sheen, real name Ramon Estevez, suffered discrimination as a result of his Spanish descent when he tried to make his break into acting. He changed his name to 'remove myself from the racism' he experienced from casting directors who thought he was Puerto Rican. Sheen's anger at injustice against people from the Latin nations makes him an important link between Hollywood progressives and the rise of anti-capitalism. The Mexican Zapatistas clearly caught his attention, because in 1997 he financed a trip to Washington for three children who survived the Mexican government's suppression of the Zapatista commune in Chiapas. The children had watched as friends and family were murdered by military forces using American guns. This fact may explain why, in the Bush Jr era, Sheen has become a spokesperson for Project Abolition, voicing their television adverts that seek to undermine through propaganda Bush Jr's nuclear missile defence programme. Sheen is the model of an anti-system protester in Hollywood and was asked by the Green Party to run with Ralph Nader for vice-president in the 2000 elections. 'I was flattered', he says, 'I believed in their whole platform, particularly with the environment, human rights and education and health care, but I don't have the ... makeup'[54] for an election campaign.

On the environmental front, actor Ed Begley Jr remains one of America's most prominent campaigners, with a brief and outspoken spell in Californian Democratic Governor Gray Davis's administration. Other Hollywood progressives who have come to life in the Bush era include Mike Farrell, who already had a track record of anti-Reagan protest but was generally quiet under Clinton. In 2003 he co-launched Artists United for a Win Without War with producer Robert Greenwald but he also runs three civil rights and anti-death penalty organisations. Farrell heads up the National Coalition Against the Death Penalty – an organisation with chapters in every American state – and is a vice-president of the Screen Actors' Guild in Los Angeles, elected on a campaigning, left ticket. Haskell Wexler organised the Bus Riders' Union which united poor workers going to work together in the morning to campaign for better transport, better working conditions and for the right of trade union recognition that had been denied them by their employers. Wexler made a documentary about his experience in this campaign and has also backed labour recruitment drives up and down the West Coast.

Alongside this, Sean Penn went to the streets of Oakland, California, in 2000 to try and encourage black people in the communities once dominated by the radical Black Panther Party to vote for new radical candidates, like Ralph Nader.[55] Director John Sayles chairs a campaign to free East Timor. Paul Newman practically came out of retirement in 2001 to oppose George Bush Jr's nuclear missile defence system in a video by Martin Sheen's Project Abolition allies. Actor Woody Harrelson funds and promotes a cannabis legalisation campaign and co-wrote as well as narrated the campaigning documentary *Grass* (1998). Meanwhile, Ed Asner keeps the flag flying about US foreign policy in Latin America by making representations to the State Department, visiting impoverished countries in the region and reporting to the press on what he sees. All of these people have become voices of dissent on the major networks – every subject interviewed for this book talks about jousting with right-wing talk show hosts on a regular basis.

To simplify this immense body of activism to a handful of salient characteristics could be misleading. This new Hollywood left, with its newfound confidence that Tim Robbins demonstrated in 2003, is just that – new! What we can be certain of is that as the new social force of anti-capitalism has emerged, so Hollywood's progressive talent has come to life, from some general observations about the current shape of progressive Hollywood it is possible to identify – with caution – three key features:

1 They take protest seriously – giving their names to campaigns, running coalitions, using the press and speaking at demonstrations.
2 They no longer trust the American state – challenging the death penalty, challenging the war, taking militant rather than electoral action.
3 A significant number have broken with the Democrats – Clinton's betrayals created a vacuum into which Seattle and then the anti-war movement emerged.

A careful approach to such statements is crucial. For example, distance from the Democrats is by no means universal; George Clooney has started campaigning for his former television-host father, Nick, to be a Democratic Senator, and Barbra Streisand – who was outspoken against the war – continues to fundraise for the party and backed Democratic presidential candidate John Kerry. However, there is a clear gulf between many in the Hollywood left and the Democrats. Alec Baldwin reflects on the experience of the last decade, concluding, 'I don't consider Clinton a progressive'. Tim Robbins made an even firmer expression of anti-Democrat sentiment during the Iraq war when he asked, 'where have all the Democrats gone?',[56] suggesting they were not involved in the campaign against Bush. Danny Glover went a step further still to argue that 'voting is a means to an end … [in] this quote, unquote, representative democracy [it's] become an end in itself … Change comes from without.'[57] In his dialogue with film journalist and author Peter Biskind for *The Nation*, Glover expressed a sense of commonality and grass roots activism that could only have been borrowed from the experience of anti-capitalist protests like those described earlier in this section. He adds, 'I'd like to be in an organisation that could set forth some sort of left agenda; that's what I want to be involved in', suggesting that Hollywood progressives like him are seeking to solidify their new confidence, to commit themselves publicly to a radical agenda for social change.

When cinematographer Haskell Wexler argues that 'all films, all productions have messages', he gives progressives like Glover one route for expressing their left politics. Wexler puts forward some sort of manifesto when he says, 'it's the business of promoting the right message, the human, collaborative message that we're in'.[58] In his work with John Sayles, we can see a conscious attempt to convey messages that fit with a collective, bottom-up, anti-capitalist spirit. Sayles's late 1990s film *Sunshine State* is a particularly good example of a character-driven narrative, shot by Haskell Wexler, that weaves a complex story with a clear anti-capitalist ideology.

The anti-capitalist aesthetic and its ambiguous brother

Sunshine State (2002) is a gently paced unpicking of several narrative strands connected by the arrival in a sleepy coastal Florida town of a major development corporation. The film demonstrates how Sayles can play with convention to produce a movie that has a strong anti-capitalist message. Wexler, who sighed and said 'wonderful' when asked his opinion on the anti-globalisation protests in Seattle, says he works with John Sayles regularly because they 'share a certain view of the world and belief in the collective humanistic solution to things'.[59] On *Sunshine State* Sayles was writer, director and co-producer with his wife Maggi Renzi. He even edited the film and produced it under the banner of his Anarchist Convention production outfit. Although the film had distribution and finance from both Columbia and Sony, there is little doubt it is *his* film, made to express the messages that he wanted to express.

In the film, Sayles sets up a number of narrative conventions: a rustic family home where the Stokes reside; a wayward daughter – Desiree Stokes Perry – returning home after leaving under a cloud; the temptation of Desiree's former lover – Lee 'Flash' Phillips; a philosophising wise old sage with gravitas in his voice – Dr Elton Lloyd; a homely daughter – Marly Temple; her new-guy-in-town love interest – Jack Meadows. To establish these conventions Sayles uses tricks he has inherited from previous filmmaking eras. The treatment of the two main female characters in *Sunshine State* demonstrates how Sayles enjoys using conventions to expose to the spectators their own hidden prejudices. In the gangster tale of a working-class Irish hoodlum who becomes a major mobster, *The Public Enemy* (1934), there are two women in the life of central character Tom Powers. One woman, portrayed as 'loose' and often wearing skimpy clothing, is dark haired. The other, a stabilising influence on Tom to whom he shows great affection, is blonde. In *Sunshine State* Sayles borrows the light and dark hair motif. He makes Marly a blonde. Marly runs her family business, is a diligent worker and is committed to keeping her parents happy. Desiree, on the other hand, suffers her mother's scorn for her promiscuity during teenage years. Desiree is not only dark haired, she is African American. Sayles appears to take the convention to an extreme that might cause some alarm. However, it is Marly who is most tempted to betray her family and sell their business to an aggressive real estate corporation, which wants to turn the town into a shopping complex complete with brand-name stores.

Marly also drinks to excess, saying, 'Shots. Tequila. I figure, you're gonna drink, why fuck around?' Desiree has instead returned to her mother's home with a respectable new lifestyle, with a partner who is a teacher and with every intention of correcting past misdemeanours – including admitting to young Terrell, who thinks he is her brother, that he is in fact her son. The effect of this turnaround is to force the specta- tor to re-evaluate the assumptions that they create based on the conventions that Sayles initially sets up. Sayles gives ample time at the start of the film to meet the characters before he begins to overlap the stories in this manner, ensuring the narrative is not confusing and that when conventions are confounded the spectator can remember what it was in the opening scenes that made them jump to a false conclusion about a character. Thus the re-evaluation isn't an epiphany, happening instead gradually as the film winds its way through a series of largely one-to-one scenes.

Each of these two-handers allows a character to meet a different per- son in the town. Whilst the dialogue tends to be about personal matters – Desiree's boredom with her present 'safe' lifestyle for example – each scene has subtext connected to the corporate attempt to take over the town. So, in a meeting between Desiree and Flash, another convention is busted when his attempt to woo her back into promiscuity turns out to be motivated by something other than physical attraction. It tran- spires that he is a real-estate dealer, working for the corporation, and wants to become close to her again in order to buy her family home. The convention of a risqué figure from a distant past that tempts a per- son on the straight and narrow back to wicked ways thus becomes something more sinister. Flash is concerned primarily with profit and Desiree reacts with high principle, expressing shock and instantly rejecting him.

Other transformations in *Sunshine State* see Dr Lloyd stop his porch philosophising and become the leader of a community action group opposed to the corporation. Marly's handsome new lover, with the fashions and dialect of a big city that she has never seen, turns out to be the head of operations for the corporation. Meanwhile Desiree's son, who is initially presented as a school truant and a vandal of local

historic monuments, turns out to be an exceptional artist. In this manner *Sunshine State* gradually becomes a study of how each character
deals with the contradictions of their relationship to the society they
inhabit. If Desiree pursues her former lover she'll be betraying the
people in run-down old condos that her mother and the old sage want
to protect. Similarly, Marly must choose whether she can really love
Jack, who has designs on the small business her family have run for
years. Dr Lloyd must find a way to generate momentum in his campaign against the developers without alienating his oldest friend –
Desiree's mother – who is considering selling up and taking the money
the developers are offering.

Through telling each story separately – giving time in the opening
to meet and learn about each character – then overlapping it with the
next, a picture of a society where corporate interests undermine real
relationships is painted. The reason for this is that, as each convention
is undermined, the corporation is shown to be the root cause of the personal dilemmas of the characters. Desiree would never doubt her new-
found security if the former lover did not try and manipulate her for
the corporation's benefit. Dr Lloyd and the mother would not come
close to falling out – having a serious argument that ends in a less than
fraternal exchange – if the corporation didn't try to buy the mother's
house. Marly would not find her positive relationship with her parents
in jeopardy if Jack did not catch her affections. In the end the only
channel for the spectator's antipathy is towards the corporation, and
our sympathy is with Dr Lloyd's campaign and with those who resist
the corporation's manoeuvres. *Sunshine State* is more than simply anti-
corporate, it is pro the people of the town, supportive of their diverse
but collaborative lifestyles, and as local an expression of the global
anti-capitalist ideology as may be possible in a Hollywood film.

This character-driven style achieves the same result as Robbins and
Lee do in their films; portraying a tapestry of typical protagonists in
complex relationships, without retreating to the representation of a
special individual hero. *Sunshine State*'s characters must each resolve
their dilemmas to bring closure to the narrative and send the spectator
away feeling that – as is the case in the film – corporate power is not
insurmountable and enough localised resistance can defeat it. A film
like *Fight Club* (1999), on the other hand, misrepresents the ideology of
anti-capitalism. Central character Tyler Durden's main aim is to blow
up banks and wipe out credit ratings. The other central character, simply called Narrator, has to give up his wealth and possessions in order
to be like Tyler. This rejection of possessions is an assertion of anti-

corporatism. However, *Fight Club*'s presentation of the theme is offset by its lack of historical specificity. The impression of sections of the film is that these are not real characters – indeed they turn out to be the split personalities of one person – and that their setting is abstract. The film confuses social and class relationships of the characters whilst sustaining a veneer of anti-capitalism.

Narrator starts off comfortable – if bored – living in an expensive apartment, employed in a middle-class profession. Tyler has several jobs – waiter, film projector and soap manufacturer. The scenes depicting his working life are minimal – we see him at the cinema once, making soap once and as a waiter twice, the second time as part of a covert operation. We never see either lead character searching for a job or worrying about money, not even when financing a small army of oddly disciplined anarchists. The film avoids signifiers of class or historical moment. Locations are anonymous, dates and times are absent and nothing is explained about the background, employment or social position of their lover, Marla Singer. This lack of specificity is quite deliberate. For example, when members of the Fight Club which Tyler has initiated join up for the anarchistic Operation Mayhem we know nothing about their previous lives. Operation Mayhem is militaristic and authoritarian. Class is ignored and an alternative, a-social, a-historical collective is assembled. Even the house that Tyler and his army inhabit is devoid of class or social specificity. The house is huge but disused. It appears early in the film to be a complete wreck, a mess of shadows and unpleasant shades of brown, with dirt and grime everywhere, a flood of water in the basement and faulty electrics. Yet when Operation Mayhem begins the place is suddenly tidied and there is a proliferation of straight and true fresh wood, especially in the basement dormitories. From that point on we rarely see the rest of the decrepit building that we were treated to previously – as if the house has metamorphosed into something new. Equally uprooted from reality is the location of the house, on a street with seemingly no other houses for miles around but yet within sight of a nearby city.

On the other hand, when Narrator is at work his office is every bit the average white-collar workplace. Everyone wears shirts and ties, photocopiers buzz, clerks sit in tiny cubicles, telephones ring everywhere. This is clearly an attempt to make Narrator a typical office worker, even the bleached colour used in the print of the film for these scenes is a metaphor for boring office nothingness. There is also an attempt at typicality in the repetition of support groups that Narrator visits in his search for genuine emotion. The characters in the support groups begin to merge into one, as their caring and sharing activities become identical. With few exceptions (Marla and Meatloaf's cancer victim standing out) these characters in dress, manner and activity become typical of an emotionally needy modern society.

The effect of this is initially to disorientate the spectator but after a while the incoherence of the film is normalised. The style comes to dominate and to mediate the spectator's relationship with the text. For example, when people join Operation Mayhem their lack of identity doesn't stand out as at all odd. This does not generate the special hero in a social context reading identified previously in *Erin Brockovich*. Nor does it produce a textured, sophisticated tapestry of social relationships as in *Sunshine State* – it is ambiguous. The root of this ambiguity, whether deliberate or otherwise, is the relationship of the film's production to the social movements discussed elsewhere in this book. Director David Fincher is not an old Hollywood liberal like Warren Beatty or even Ed Asner, nor is he connected to the independent revival in the early 1990s through association with Steven Soderbergh, as actors like George Clooney have chosen to be. Fincher is also disconnected from the anti-globalisation movement and appears on none of the lists of campaigns or activities that Tim Robbins, Susan Sarandon, Danny Glover or Sean Penn have been involved in. During the recent war with Iraq in 2003 Fincher remained decidedly silent when the rest of Hollywood seemed to be on the streets against George Bush Jr's foreign policy. Fincher is a son of corporate Hollywood who cut his teeth directing top-end music videos for stars like Madonna and began his life in cinema working on the mainstream sequel to a successful franchise launched by an inventive Ridley Scott film in 1979 – *Alien*. Fincher's first film was the highly unsatisfying, special effects driven and narratively confusing *Alien³* (1992). In terms of directorial influence *Fight Club* had no one at the helm with a vision shaped by direct connection to the crisis of liberalism or the re-invigorated Hollywood left that emerged in the late 1990s.

In the film's production this disconnection is even more apparent. This was a Twentieth Century Fox film, big budget and with no influence from the independent or left filmmaking sector. *Fight Club* is a prime example of an attempt by the big studios and their own cadre of talent to create an anti-globalisation niche market and sell films to it that captured something of the mood of a politically engaged Robbins, Lee or Sayles film. This strategy of niche marketing by global media corporations is what alternative media expert Norman Solomon has called 're-packaging and exploiting the grass roots'.[60] It is a practice that Saul Landau, radical documentary maker and life-long friend of Haskell Wexler neatly summarised as 'incorporating a product because you can turn a profit from it'.[61] When *Fight Club* was released in 1999 it marked the turn of corporate attention to the potential of an anti-capitalist product and away from the previous niche market that the studios had created by borrowing themes and styles from independent-minded talent. That niche was a particular brand of movie violence, for which Fincher had equal responsibility in creating.

Copying the independent gun movie

Fight Club is a fantastically violent movie and there are three possible explanations for the style and quantity of violence. Firstly, David Fincher uses grotesque violence in previous films. *Alien 3* features humans on a prison planet shooting hundreds of bullets at rampaging alien beasts who generally catch, kill and eat the humans, splattering their blood and body parts around. In *Se7en* (1995) a psychopathic killer stalks a major US city, devising foul ways to kill citizens, like tying them to a bed and starving them slowly, forcing them to eat and choke on their own vomit, creating a sick-making phallic blade which a prostitute is forced to use at gun point, and so on. It is part of Fincher's film form to portray the most gruesome of violent acts towards human beings. Secondly, violence has a precedent of pulling in profits at the cinema. Among the top ten grossing US films of 1998 were violence-heavy features including *Armageddon* – picturing the death of hundreds of people in a meteorite storm, *Rush Hour* – where Eastern martial arts expert Jackie Chan fist fights innumerable bad guys every five minutes, and *Godzilla*, where a giant reptile stomps all over the people of New York. The films shared $700 million at the box office. The same was true of the box office top ten in 1997 with *Men In Black* featuring shoot outs with aliens, *The Lost World: Jurassic Park* showing humans devoured by genetically modified dinosaurs, *Air Force One* pitting a family-guy president against a gang of Russian terrorists, and *Face/Off* being one of Asian director John Woo's first chances to make a gun-toting, high-kicking US-based action movie. Major corporations such as Columbia, Paramount and DreamWorks produced these films. So *Fight Club*, produced by Twentieth Century Fox, may just have been cashing in on this big profit maker.

Thirdly and more complexly, a certain style of violence was used in the 1990s by a set of 'independent' films, to which Fincher references his work. Among the independent movies benefiting from the brief boom in non-studio production in 1992, for example, were *One False Move, El Mariachi, Reservoir Dogs* and *Laws of Gravity*. The first is a Metro Films production, directed by African American Carl Franklin and written by Billy Bob Thornton. It's a road movie and thriller about two killers and their black girlfriend on the run in Alabama. Jami Bernard wrote in the *New York Post* that the film gave 'that special jolt' that comes from suspense and slick shoot-'em-up sequences. *El Mariachi* was Robert Rodriguez's – who went on to make the huge box-office success *Spy Kids* – movie shot for a $7,000 budget, about a Mexican hitman who carries his guns in a guitar case. Somehow Rodriguez squeezes car chases, huge gunfights and a lot of slow motion blood spilling action out of the most limited of resources. In *Laws of Gravity* a semi-documentary style tells the story of childhood friends caught up in gun running in Brooklyn. Made by little-known Oasis Films and featuring Edie Falco (who was also in *Sunshine State*), this film concludes in stylised violent skirmishes and shares a penchant for funny dialogue with Quentin Tarantino's debut feature *Reservoir Dogs*. Tarantino is these days a cinematic institution, respected enough to run the jury at Cannes in 2004 and give an award to Michael Moore's anti-Bush *Fahrenheit 9/11*. In *Reservoir Dogs* there is perhaps the best example of the one characteristic that all these 1992 movies have in common – firepower.

These 1992 films are of the Tarantino ilk, made by unknown directors – including Tarantino himself – with little-known stars or one big name cameo. In setting up his Band Apart production company in 1990, Tarantino was working on the assumption that he might only get to make one movie. He relied heavily upon the personal support of big-screen star and one the generation of actors who emerged in the bitter social critiques of the 1970s, Harvey Keitel. *Reservoir Dogs* is an ensemble production that revolves around a bungled robbery and the scenes of confrontation and violence that follow. Like *One False Move, El Mariachi,* and *Laws of Gravity*, it features men with guns in sequences of personal dilemma and collective confrontation with other forces, such as the police or rival gangsters. All the films show copious amounts of thick red blood being spilled, spend more time watching people die than is commonly accepted and use stylised camera work (odd angles or movement) or music (a funky song plays while a robber cuts off a police officer's ear in *Reservoir Dogs*) during the most gruesome moments. What is interesting is that David Fincher makes similar stylistic choices in his treatment of violence for *Fight Club*.

Fight Club is different from a film like *Godzilla*. In the latter the camera pulls away at the moment of pain or death. The spectator only sees horrified expressions or hears screams. *Air Force One* and *Face/Off* feature gunfire and explosions but there are no close ups of bullet wounds or charred bodies. *Fight Club* repeatedly shows bloodied faces. In one instance Narrator smashes another character's face, sitting astride him and raining down rhythmic crunching blows. The basement under a dingy urban bar where Fight Club has its home falls silent, the sound of knuckle upon bone filling out the spatial dimension. There are no background sounds and we are not edited away from the action. Subsequently, the beaten character is lifted to his feet, his shocking injuries filling out the frame. The faces of the club members supporting him are not visible, nothing distracts from the injuries. Later the same character returns disfigured. In this respect *Fight Club*'s violence borrows from Quentin Tarantino.

In Tarantino's 1996 Palm d'Or-winning non-linear narrative of overlapping individual stories, *Pulp Fiction,* gangster Vincent Vega and his partner (accidentally) blow off the head of a passenger in their car. Blood, skull and brain splatter them and the white leather of the car's interior. This gory killing remains in the foreground as the gangsters recruit 'the cleaner', a mister fix-it played by Tarantino's old pal Harvey Keitel, to clean the car. *Reservoir Dogs* presents the same kind of stylish violence. One character is shot in the stomach and spends the film on the floor of a warehouse, bleeding slowly to death. His wound isn't hidden from view and we see the blood spurt forth from his flesh. In perhaps the film's most controversial scene, a police officer has his ear removed with a razor to the song 'Stuck in The Middle With You'. We actually see the ear and the officer's blood-soaked, sweating head. Michael Madsen – the actor who dances and sings as he cuts the policeman's ear – claimed later that Tarantino was so intent on making the violence real for the audience that he locked the actor playing the policeman in a car boot and drove him around till he was panicked enough to look really scared of Madsen's knife wielding. The rhythmic beating in *Fight Club*, the refusal to pull away from blood and guts is not identical to Tarantino's style but close to it. So much so, in fact, that *Fight Club* made some reviewers most uncomfortable.

The major critical debate about *Fight Club* at the time of its release concerned the way the whole text was soaked with violence. Mike Clark said in *USA Today* that the film was 'disgusting and possibly even diseased … fun to talk about … but the price you pay is enduring its excesses'.[62] Critic Jim Chastain was much sharper in his criticism, suggesting that 'while this film is strong in most of the critical areas, its overall vision is so violent, so bloody, and so hopeless, I simply cannot recommend it to anyone, myself included'.[63] Kenneth Turran of the *LA Times* even argued the Motion Picture Arts Association were too lenient when assessing the film, proposing that 'its stomach-turning string of bloody and protracted bare-knuckle brawls, make it more than worthy of an NC-17 if the MPAA could ever work up the nerve (don't hold your breath) to give that rating to a major studio film'.[64] Even James Sanford of the *Kalamzoo Gazette* found it hard to place the film in some sort of historical context without getting caught up in its superficialities of fists:

> Those with long memories will recall there was once another picture which earned the same kinds of criticisms when it was first released: Stanley Kubrick's 1971 masterpiece 'A Clockwork Orange.' If 'Orange' was a bitter answer to the 'all you need is love' message of the late 1960s, 'Club' is a brass-knuckled slap in the face to yuppiedom and its 'greed is good' mantra.[65]

Why were so many critics, in such a diverse range of publications, so worked up? David Fincher is not a radical and possibly not even a liberal. His film does not engage fully with anti-capitalism, but there is something about the quality of violence in *Fight Club*, the way it appears in different forms in every aspect of the gloomy consumerist world Fincher has created, that locks into a debate Oliver Stone started in 1994 with his equally violent and probably more controversial film *Natural Born Killers*.

Natural Born Killers was the subject of a lawsuit against Warner Brothers by the family of a shooting victim. Two 18-year-olds on a crime spree in Louisiana had claimed to be inspired by Stone's film. The author of many legal thrillers later adapted by Hollywood, John Grisham, even got involved, demanding that filmmakers be held accountable for violence that 'incited' kids to kill. The whole affair led to the film being cut drastically in some states in order to get released, and Stone was not responsible for choosing what stayed or went. The film was even banned in the UK. Eventually, after a protracted legal case a Louisiana judge ruled the film to be protected under the First Amendment of the American constitution. However, the furore around the film had already indicated the sensibilities of the American establishment upon which Fincher touches. Again, the violence in *Natural Born Killers* was no worse than that in many studio productions. One of the central characters, Mallory, kills her parents, a prostitute is strangled and a petrol station attendant is shot, as are a Native American, a shop worker and an Australian TV host. That makes seven deaths in all, roughly equivalent to the number of killings in the *The Godfather*, with the addition of some scenes of sexual violence. What was different about Stone's film was that it flouted narrative convention, stylised its action and was unrepentant in its representation of the mass popular media. The film opens with a sitcom-style presentation of Mallory's abusive family and closes with her and crime-partner Mickey starting a new sitcom in their trailer. The exploits of their crime and murder spree are both the subject of the film and a vehicle for demonstrating the manipulative nature of capitalist culture. Celebrity crime-show hosts and police officers are both lampooned and shown to be perverse: witness Jack Sagnetti's hooker, chosen because she looks like Mallory and dispensed with brutally when she doesn't meet his sadistic standard. Stone gets in his compulsory reference to American football, which would later work itself up to be *Any Given Sunday*, by depicting a producer desperate to get his interview with the 'natural born' killers on prime-time TV after the Super Bowl. The producer gets his just deserts, killed in front of the audience he was so determined to lure. The wider American establishment is complicit in this twisted media circus – the warden of the prison is keen to get Mickey and Mallory on to TV in order that he can subsequently kill them.

Stone was the epitome of the anti-Reagan liberal in the 1980s, taking outings to Central America and producing the fiercely critical *Salvador*, which we have already placed as the filmic pinnacle of liberal Hollywood activism. With *Any Given Sunday* he is transformed into the anti-corporate new liberal, hanging on tight to his special hero, dabbling in historical specificity and almost presenting a class analysis. *Natural Born Killers* is the exception to the rule of his trajectory. Stone, it is fair to say, fell out with Clinton before others such as Beatty. He never slept over at the White House and stated equivocally in *The Nation* in 1999 that he had never been a 'Clinton man'. The point here is that in 1994, as his own words show, Stone was not enamoured by Clinton and was not about to be an FOB. If we put *Natural Born Killers* in this light, then it becomes a bitter anti-establishment film – even a radical one.

Natural Born Killers set the precedent for the critical reception of *Fight Club* because it held a radical mirror up to the American media. Is it any surprise that the biggest critics of *Fight Club*'s violence were just that, media critics? *Natural Born Killers* was accused of glamorising violence but its mannered style and iconographical references, in fact, attacked the media for making killers media stars. *Fight Club*, however, is not a radical film. The media are not implicated in the generation of violence. The complicity of the capitalist system in Stone's film is reduced to consumerist emasculation in Fincher's. The fact that *Fight Club* was interpreted by some critics as sharing its screen space with *Natural Born Killers* says more about Fincher's clever referential use of violence, and his marriage with studio economics, than it does about his politics. Furthermore, Fincher's treatment of violence gives his film the 'independent' tag which Stone carries historically from his early productions like *Salvador*, which were produced outside studio influence and were direct attacks on the American government. Deliberate or otherwise, Fincher's film appears on the surface separate from corporatism, stealing the clothes of early 1990s independents. However, by choosing the gun-toting half of the independent revival as his model he steers away from those early 1990s independent films tackling real social issues. This helps explain the major difference between ambiguous, studio-made films and the work of Tim Robbins or John Sayles. Ambiguous films borrow from the less political independent scene but distort the political message of the anti-capitalist film, because they are produced by an alliance of talent with the corporate Hollywood machine; a corporate machine that George Bush Jr was helping to grow stronger.

Trans-national Hollywood business

Fight Club's use of violence is often shocking. Consider the moment in the final sequence when Narrator puts a gun inside his own mouth without warning. The barrel of the revolver stretches the rim of his lips. His pale and heavily bruised face fills the frame as he pulls the trigger. His head flings backwards, blood squirts from his cheek and smoke rises from the side of his head. For several seconds the mise-en-scène is reduced to a contrast of contorted smoking pale flesh, festooned with crimson speckles, and a black emptiness like a vast hole in the background. Yet the film was popular, as can be judged by its position at number 35 in the 2002 Internet Movie Database's poll of the all time best movies.[66] Its reception from critics was massive, and on the same website – which has over 10,000 visitors a day – 225 newspaper reviews are listed, more than are listed for any other film. *Fight Club* also received 19 award nominations from 10 different bodies in the year of its release.

As well as being popular, *Fight Club*'s use of an independent movie-maker's style of violence did not put it outside the Hollywood machine. In profit, production and recognition it is a corporate film. *Fight Club* featured stars (Brad Pitt, Meat Loaf, Edward Norton) and was financed by Twentieth Century Fox at a cost of $63 million. However, between the birth of the 1990s violent independent film, in the form of Quentin Tarantino's crime story *Reservoir Dogs* (1992), and the release of the corporate-made *Fight Club* (1999), it can be argued that the term 'independent film' was redefined.

Reservoir Dogs made $22 million worldwide, from a budget of just $1.2 million.[67] An astounding $22 return for each $1 invested. There is an absence of any major studio from the credit sequence, having been produced by Dog Eat Dog productions, a temporary company Tarantino set up. Tarantino was ready to shoot on cost-effective black-and-white film, using a cheap 16mm camera, with props picked up for free and using a few of his friends to play the criminal cast. Then, through a friend of a friend, the script found its way to respected Hollywood star Harvey Keitel and he offered a $1 million investment. Such a small production was the film that there wasn't enough money for all the costumes and the cast had to provide some of their own, including Mr Pink's black jeans, Mr Blonde's cowboy boots and Nice Guy Eddie's jacket. To further establish the film's out-of-Hollywood credentials it is worth noting that actor James Woods was asked to play a leading role but never got the opportunity to say no for himself because his agent simply ignored the offer as it was a little under one-tenth of his usual fee. Furthermore, Tarantino shuns the corporate aesthetic in the construction of his fiction.

For example, in the meeting scene at the start of the film – when the gangsters are given their colour-coded secret identities – one smokes a packet of 'Red Apples' cigarettes. This is a brand that was taken off the market in the 1970s and its use suggested that Tarantino wanted to avoid unintentional product placement. For the same reason a cereal packet in one the film's flashback sequences is called 'Fruit Brute', another dead product. The same deliberate use of outdated brands appears in the director's subsequent films. However, despite the film's origin and independent aesthetic, Tim Roth – who played the undercover cop, slowly dying from excessive blood loss caused by a shot in the stomach – told an *LA Village Voice* journalist in 1998 that he felt he'd been disadvantaged by the success of the film. He had not had the most prosperous of careers since *Reservoir Dogs* and had chosen to stay predominantly within the independent film sector. The success of the film exceeded his limitations as an actor and left behind him and most of the shoe-string company of talent gathered by Tarantino. Roth said, 'the studios, they're looking and going: "Hmmm. Wait a second. We're missing out on some cash here ... We've got to pay attention to these people"'.[68] That attention was paid very closely indeed.

Over the course of the mid-to-late 1990s major corporations bought out independent production companies and independent producers. PolyGram International took in distributor and producer Gramercy. USA Networks Inc., a multi-media entertainment group, swallowed them both in 1993. Then in the late 1990s a USA-, Japan- and Europe-based giant, Vivendi, bought up USA Networks as well as Universal Studios, Focus Features and major European producer and distributor Canal. Following suit, AOL Time Warner bought New Line in 1995. Fox, bought by Australian mogul Rupert Murdoch's international News Corporation in the mid 1990s, now own Searchlight and Regency. Around the same time, MGM swallowed United Artists and bought controlling stakes in the Independent Film Channel and AMC (American Movie Classics network). Disney own Touchstone, Hollywood Pictures and Dimension Films, as well as the leading light of 1990s independent distribution run by the Weinstein brothers – Miramax. International media giant Viacom also acquired Paramount and Paramount Classics in the late 1990s. Hollywood talent cannot enter the process of film production without bumping into an executive connected to at least one of these corporations. Tim Roth's observation that major business wanted a piece of the independent dollar that *Reservoir Dogs* had shown was out there is proven by the fact that these acquisitions started in 1993, when the Disney–Miramax deal took place. Ultimately these buy-outs acclimatised the formerly independent Weinstein brothers, who ran Miramax, to corporate lifestyle and ideas. So it was that Bob Weinstein began to produce bigger budget, lowbrow and frankly un-funny but big box-office hits like *Scary Movie* and its sequels.

Meanwhile the parent companies merged with rivals or sister organisations to spread their tentacles into every media marketplace and to sell on every continent. What emerged by the start of the twenty-first century were trans-national mega businesses competing on a grand scale for audiences at the cinema, on television and radio, in the computer games market and at the rental store. Eight big corporations and their franchise operations today control the process of movie production, distribution and exhibition: AOL Time Warner, Disney, News Corporation (who own Twentieth Century Fox),

Viacom, Sony (who own Columbia Pictures), Vivendi, MGM and the newest addition, DreamWorks SKG.

By 2000 just 255 films were officially recorded as independent by the Dodona Research publication *Hollywood: America's Film Industry*.[69] Of these, all were in fact produced by a major corporate subsidiary, with the exception of eight which were distributed by Artisan who rely upon the major studio cinema chains – such as United International Cinemas, owned by Viacom – for exhibition deals. The average budget for an American film in 2001 was $90 million, close to a hundred times what it cost to make *Reservoir Dogs* – indicating that the dominant force in production was the big-budget Hollywood copy of the independent film, in the mould of Fincher's *Fight Club*. The very process of bringing a film to life is studio dominated. Even a film concept requires registration with the Motion Picture Association of America's Title Registration Bureau.

The studios, with more staff and more financial capacity, can regularly register hundreds of names of potential films and block smaller companies or individuals from titling their film appropriately, and being able to sell it as a marketable product to distributors. The MPAA is a corporate business association set up in 1922. Jack Valenti, CEO of the MPAA since 1966, is now the model of a Bush era business lobbyist. He earned $1.5 million in 2000, has been a White House adviser to Republican administrations and has made a point of speaking out about trade relations, copyright laws and piracy issues. He told the White House in 2002 that 'copyright issues are responsible for some five per cent of the GDP of the [American] nation … the movie industry alone has a surplus balance of trade with every single country in the world'.[70] Another way to express this might have been, 'Hollywood is profiting more than any other industry from the globalisation dream by using World Trade Organisation international deals – which you, Mr Bush, helped to broker – that guarantee media corporations copyright on ideas, not just on products, thus preventing small national film industries making similar films in their mother tongue'. A successful strategy that, according to the ex-studio executives Peter Bart and Peter Guber, made the American media industry worth $3 trillion by 2003 – equivalent to 6 per cent of the global economy.

The MPAA is in charge of giving ratings certificates to films and has the power to limit a film's audience to the R – over 17 only – category or even refuse to give it a certificate altogether, thus encouraging cinemas not to exhibit the film. This system, which in the UK is administered by a non-profit, government-supported board of film classification with an elected steering group, demonstrates how the American movie market is utterly integrated. Agents, supposedly there to represent talented creative individuals, collude in this integration. The Creative Artists' Agency (CAA), for example, organised the sale of Columbia to Sony in the 1990s. Its chief executive Michael Ovitz is largely responsible for creating the package-deal model of movie making – where a concept, director, actors and crew are sold as one deal to a corporation. Agents like Ovitz have become vital cogs in corporate production processes, even earning producer credits. Ovitz is even credited with being the real production head behind the creation of 1990s dinosaur hit *Jurassic Park*. CAA also markets Coca-Cola to Hollywood and ensures that any films in which they have a say feature Coke products. The company's deals earned them $200 million in 1999 alone. Subsequently Ovitz had short tenures as a head of production at Disney and Universal. Agents and managers are now creating their own production companies based on existing corporate models. Brillstein Grey Entertainment and Artists Management Group are two as yet unsuccessful examples – a clear attempt to take the production mantle away from studios altogether. Agents have already begun to negotiate deals where stars are bound to certain studios and certain inter-dependent production units. Such PACT deals are ongoing partnerships between corporations and leading talent, mediated in most cases by an agent.

Disney has producer Jerry Bruckheimer and writer stars Ben Affleck and Matt Damon on its roster. DreamWorks has comedy stalwart and producer of at least one film a year, Woody Allen. Fox have Mel Gibson, *Gladiator* director Ridley Scott and his brother Tony, as well as the director behind the biggest grossing cinema hit of all time – *Titanic* – James Cameron. Universal have an exclusive deal with comedy- and family-film actor Danny De Vito's production company Jersey Films, which produced *Erin Brockovich*. Even the father of early 1990s independent film, Steven Soderbergh, who directed *Erin Brockovich*, has his Section 8 production company tied to AOL Time Warner. There is virtually no production company on an American film credit that is not financed by or locked into a deal with a big corporation. As a result the big eight have a 95 per cent share of the global exhibition market and are similar to the 1920/30s Hollywood studios who produced, distributed and exhibited films. They are also eliminating competitors in TV broadcasting: AOL Time Warner are combining TV, film, audio and electronic markets. This picture demonstrates how the power in Hollywood currently remains with the corporations and that agents' machinations are, at the present time, only assisting in maintaining corporate control by chaining talent to the corporate mangle. The corporations would have to choose to withdraw their power from Hollywood for agents like Ovitz to take over. The expansion of digital technologies, the Internet and merchandise, like computer games, is unlikely to turn them away but they have threatened to leave before.

Bart and Guber observed during the 2001–2 potential actors', directors' and crew strike in Hollywood – when talent threatened militant action in order to get a marginally bigger slice of corporate revenue – that corporations complained 'that the profits from the production of TV and film are wafer thin, having been eroded by … talent costs'.[71] That didn't stop them settling the dispute and hadn't stopped Vivendi spending $30 million in one day to acquire the film production company Universal just one year earlier. If anything, the corporate interests in Hollywood are more entrenched today and have used the agents to outsource the cost of brokering deals with stars and of finding ideas to make into films. Agents today are the main source of scripts and concepts for Hollywood and most writers find themselves needing an agent just to get a studio to see them. Agents like Ovtiz may wish to run Hollywood but they are merely a part of the machine controlled by powerful corporate CEOs.

Producer of *Crouching Tiger, Hidden Dragon*, James Schamus, wrote of the AOL–Time Warner merger: 'Gerald Levin, the head of Time Warner … told CNN that global media companies are "more important than government … they have the resources, they have the reach, they have the skills base" … AOL Time Warner will most likely control half of all U.S. internet access and a quarter of its cable market'.[72] The concern implied in Schamus's remark is the same one that motivated many Seattle protesters, and it seems to have justification. AOL Time Warner, for example, own over 40 television networks, including the HBO company that produced *Six Feet Under*. They own 26 film production or distribution outlets, including Castle Rock Entertainment. They have control of over 15 music companies, more than 50 publications and 10 television channels. They operate in North America, South America, Europe, Asia and the Middle East, where they own the Al Jazeera television network that has copied the rolling-news style of American 24-hour broadcasters, like CNN but with an added element of Islamic religion. From filmed entertainment alone AOL Time Warner made $8,759 million in 2001.

Disney has a similar make up, owning a major local television station in every American state capital and 10 others besides, as well as 12 production or distribution companies in Hollywood. Disney owns Buena Vista International – *the* biggest cinema and video distributor in the world. Disney also made a considerable part of their $25.3 billion turnover in 2001 from toys, computer games and parks or resorts. News Corporation is the dominant force in global television and newspaper markets with nearly 30 networks in the USA alone, including many sports networks and specific cable channels for the New York Nicks basketball team and for Madison Square Garden, the team's home venue.[73] Where such companies do not own actual venues for exhibiting or renting movies, they do own the channels of movie distribution to cinemas, to home rental stores and the television channels that films are shown on. Through distribution deals the big eight can make money from theatrical exhibition (90 per cent of the gross box office goes to the studio), video rental (as a study of the exhibition system concluded in 1992, the studio 'puts 80% [of video revenue] in its pocket'[74]), pay television (where studios usually get 50 per cent of the fee), free television (where the station must pay for rights to show the movie) and a vast range of merchandise and follow-on products like computer games or music CDs.

This situation led Peter Bart, now editor of *Variety*, to tell the Public Broadcasting System in 1991, 'they're sort of nation states, AOL Time Warner is a nation state, so is Vivendi'. Only one relatively small constituency of these nation-states deals with film production. British television producer and one-time Hollywood director Tony Garnett comments that 'they won't make more than six or seven studios, the corporations think its too expensive to set up a new one. The corporations that own the studios don't just represent capital, they are capital.'[75] Bart calls the situation of being a 'vision keeper' – the person or people creating a film – a 'high wire act'.[76] Writers produce a script or re-work someone else's but they have to balance their own wishes with the corporation's, who negotiate to buy the concept, usually through an agent, from the position of owning the production company, the distribution wing and controlling any future budget. The producer – if not a corporate executive – has to balance the pressures of meeting a studio-set budget and corporate marketing objectives with the wishes of the writer, director and actors. The director has most control over the aesthetics of a film but has to negotiate with the studio, again usually via an agent, and it is the studio that owns either the film's concept as bought from the writer or the means of funding and distributing a film based on the director's own concept. If directors balance studio interests with their own to get the right to develop the concept of their choice, then the marketing department gets involved. Marketing a Hollywood film in 2003 averages a cost of $27.3 million – 11 per cent more of the total budget than during most of the 1990s. On bigger budget films 60 per cent of this cost is television advertising alone, which is, in a manner of speaking, one department of the nation-state paying another to raise its own profile. Like agents, the marketing experts are, in the new millennium, a significant part of the Hollywood machine. Moreover, they increasingly dictate what gets made and what gets distributed, as well as what the potential viewing public is told about a film.

For example, in 2000 Marc Schmuger, a marketing executive, became the vice-chairman of Universal with overall budget and green light authority. Underneath him marketing chief Buffy Shutt describes how all films made by Universal are now seen 'merely as product', not as a concept or a story.[77] Shutt or Schmuger might even get a credit if their influence, which – if not felt in their green light decisions – is felt from the first production meeting, changes an aspect of the movie to meet audience profiles. Bart and Guber observe that marketing executives and film distribution chiefs at Disney, Vivendi and Warner Brothers were often based in the same physical space and are increasingly becoming the same person. In this way the corporate executives influence what is made and how it is sold in one swoop, ensuring that a 90 per cent return from the box office can be negotiated for the company and that theatrical exhibitors who don't play ball – i.e. want to show work by other companies or exhibit shoe-string funded independent cinema – are starved of the most popular, best advertised and revenue generating films.

In this context of profit-focused corporate power it is logical to ask why the corporations have not closed down the anti-corporate themed films that emerged in the late 1990s. Why have they invested in films like *Fight Club*? As well as its penchant for violence *Fight Club* features an anarchist army – Operation Mayhem – that consciously seeks to undermine corporate influence on modern life. Charismatic leader Tyler Durden's black-clad foot soldiers deface corporate emblems and destroy credit card databases to free ordinary citizens from commitments to the banking industry, to 'return everyone to zero' as Tyler puts it. This anti-corporatism proves how important the independent mentality has become to Hollywood's market manipulation. The crucial fracture in the corporate strategy of power is that each film must be sold as its own mini-brand. The logo at the start of a film alone does not sell the product for the corporation, it does not pay the marketing executives or the agents locked into the corporate media structure by their increasing back-end – a cut of the box office – deals. The stars, name recognition of the director, the special effects and the quality of the story sell the film. There must be some aspect of the film's content that attracts the audience. This means that the shrewd socially engaged filmmakers can create a space for their concept, and win themselves directorial control, if they can convince someone in the corporate-owned process that their idea will sell.

Tim Robbins explains the situation this way: 'you have to under-stand first and foremost that it is a business that you're dealing with, and if you can create a product that's potentially profitable, that's what they're looking for'.[78] This is what Robbins did with *Cradle Will Rock*, persuading Disney executive Joe Roth that his concept was marketable enough to be worth funding and distributing. Robbins employed one of three basic strategies for progressive filmmakers in present-day Hollywood: he sold his idea to the corporate machine and let them exploit it for profit in order to get his film made. A second strategy might have been to work with a corporate satellite company, like Joe Roth's early 2000s-founded Revolution Films. Such intermediaries can broker a deal where they pay a third of production costs, the other two-thirds coming from the lucrative European exhibition market control-led by a major corporation with whom the satellite has a permanent distribution deal. Tony Garnett – who returned from Hollywood to work in British television in the 1990s and whose World Productions outfit has a satellite deal with Sony, via their subsidiary Columbia – outlines a third strategy. Individual filmmakers can negotiate in what Garnett calls the 'interstices of the system'. This strategy is concerned with manipulating the minutiae of relations, business and personal, so that an executive will green light a film 'for a friend or to ensure future relationships', as Garnett puts it. Having worked with Joe Roth during the 1980s, Garnett supposes that he is both 'a democrat and a liberal'[79] who may have sanctioned *Cradle Will Rock* to nurture the personal alle-giance of Tim Robbins.

In using all three of these tactics, filmmakers have to negotiate with care, being a good self-publicist or already having widespread name recognition and being able to keep their eyes on the prize that they originally set out to win – the hearts and minds of the audience. Michael Moore, the radical documentary maker, has become the mas-ter of this art and in the process has made perhaps the most important film of the last decade: *Fahrenheit 9/11*.

Michael Moore's
radical documentary phenomenon

In 1989 Michael Moore made a film about the closure of a General Motors factory in his hometown of Flint, Michigan, which appears as a case study of American life in all his subsequent documentaries. Moore's films have a number of hallmarks. He always talks to ordinary citizens in homes and workplaces, such as Geraldo Rivera, a laid-off worker in that 1989 documentary, *Roger and Me*, or the teacher who witnessed a six-year-old shoot another student in the tale of gun crime and global weapons production that is *Bowling for Columbine*. In his latest film, *Fahrenheit 9/11*, exploring the aftermath of the World Trade Center attacks in 2001 and blaming the Bush administration for using them to political advantage, Moore interviews diminutive Lila Lipscomb in her kitchen. Lila is a Flint resident and a parent of a soldier who fought in the 2003 Iraq war. Other Moore-isms include establishing shots of heavy industry plants and credits that appear to make no sense – such as 'Mike's Militia' in *Columbine,* a reference to Ohio University students who viewed and suggested re-edits for the film before release. Moore certainly makes films that conform to his own ambitions and aesthetic.

Moore also uses archive footage of politicians – Bush in *Columbine* and *Fahrenheit* – with an acerbic Moore voiceover, and scenes in which the filmmaker or one of the real-life people in his film are blocked from a building of a major corporation or a powerful agency. Security guards in pressed shirts with black epaulets appear in the background as a threatening presence just picked out by the swaying of a hand-held camera as the crew retreat. In *Fahrenheit 9/11* it is Bush's reading of a book in a Florida school classroom after hearing about the 9/11 attacks that gets the voiceover, and it is uniformed secret service officers who stop Moore outside the Saudi Arabian Embassy for doing nothing more than filming the street.

There's also a tendency in his films to reinforce Moore's social commentary by following comic dialogue with an instantaneous image, interview or press cutting that reminds the viewer of the devastating effect of a factory closure, a gun crime or a war on a person's life. In *Fahrenheit 9/11* this takes the form of real images from the Iraq war of the shattered limbs of soldiers and Iraqi civilians, in the kind of footage that stirs memories of every Vietnam film ever seen. Then there's Moore's willingness to shake up his own use of form, to move from

conventional television documentary style – point the camera at someone like Lila Lipscomb and ask questions – and inventive techniques,
such as knocking on doors and asking residents if they own a gun, having a 10-minute cartoon sequence to explain a historical issue, or
turning up at acting legend and National Rifle Association president
Charlton Heston's gate and asking for an interview. These elements in
Bowling for Columbine give Moore's social documentary a unique narrative quality.

Time magazine has gone so far at to call these motifs the 'Moore
method'. This method has five elements: comedy – like driving round
Capitol Hill in an ice-cream van to talk to congressmen through its
loudspeaker; tragedy – Lila Lipscomb's tears outside the White House
for the loss of her son; infiltration – finding an un-doctored copy of
George Bush Jr's military record; confrontation – visiting the K-Mart
headquarters to return bullets used in the Columbine school shootings;
speculation – asking what Bush is thinking in footage where he is sitting in silence. Arguably, if Moore's films weren't documentaries these
motifs could be sighted as the artistic threads of an auteur's oeuvre.
Instead, as Moore himself put it to MSNBC reporter Jeanette Walls in
2002, these films are discussed as 'provocative, controversial … going
to make a lot of people angry. That is not my intention.'

Moore's intention is, as the official website for *Fahrenheit 9/11* pro-
claims, 'to make people consider the future of their country'. His films
are documentaries but also carefully constructed movies that tell a
story Moore wants to tell, consciously conveying the social messages
that Haskell Wexler says all films contain in some form. Moore is mas-
ter of his art – injecting feature-length cinematic experiences with anti-
government, pro-democracy venom – and he deserves credit for his
ability as well as for his ideals. Sean Penn, as mentioned earlier, had
demanded that all Hollywood filmmakers take such a stance in their
work, and in Michael Moore Penn and other Hollywood anti-
capitalists could find their greatest inspiration. In a time when Hollywood has become a globally integrated economic media machine,
Moore has exploited the space created by corporate attempts to catch
the independent market with a new brand of politically engaged
movie that has been massively popular.

When Moore made *Roger and Me* he did so with his own camera and
funded it by holding bingo games in his front room. The film received
no studio distribution and was seen by a tiny audience, premiering in
a Flint cinema at an event that Moore himself had to organise. Moore
worked out of his tiny personal company, run for years from his home

in Flint and only since *Bowling for Columbine* from a New York office, where his website, michaelmoore.com is hosted and where volunteers are able to send him information that assists in his quest to present the American progressive agenda.

Bowling for Columbine, unlike *Roger and Me*, has 10 producers on its credits, was backed by the United Broadcasting mini-corporation based in California and had distribution deals from United Artists, Atlantis International and MGM. The Cannes Festival panel of judges created a special 55th Anniversary Award for the film and it went on to win other awards, like the Vancouver International Film Festival. It also made history by becoming the first documentary to win the Writers' Guild of America Award for Best Screenplay. In October 2002, MGM announced that *Columbine* had been one of its five most profitable distribution deals of the year. By November this film about American life and politics had even made the corporations $10.3 million from cinema exhibition in Europe, according to *Screen International* magazine. Amazingly, the film ran at theatres for almost a year and in February 2003 MGM said its $106 million profit from American releases over the previous 12 months was due to the success of four films, of which *Columbine* was the third-biggest earner. From a budget of just $4 million the film grossed $21.25 million by the end of its run in early 2003.[80] In March 2003 Moore then won the Best Documentary Feature Oscar and he chose to question the legitimacy of Bush Jr's presidency in his acceptance speech.

'We are against the war Mr Bush ... shame on you, shame on you, shame on you', he called, with the support of all the other documentary Oscar nominees who joined him on stage. Oscars producer Gil Cates told the orchestra to start playing, lowered the stage microphone to stop Moore and turned up the volume of a small section of the audience that booed Moore – up on the balcony – but by a 60 to 40 per cent majority Moore estimated the audience was behind him. Indeed, Susan Sarandon and Tim Robbins gave peace signs to protests outside the ceremony, Andy Serkis – the slimy creature Gollum in the *Lord of the Rings* films – carried an anti-Iraq war placard with him into the theatre and A-list acting stars like Colin Farrell pleaded for an end to war by going off-script in their presentations. By mid 2003 Moore was more than just a progressive, more than just a documentary maker. Arguably, he had become the world's leading documentary maker, with an artistic flair to his work, recognition among Hollywood's glitterati, a reputation for controversy that tabloid media worldwide could be persuaded to cover and was giving confidence to the growing progressive

10. Michael Moore declared his Oscar for *Bowling for Columbine* the 'people's Oscar' (*copyright Marissa Hauptman*).

element among Hollywood's talent. On a commercial level Moore's popularity and profile make it no surprise that Icon Productions – already mentioned as being closely associated with arch Republican Mel Gibson and Rupert Murdoch's News Corporation – offered Moore the money to make *Fahrenheit 9/11*.

When this deal was announced in April 2003 it demonstrated how quick the corporations have become in jumping on the progressive bandwagon for the sake of profit. *NewsMax* cited a Hollywood insider as saying that President Bush had 'always considered himself on good terms with Gibson and even invited him to a private meeting at the White House. He can't expect more White House invites if he's backing Michael Moore.' In the end Gibson's company withdrew support, but Disney subsidiary Miramax stepped in, as did Lion's Gate. *Fahrenheit 9/11* proved to be an even better investment for these studio inter-dependents. It became the first documentary since 1953 to win the coveted Palme d'Or at Cannes in 2004, receiving a 15-minute standing ovation from the audience. It had the highest grossing documentary opening weekend of all time in America, making $23.9 million. It made that from just 868 screens, but the cinema exhibition chains soon realised they could make money and bumped this up to 1,725 in the second week of release, setting a new record figure for a documentary feature release in the USA. The film was the first documentary to feature in the American top five grossing movie list during its opening two weeks and even made it to number one in its first weekend. Moore's film had tapped into a previously unknown or unused audience, and this despite the studios getting cold feet because of the film's clear anti-Bush message.

Time accurately described what Moore was trying to achieve in making *Fahrenheit 9/11*; after interviewing him in July 2004 they concluded he wanted to make 'a nationwide rally point for Bush opponents, a red flag for Bush supporters, a cinematic teach-in for the undecided and a potential factor in the '04 presidential race'.[81] *Fahrenheit* has not just done well with a liberal or progressive audience, it packed out cinemas in Republican heartlands like Bartlett, Tennessee, and in Memphis, where audiences reportedly clapped, booed and laughed as if there were television studio cue cards on view. Having asked Republican officials for a response, *Time* concluded that 'for months to come pollsters and political consultants will be analysing and focus grouping the viewer/voter response to *Fahrenheit 9/11*'.

Initially, however, Disney, Miramax's owners, had cold feet. When he won the Cannes Palme d'Or, Moore announced that Disney had instructed Miramax to stop the distribution of his film. They argued that the film was designed to interfere with the 2004 presidential election, something Moore has never denied. Fahrenheit911.com, which features an amusing fake picture of Moore in trademark baseball cap and t-shirt on the White House lawn hand-in-hand with Bush, also has an 'OK I've seen the movie what do I do now?' section, giving advice and links that assist citizens in rubbishing the president's name and promoting alternative candidates in the election. The film opens with the line 'was it all a dream', and begins by taking apart the 2000 election win for Bush, exposing potential corruption in Florida that probably won the president his office. There can be little doubt that Disney was right, it was their motivation that Moore attacked in Cannes. He pointed out that they get a special tax break from the Bush government for their theme parks and hotels in Florida. In the end, much as in the Robbins versus the Baseball Hall of Fame incident,

Moore's exposition of the vested interest of the corporation won and Disney allowed Miramax to release the film. Their pay-off was the prediction by Miramax chief Harvey Weinstein that the film would gross over $100 million in around a month. The popularity of the film's political message proved him right, paid Disney the profits, but also ignited a flame of anti-Bush sentiment across the USA and further fuelled the confidence of progressives within Hollywood's creative ranks.

Producer and anti-war activist Robert Greenwald, for example, said in July 2004, 'we've underestimated the audience's desire to see [political] material ... I don't think it's about hating the President ... the issues in it are larger than that'. Moore's success has not won people like Greenwald to the Democrat banner. Indeed, Moore makes a strong criticism of the Democrats in *Fahrenheit 9/11* in a scene where he exposes exactly who voted for the war in Iraq in Congress and shows no Democrat voted against. Inspired to think of future activism and filmmaking, Greenwald concludes that Moore's success makes it possible for him to operate politically with more success than before: 'When Clinton was President, I went after him. And if Kerry's President, on Day Two I'll be on him.'[82] There are even some people in and around the Hollywood left who see little distinction between Bush Jr and John Kerry. 'The difference is one of tone', says British producer and veteran of 1980s Hollywood production Tony Garnett. He goes on, 'most people in Hollywood would doubtless prefer Kerry's rhetoric to Bush's but the generation coming up now care very little about electoral politicians'.[83]

This indicates that the new Hollywood progressive generation, inspired by Moore's political exploitation of the development of corporate media, were not drawn back into supporting the Democratic Party as a result of their Bush hatred. Bill Clinton had assisted the initial development of trans-national corporate Hollywood. The 1996 Telecommunication Act had, as Bill Moyers on the Public Broadcasting Service's *Now* programme calculated, helped eight corporations take control of the media by 2002.[84] Under Bush, that market exploitation by corporate giants had simply taken on a more ideological dimension. In broadcast radio Clear Channel Communications used the 1996 Act to buy out two-thirds of all American radio stations. In 2002 and 2003 Clear Channel organized pro-Iraq-war demonstrations, was rumoured to be bussing its own staff to rallies under threat of censure and to be paying people to boo and throw debris onto the stage at concerts by the Dixie Chicks. When a member of the country music group said she was ashamed to be a Texan because George Bush was too, Clear Channel executives removed their records from all play lists. Speaking to the National Press Club in 2003 Tim Robbins told the story of a high-profile American 'rocker' who called him to thank him for speaking against the war, 'only to go on to tell me that he could not speak because he fears repercussions from Clear Channel. '"They promote our concert appearances", he said, "They own most of the stations that play our music. I can't come out against this war."'[85] The strategy of the Bush administration from day one had been to open up the entire media industry vault to the pro-Republican corporations.

In the first week of his presidency Bush appointed Michael Powell – son of Secretary of State Colin Powell – to head up the Federal Communications Commission (FCC). The commission has the power to review and monitor the shape of the media industry, and is supposed to do so in the public interest. Hollywood progressives must have wondered how it served the public interest when, on the second of June 2003, Michael Powell forced a vote in the FCC committee overturning rules spanning 50 years that had prevented corporations having an absolute monopoly of the broadcast industries. The broadcast and newspaper rule (1975) stopping a company owning a newspaper and television or radio station in a locality was scrapped. The television-radio rule (1975) that prevented ownership of multiple television and radio stations and preserved the presence of independent broadcasters was also torn up. The television ownership rule (1941) designed to stop national networks buying up local stations was changed so that the nationals could own 45 per cent, the equivalent of a controlling stake. Whilst these were Republican changes, the crowbar used to open the media vault had been left behind by Bill Clinton.

The 1996 Telecommunications Act mandated the FCC to review its rules every two years, and it was this stipulation that Michael Powell used to make his changes. Indeed, he'd already used a clause in the Act to let him re-word the dual network rule (of 1946) from saying no company or individual could own more than one of the major four television networks – ABC, CBS, NBC and Fox – to saying they could buy each other under certain circumstances. What is markedly different between the Bush era and the Clinton era is that Bush's administration made no apology or justification for its actions. Where Clinton talked of a 'third way' and of 'inter-dependency' between corporations and government, Michael Powell said 'the market is my religion'.[86] When the House of Representatives voted 400 to 21 against some of Powell's ideas in July 2003, Bush announced he would use his executive powers to veto their decision.

It is this riding roughshod over any opposition which has led to a deep pool of anger at the Bush government among personalities like Ed Asner, Kate McArdle, Martin Sheen, Tim Robbins and Sean Penn. So murky are the depths of this dislike that Jonathan Chait wrote in the *The New Republic* about, 'a viscerally hostile reaction to the sound of [George W. Bush's] voice ... his existence [is] a constant oppressive force'.[87] In a moment in *Fahrenheit 9/11* Bush is pictured on a golf course with his father George Bush Snr. Baited by television cameras, Bush said to the press, 'I call upon all nations to do everything they can to stop terrorist killers'. Then, as if believing that was enough politics for the day, Bush turned away, golf club in hand, saying 'now watch this drive'. Bush and his policies are buffooned in Moore's film, and the particular emphasis is on the 'war on terror'. Moore suggests the conflict with Iraq in 2003 was politically and economically motivated. That war resulted in the biggest anti-government revolt in recent Hollywood history. A revolt involving all of the personalities on the new Hollywood left.

War, resistance, unity

The 2003 Iraq war was the most vehemently opposed conflict since Vietnam. The crucial difference between opposition in the 1960s and 1970s and opposition to the 2003 war was that the latter began *before* the war itself started. In the case of Vietnam the war had been underway for years before the major demonstrations of opposition took place.[88] In the case of the Iraq war American opposition first seriously manifested itself in October 2002, when in the region of 100,000 people marched against war in Washington and San Francisco. The largest anti-Vietnam demo in Washington was of equal size. Danny Glover, Tim Robbins and Susan Sarandon spontaneously attended such protests. Bob Polizeros, an organiser from Act Now to Stop War and Racism – set up by the tiny World Workers' Party and central to the early protests – explains, 'we didn't invite them, they just turned up and then they made great speeches'.[89]

Further protests took place in Washington in January 2003, achieving a 250,000 turn-out. In between the major events small protests, rallies, weekly events and conferences, training camps for non-violent direct action activists took place in communities as far-flung as San Diego (the most militarised city in the US), Pittsburgh and New York.

Fifty municipal authorities voted to oppose the war, including Chicago. In Oakland – the birthplace of the Black Panthers in the 1960s – teachers organised high-school teach-ins on war on the birthday of Martin Luther King. Trade union hierarchies were slower to move, but US Labor Against the War had support from 76 local and regional unions, successfully organising a national labour conference against war in Chicago in January 2003. The Bay Area Labor Committee for Peace and Justice claimed, 'labour opposition has emerged faster, with more clarity and greater influence than to any other war'.[90]

It is significant that the last quote is from Michael Eisenscher, the organiser of Medea Benjamin's election campaign in California in 2000, which had won significant support in Hollywood. This shows that the very people who organised Seattle and other anti-globalisation protests were now organising opposition to the war. Indeed the anti-war movement had a global resonance: London saw protests of 100,000, then 400,000 before the peak of 2 million; Barcelona saw 500,000 march; Rome saw 3 million protest against President Silvio Berlusconi's compliance with America; and 200,000 joined a day of action across France. These protests embodied the energy, methods and political consciousness of anti-capitalism. Pictures of a San Francisco protest feature huge puppets of George Bush Jr brandishing missiles, and drag queens marching next to fire fighters. Slogans damning the global system behind the war were present: 'regime change begins with Bush', 'no blood for oil'. What it took to organise these many actions was what alternative media expert and friend of Sean Penn, Norman Solomon, called 'painstaking organising among progressives, including religious organisations and many other constituencies, at the grassroots'.[91]

That grass roots anti-war work ran in the opposite direction to the beating of war drums at the top of American society, something the media conglomerates now running Hollywood were complicit in. In September 2001 two planes hijacked by – mainly Saudi Arabian – terrorists flew into the two towers of New York's World Trade Center. The buildings collapsed, thousands of office workers, domestics, firemen and policemen died in the most horrific of circumstances. This book need not explore in detail that fateful day, which was the biggest attack on American soil in the country's history. Pictures of the carnage were featured again and again on news channels around the world. Bush Jr quickly felt a response was needed and chose to bomb, then invade, Afghanistan, where the Al Qaeda terrorists behind the attack were said to be hiding. The invasion did not find them but it did result in the immediate installation of a new Afghan leader who quickly signed an agreement to put a natural gas pipeline through his country and help transport the fuel west. Over the next year and a half the Bush administration and the major media businesses in America worked together to present the idea to the American nation that Iraq was connected to the 9/11 attacks, was a terrorist country and should also be attacked by America.

CNN, owned by AOL Time Warner, whose CEO Bernard Levin had argued that corporations were more powerful than government, gave a regular platform to Kenneth Pollack. In 2002 former CIA analyst Pollack wrote a book in 2002 called *The Threatening Storm*.[92] He toured America, with CNN's help and appeared almost once a week in the second half of 2002 on their news programmes. CNN news anchor Wolf Blitzer called *The Threatening Storm* 'an important new book' and Pollack stated that 'after September 11th the American people are willing to make sacrifices to prevent threats'.[93] Blitzer and Pollack talked about Iraq's perceived ownership of dangerous weapons in definite terms. CNN ignored the United Nations weapons inspector Hans Blix when he visited Baghdad in November 2002 expressing his belief that a 'zone free of weapons of mass destruction' was becoming a reality in the country. Of all the corporate-owned American media, only the *Washing Post* quoted Blix – an unrivalled expert in his field. Indeed, the *Wall Street Journal* wrote in December that Blix 'doesn't inspire confidence' because he was 'seventy-four' and might let Iraqi leader Saddam Hussein 'make a fool of him'. The *New York Times* had written in November that any 'proof that Iraq has lied' would justify going to war.

The news media, owned by corporations of which Bush was an ally, helped in the war drive by ideologically undermining peaceful routes to disarming Iraq, by demonising the country and by repeatedly showing emotive footage of 9/11. Then, during the war itself, all the news channels embedded journalists in the armed forces; pictures showing US soldiers dying or in coffins were never shown on American mainstream television. Fairness and Accuracy In Reporting (FAIR) studied the news media during the war and found that only Middle Eastern networks showed the bodies of Iraqi civilians lying dead after attacks on their homes – the US media only showed a dead Iraqi twice. It was not until Michael Moore's *Fahrenheit 9/11* that Americans would get to see the real pictures. Video footage of dead and maimed civilians or US soldiers is given equal status in the film. Moore shows the behind-the-scenes preparation for battle; both the recruiting of impoverished urban black American youths, and the psyching-up of soldiers with rock music before going into battle. The picture is bloody, bloodthirsty, exploitative and shocking. Flint resident Lila Lipscomb then reads the last letter from her son who died on active service in Iraq. He says the war was pointless, that he wants to come home and, crucially, that George Bush Jr lied to the American people, wanted only Iraq's oil and is sending boys to their death unnecessarily. *Fahrenheit 9/11* is hate mail for George Bush, it is an anti-war message, it is the story of how the war happened, the media complicity in its preparation, the effect of it on ordinary American kids. The film captures the anger at Bush and the anti-war sentiment that had emerged in Hollywood even before the war began.

Two scenes in two films demonstrate that war, the dragging of the urban poor into the military – on which subject *Fahrenheit 9/11* spends several minutes following salesmen-like army recruiters – and the response of 'good people' to war were already subjects of concern in Hollywood a year before Bush attacked Iraq. In *Ali* (2001) a pivotal moment in the great boxer and orator's life is portrayed in dramatic style at the film's half-way point. Muhammad Ali refuses to fight in Vietnam and says to the media and the government: 'You wanna send me to jail. Fine. You go right ahead. I been in jail for 400 years. I can be there 4 or 5 more. But I ain't goin' no 10,000 miles to help murder and kill other poor people.' It's a highly dramatic scene with Will Smith, playing Ali, stomping through a court-house, surrounded by cameras and microphones and a gradual build-up of a rumbling orchestral sound underscoring his dialogue. In *Fahrenheit 9/11* an African-American marine lieutenant tells Michael Moore he will not return to Iraq and is willing to face prison because 'I won't go and kill other poor people'. Did the soldier watch *Ali* before he met Moore for filming that day, or did director of *Ali* Michael Mann – a veteran of anti-Vietnam protests in the late 1960s – sense the mood after 9/11, realise that war was on the cards and recognise the contemporary significance of Ali's historical speech?

The second film is *The Quiet American* (2002), in which British journalist Fowler, slipping into middle age in Indo-China – later to be called Vietnam – gets mixed up with the country's internal conflicts. American 'scientist' Pyle then appears, befriends Fowler and saves his life in a raid by guerrilla soldiers. Fowler discovers that a Vietnamese businessman is importing a plastic explosive from America under the guise of medical supplies. The sense of impending war is strong, in muddy forests villages are sacked and innocents murdered. A bloody sequence in a city square is reminiscent of the real war scenes in

Fahrenheit 9/11. Explosions rip limbs from bodies, women cry over children, men with burning flesh beg for help. Fowler tries to assist as tears soak his face. Lasting for four minutes, this sequence is stomach turning. With blood still on his face, a local man, who has been assisting Fowler with his journalism, approaches him and it is explained that Pyle is a CIA agent doing the American government's business in the country. Fowler feels cheated by the arrogance of the American government that they can ride roughshod over whatever global situation they wish. The local man says to Fowler, 'sometimes you have to take sides' and Fowler does, helping Vietnamese nationalists try to kill Pyle. Fowler and his historical situation are a metaphor for the position of Hollywood progressives during the build-up to the Iraq war of 2003 – they were angry with the American government and wanted to take a side against it.

Ed Asner describes how, 'there was a good cadre in the creative community ready to pick up the cudgels and campaign.' After listing 20 names Ed says 'but I'm leaving a lot out. And we worked with the organisations out there who have been wonderfully mobilised, all of them – Move On, ANSWER, Not in Our Name. Thorough and well developed. They all have great credit.'[94] As early as June 2002, before any protests took place, this Hollywood cadre was in action with its activist partners. Some helped launch the Not In Our Name group, as actors Ossie Davis and Ed Asner, writer Jeremy Pikser (*Bulworth*) stood alongside Mos Def (rap artist), Noam Chomsky and African-American novelist Alice Walker to read a statement that criticised 'a new openly imperial policy towards the world'.[95] Jessica Lange used her lifetime achievement award at the San Sebastian Film Festival to explain why she 'despises George Bush and his entire administration'.[96] She went on to make the same speech, attacking America's 'imperialism' over 15 times in other locations. Veteran producer Saul Zaentz used the receipt of his British Academy of Film Fellowship to call for all war preparations to stop. Oliver Stone applauded celebrities for speaking out, saying 'I'm heartened to see so many intellectuals and people in my business saying the same thing'.[97] Danny Glover told *The Nation*, 'this starts with Iraq but it can go on and on'. George Clooney told PBS viewers that Bush was like Tony Soprano, 'ready to jump in and kill people first'.[98] Alec Baldwin, Kim Basinger, David Clennon, Hector Elizondo, David Duchovny, Mia Farrow, Screen Actors' Guild President Melissa Gilbert and countless others used public appearances as opportunities to attack the war. At least 89 Hollywood celebrities made separate anti-war statements.

In the early stages Ed Asner became worried that 'certain people in the movement did not want to unite with ANSWER or Not In Our Name' because of the radical leftist groups in those organisations. 'They set up some rival organisations – I think Artists United may be one of those – and that disturbed me because what we needed was unity.'[99] To a certain extent Asner is correct, but what his theory alludes to is the attempt by traditional Hollywood liberals to catch up with the growing anti-war movement. Artists United for A Win Without War organiser Kate McArdle explains how her organisation came into being. 'It was when the drums of war were already beating ... Mike Farrell [actor] and Robert Greenwald [producer] thought, "we don't know that much about what is going on, perhaps we can have a teach-in"'. Farrell and Greenwald organised this themselves, almost on a whim, 'they said, "lets open our rolodexes and call some friends" ... between them they had a hundred people ... Then they just wanted to have a press conference and draw attention to the view that the inspectors should be left alone and there should be no pre-emptive strikes. No one wanted to form a new organisation.'[100]

However, when they put forward a simple letter to the president 'every press outfit in the world seemed to turn up' according to McArdle.[101] Simply by taking a stance, however radical, Greenwald and Farrell became organisers in the movement. Along with the MoveOn.org website, they began to push anti-war adverts onto mainstream networks and their affiliates became organisers of protest. Ed Asner concedes that from then on, in the eyes of the public and the mainstream press, there was no distinction between softer and harder anti-war opposition. In this way the anti-capitalist radicals in Hollywood profited.

Sean Penn visited Baghdad in December 2002 as part of a goodwill mission led by Norman Solomon's Institute of Public Accuracy. He also took out a newspaper advert in the *Washington Post*, suggesting the war was stoking up anti-American feeling around the world and would be a 'most temporary medicine' for terrorism. As the war began Penn went further, saying the US flag was 'waving ... in servicing a regime change that is significantly benefiting US corporations'.[102] Through Penn's statements the themes of anti-capitalism were pushed to the forefront of anti-war activity, as a second newspaper advert in the *New York Times* in 2003 made clear. Indeed, when Tim Robbins and Susan Sarandon spoke to protesters in New York they made the anti-capitalism/anti-war connection explicit, arguing, '[American] fundamentalism is business, the unfettered spread of our economic interests

throughout the globe ... Our resistance to this war should be our resistance to profit at the cost of human life ... this is about business ...
Enron and Halliburton.'[103]

So significant was the impact of anti-capitalist rhetoric from Hollywood progressives that Kate McArdle commented, 'the globalisation
movement is very important in terms of the war because if you believe
it was for ... ideological reasons, there's also Halliburton and business
interests, and there's the advancing of the conservative agenda which
is tied in to the corporate profit. It's all very intermingled.' One figure
who had stood up against the inter-mingled strands of American capitalist society with verve and passion was Martin Sheen. During the
Iraq war Sheen came to be a figurehead who epitomised the way
Hollywood's anti-system next generation progressives led opposition
across America.

Martin Sheen became a central figure on the West Coast. Demonstrations in January and February 2003 attracted tens of thousands and
had him at their head, he called a 'virtual march on Washington' in
December 2002 which snarled up White House communications for 24
hours; he wrote an opinion piece in the *New York Times* and strapped a
cross to his back as well as taping his mouth shut to symbolise the
attempts of NBC (producers of his hit show *The West Wing*) to silence
him. The result of this militancy was to turn Artists United into a new
coalition, which echoed the shape, if not the hardcore politics, of anti-
capitalist groupings. McArdle describes its make up as involving
'everybody from the American Friends Community, Rainbow Coalition, National Organisation of Women, Sierra Club, to Physicians for
Social Responsibility ... that's kind of what we've transformed Artists
United in to, an organisation that provides coalition for lots of other
groups'. Organisation of opposition in Hollywood was now utterly
infected by the Seattle spirit and the politics of radicals like Michael
Moore. Even organisations that is was feared might retreat into liberal
individualism, which was progressive Hollywood's weakness in the
anti-Reagan activity of the 1980s, found themselves drawn into the collective, diverse and broadly political combat that was the main feature
of anti-capitalism. This contradiction of the new collective spirit of
opposition to Bush Jr's presidency with the old style of individualistic
Hollywood liberalism found an expression in a number of Hollywood
movies.

Individualist film and the collective spirit

The Last Samurai (2003) was produced by and starred Tom Cruise, and directed by Ed Zwick. Together they explicitly sought to express liberal ideology about war in a 'popular action film'. Cruise was married for many years to the anti-war Nicole Kidman and is a member of the Church of Scientology – a refuge of mysticism for disgruntled Hollywoodites. Discussing *The Last Samurai* Cruise says, 'some great values are … embodied in this picture … themes that are very dear to me as a man – loyalty, compassion'.[104]

In this way Cruise calls on the legacy of liberalism: the ideal of loyalty underpinned the hero's quest in *Anti-TRUST* and *Bulworth*; the ideal of compassion motivated George Clooney's outbursts against a perceived racist news media after the 1992 LA riots. In their 'Conversation' documentary[105] Zwick and Cruise talk of passing on such values to their children. During their discussion Zwick also suggests that this film shares the major concern of Hollywood progressives in the new millennium – the horror of war.

In *The Last Samurai*'s major set-pieces, Samurai warriors, loyal to each other and their moral code (Bushido), do battle with heavily armed modern soldiers. The implausible relationship between enemies, American Captain Algren and Samurai Katsumoto, is predicated on honour. In keeping with liberal aesthetics the narrative is driven by Algren: from his lowest ebb, through his acceptance of a commission in Japan, to defeat on the field, to the study of his captors, to entering battle as a Samurai. The film begins with the line, 'Japan was made by a handful of brilliant men' and ends with Algren changing the future of the Japanese empire by personally persuading an emperor he has never previously met to end his relationship with a business-driven, imperialist America. The film is punctuated by Algren's diary entries, including the line, 'what does it mean to be a Samurai but to commit yourself to a set of moral principles?' There is not much more evidence needed that in Captain Algren the film has a hero who learns to adhere to the ideals of liberal individualism. Besides these liberal references, the film contains metaphors for contemporary situations: trade treaties are proposed to give exclusive rights to American companies in Japan; the stiff-collared and suited Japanese government officials are as obsessed with business as any Clinton or Bush minister; the American diplomats demand their requests are met, much as Bush's envoys demanded that the United Nations back their war with Iraq; and Eastern traditions are oppressed by Western culture as, it could be argued, the expanding Hollywood media empires have done or as the imposition of an American-led administration in post-war Iraq may have done.

However, where life-long liberal Warren Beatty's 1999 film *Bulworth* created an un-real hero in a real context, or independent figurehead Steven Soderbergh used social specificity in *Erin Brockovich* to create a real hero in a real context, *The Last Samurai* fails to do either. Despite Zwick's professed aim of representing the 'political culture'[106] of the era, there are only brief glances at Japanese social structure. Historian Geoffrey Warne says Zwick does 'a great job of re-creating Meiji society' through a richly constructed mise-en-scène but fails to make clear the Samurai role in society or how the emperor's government runs the country. So many questions are left unanswered by the film, and we have no way of challenging Warne's view that it is a 'real Hollywood-isation because, let's face it, the Samurai in 1876/77 were the bad guys trying to go back to a bygone era when women didn't have rights, when there was no hope of democracy'.[107]

In *Erin Brockovich* the spectator is clear who has power (the corporation, its lawyers), how decisions are made (board meetings, lawyer negotiations) and where the pressure points are for change (mass petition to the courts). In *The Last Samurai* all we can be sure of is that Algren is a broken man who fixes himself fighting for the Samurai in a fatal battle. Algren's salvation is the main driver of the film, so his survival in the final battle is more significant than the fact that all the Samurai are dead. Algren is a de-socialised hero in a colourful setting, following a narrative that fleetingly touches upon weighty themes, only to render them utterly abstract.

The Last Samurai did not make as much in overall box-office or video returns as *Fahrenheit 9/11*. This might suggest that the more conventional mainstream film exploring contemporary political situations is today a failure in both audience popularity and its generation of accurate, relevant and collective meaning. Whilst this appears to be true in the case of *The Last Samurai*'s backward-looking individualist narrative – that was out of step with the grass roots organising and political outlook of most Hollywood progressives in the early 2000s – there is another type of mass-audience film that has significant potential for generating anti-capitalist influenced progressive meanings. *Hey Arnold the Movie* ran at US and UK movie theatres for nearly a year. Like many cartoons, the film caricatures real situations, but through a figurative animation style and simple narrative its meanings take on a generic quality. However, unlike live-action comics such as the *Matrix* movies,

Hey Arnold does not create a de-socialised reality. The places that are figuratively rendered are tenements in a modern American city, where the people wear clothes typical – in rudimentary shape and colour – of contemporary street wear. In narrative the film engages with globalisation; a multinational corporation threatens to demolish an impoverished community. Furthermore, a back-story connects the corporate developers to a past imperialist era. In this way *Hey Arnold* draws in complex contemporary and historical concerns.

In its treatment of heroes the film is notably influenced by the activism in Hollywood in the last four or five years. Arnold, despite donning spy wear at one point, fails repeatedly to undermine the corporation. The same is true of a collection of geriatrics working with his grandfather, the girl-next-door who loves him and his buddies on the block. What eventually undermines the corporation is a collective uprising involving explosions, running battles with police and an impromptu media exposé.

This is a marked contrast to *Fight Club* which, as our classic example of a corporate copy of the 1990s independent film, distorts visions of a collective of people in an attempted struggle with corporations. Tyler Durden becomes a special individual through his off-the-wall actions, through being consistently centrally placed in the frame as well as via his bright and stylised clothing. *Fight Club* adopts this style without understanding contemporary social reality. Why does Narrator never leave his middle-class, corporate job? Why do the pressures of work and money never get in the way of Operation Mayhem? *Fight Club* creates two polarised worlds. The shiny office and flat of Narrator and the windowless, shadowy, dirty Fight Club basement. But we do not know why Tyler's home has grimy décor. Furthermore, instead of trying to change this world through struggle, Tyler and Narrator actually adopt one-half of it – their final act of destruction being to try and destroy the other half. In effect, instead of fighting corporations, they only change their cultural practice – they join Fight Club.

Another confusing representation of resistance to the modern capitalist system is present in the studio-produced *Three Kings* and *The Perfect Storm*. Both films are about conflicts. The former concerns the first Iraq war of 1990, the latter the battle of fishermen to make a living against the elements. In *Three Kings* there are some startling visuals involving the internal path of a bullet through a body and a washed-out colour scheme that lends a paleness and coldness to the heat of desert warfare. In this film a band of four soldiers – one of whom is killed – decides to rob gold from a Kuwaiti store as the war comes to an end. They wind up captured by Iraqis who think the war is still on and subsequently they rescue a number of refugees and lose the gold. There's a great humour between the three soldiers, led by George Clooney as Major Archie Gates, and a sense that they care very little for the war is created through dialogue that questions why they were sent to Iraq in the first place, their total disregard for incompetent senior officers and their genuine compassion for the ordinary Iraqis they meet. However, the fact that they are engaged in robbery, that Archie assumes command of their robbery operation in the manner of an officer, that they have to lie to everyone they meet and they kill Iraqis without much sympathy – especially at the film's opening – undermines the sense of resistance to their situation that is initially conveyed. They come across as a hearty and likeable gang of bandits with their hearts in the right places and who ultimately do the right thing by helping the desolate refugees.

The manner in which *Three Kings* develops and then confounds a vision of collective resistance is partly a result of tensions placed upon its director and acting talent by AOL Time Warner, who funded the production. Director David O. Russell was a maverick responsible for *Spanking the Monkey* (1994), a family drama featuring a great deal of teenage masturbation. He was on contract at Warner Brothers and found an average action script about the 1990 Gulf War in the studio archives. He worked it up into a deliberately chaotic mix of action, heist movie and war film, with a subtext of criticism of the way the US forces had left innocent Iraqis to be murdered by the country's dictator Saddam Hussein. The film only went into production because Lorenzo di Bonaventura – production chief at Warner Brothers – and deputy CEO Terry Semel casually backed it. Once in production it was the power of leading actor George Clooney that kept marketing and production executives from changing the film's shape. Clooney says, 'there was a great fear we were … taking Time Warner into a dangerous place'.[108] In response to various attempts to change his script, which Clooney fended off, David O. Russell did moderate his script and prevented *Three Kings* from indicting the American government with dialogue that directly attacked the then president, George Bush Snr. In so doing Russell created a film that 'surprises you and then at the end you realise … this was a political exposé', or so he argued.

Indeed, the film features a remarkable scene in which the Rodney King beating by police in Los Angeles, which led to the riots that Clooney spoke out about in 1992, plays in the background as thick, black oil is poured down the throat of a young US soldier and angry

Iraqis tell him this fuel was the real reason for the war. However, when Warner Brothers saw what Russell and Clooney had made they tried to sell the film as a pure action movie, using their marketing power. Clooney complained that everywhere he went, people told him this was not the movie they had expected to see.

The scene is in fact so powerful that it is the abiding memory of the film and, whilst the sense of banditry and deceit in *Three Kings* is not lessened, the spectator cannot help but keep returning to the message contained in that one moment. *The Perfect Storm* has a similar effect, sending a team of fishermen – again led by George Clooney – on a desperate and fatal fishing mission in a terrible storm. They go because of the financial pressures of their industry, to try and earn a living in desperate times and their desperation is rendered in a slow build-up of family and social scenes that take up the first half of the film. Again, this is a gang, breaking the rules and taking risks when no one else will go out in the storm. Again Clooney is the leader and orders his boys about the boat. Again there is a sense of collective endeavour, only to be undermined by the way the men deceive their families about the risks of going out and deceive each other about their own objectives – Clooney, for example, is about to lose his boat but does not tell his crew. In this way both films play with the collective notions of more radical offerings like *Cradle Will Rock* but fail to deliver the same final message, instead offering memorable moments of radical content.

These films fail to achieve the effective combination of form and narrative, creating representative social situations and generic protagonists as in *Hey Arnold*; something *Cradle Will Rock, Dogville* and Sean Penn's contribution to *11/09/01* (2002) do repeat in live-action. *Cradle Will Rock* features a steel magnate who is funding Mussolini. Though he is an invented character, he meets with Margherita Sarfratti (a real-life go-between for Mussolini), Nelson Rockefeller and William Randolph Hearst. These real figures from the corporate world indirectly cross paths with Mark Blitzstein, the writer of *The Cradle Will Rock*, in a restaurant and outside a theatre. Later, in the play itself, steel workers go on strike. The effect is to throw real historical events and figures into question – to ask: what if this happened? In his book about *Cradle Will Rock*, director Tim Robbins intersperses factual evidence about real events with extracts from the film's screenplay.[109] The real social context, rendered by newspaper cuttings and still pictures, is compared and contrasted with snapshots of fictional characters from the film. The book reflects the lyrical narrative movement of *Cradle Will Rock* – an ensemble of narratives generating what film professor Hilary Radner has called 'a sense of how collective social and political structures might be understood as forming individual destinies'.[110]

This distinguishes *Cradle Will Rock* from failures like *The Last Samurai*, echoing the radical collectivism of the movement of anti-globalisation and against George Bush Jr's war with Iraq that Tim Robbins has been part of. In Robbins's film there are essentially no heroes, although individuals do dramatic and stimulating things – such as the moment that one of the actors in Orson Welles's troupe chooses to abandon his family after he has heard them singing fascist songs. In this way the spectator is not permitted to identify too closely with a single character, and the characters' values are interpreted within the context of the whole society on display in the film. It is the multiple strands of the narrative, the manner in which the film from its opening weaves in and out of each strand, that makes this possible. So, an anti-Communist working in the labour exchange can report possible 'reds' to the authorities, which has the effect of putting otherwise unconnected Federal Theater employees on trial, which in turn causes lack of employment and emotional breakdown for a vaudeville performer. The consequences of individual action are always shown to be social, and narrative is shown to be the product of decisions by individuals and organisations. Where Captain Algren's choice to join the Samurai ultimately only makes a difference to him, or Erin's decisions to fight Hinckley's case makes a difference to everyone but is shown to the spectator only through her eyes, in *Cradle Will Rock* a personal decision can effect countless others and each effect is shown on screen.

This representation of heroes, or ensembles of characters, in complex socio-political structures does not leave room for mysticism. Something similar is achieved in Sean Penn's short film, contributing to *11/09/01* – an eclectic collection of shorts responding to the attacks on the World Trade Center. Penn's film comprises a dishevelled old man in a compact apartment and minimal dialogue. The man eats, watches TV and talks benignly to aged dresses as if they still contain his absent wife. 9/11 makes a background appearance through the television, a telephone bell escalates to crescendo and the man collapses into tears, suddenly conscious of the charade he is living. This is a man in a recognisable world – a familiar apartment – but a range of camera angles (including shots from outside the apartment window), odd jerky movements and natural lighting (creating a time-lapse feel) generate an observational sensibility. We are not complicit in the fiction of the wife's presence but can still empathise with the man's situation. Therefore, when the false serenity of the apartment is disrupted we are both unsurprised and saddened.

Penn avoids binary opposites; the observational quality allows us to judge the man's fiction as wrong, but the emotional effect of shattering his fiction seems equally wrong. As with *Cradle Will Rock*, there is no special hero in Penn's film, just a self-delusional man affected by wider social forces – the phone and 9/11. In a metaphorical sense this could be any American, deluding themselves that all is well, until the rest of the world interjects and shatters their illusion of peace. By different methods *Dogville* reaches the same conclusions.

Here a small American town in the Depression is created through costume and a minimalist set laced with motifs like American flags, rustic trucks, etc. *Dogville* was filmed in a former machine hall in Sweden on an entirely indoor set; there are no walls, just white lines painted on the floor to create a plan of the town. With the exception of their period clothes and the occasional piece of furniture there is nothing on the set of *Dogville* that denotes historical moment. Indeed, there's an otherworldliness, a distinct lack of reality that director Lars von Trier serves up through a set where the inside of three homes is visible in one shot, and the lack of external lighting makes it hard to know if it's night or day.

What von Trier achieves is a mix of social specificity and universality that leaves the viewer in no doubt of what *kind of* place this film occurs in. A Thanksgiving dinner, the harvesting of particular kinds of crops, the rhetoric used in the town church, even the choice of actors (iconic stars Lauren Bacall, James Caan, big-name Hollywood talents Nicole Kidman and up-and-coming British Hollywood star Paul Bettany) root the film in America. But this could be any town in the USA. In this almost universal location, a young philosopher struggles to retain his abstract belief in the 'goodness of human kind' when his neighbours exploit a young woman who has fled from the big city. No character is given special qualities, each is flawed – the young woman compromises in every way to avoid being given up to the police and each townsperson manipulates her desperation. *Dogville* does not allow the determination of any protagonist to win out. The philosopher's determination to make the young woman part of the community fails miserably as she becomes everyone's dogsbody.

The fact that von Trier has stated his desire to make films about America's corporate and political failings,[111] that he is a public supporter both of independent cinema and of anti-globalisation, is evidence that *Dogville*'s critique is deliberate. *Dogville* demonstrates the range of techniques available to those intent on challenging the order of American society and stripping bare its class dimension. It also shows that that cinematic critiques of the American social class system are today generated across the word, and are in some cases exceptionally severe. As *Sight and Sound* put it, 'Is *Dogville* clever? Extremely ... exposing the self-interest lurking behind ... a reductive, paranoid model of humanity ... take a look at the closing credits [laden with images of poor Americans] or the spine-tingling moment when the citizens break into a spontaneous round of "America the Beautiful"'.[112]

Furthermore, *Dogville* stresses the interconnected nature of American society. The apple farmer, for example, needs the haulage operative to sell his wares. In town meetings the property owners hold sway. As in *Cradle Will Rock* but in episodic style *Dogville* does not single out a unique hero, instead spending time identifying each *type* of person in the town. Combine this treatment of characters with a proliferation of icons of American life – like an Independence Day celebration – and *Dogville* could be a metaphor for the exploitation of women and the working poor in present-day America. Then, when a dark force suddenly murders the townsfolk, claiming to retaliate against their social crimes, parallels with 9/11 can be perceived. By socialising its characters, eschewing special heroes and focusing on social relations, *Dogville* presents America as a tortured, exploitative and dangerous place. Put *Dogville* alongside Michael Moore's *Fahrenheit 9/11* and you have the factual deconstruction of American corporate and political power mirrored by its fictional version.

Moreover, in films like *Cradle Will Rock* the centrality of collective action to the new Hollywood progressives is asserted. The Central Park crowd scene in *Cradle Will Rock* demonstrates how important collectivism had become to Tim Robbins. Whilst the unemployment rally goes on around him, Mark Blitzstein composes music for *The Cradle Will Rock* in his head, and the camera moves around the park. We see the speaker at the rally and faces in the crowd. These shots are not from Mark's perspective and he has disappeared from the frame, though the music he was composing continues to play. The workers' rally becomes more tense and angry. We suddenly return to Mark, who is now having a conversation with an imaginary Bertholt Brecht. It seems that this 1930s America-based writer has taken the 1920s Communist German playwright as a pretend spiritual mentor. A quick edit transports us to a queue of depressed and dishevelled people outside the local labour exchange. All the while Mark's music continues. Swiftly we return to the park where Mark is now playing an imaginary piano. As he does so the police move into the crowd around him and Brecht re-appears commentating on the action. Brecht directs Mark to bear witness to what is happening, to the plight of ordinary people who are forced to 'prostitute' themselves to the corporate American machine. Immediately Mark breaks from his music and screams at the police.

At the end of this sequence a speaker at the rally is heard to shout 'the cradle of power is rocking'. As the film develops this line becomes a feature of Mark's play, it leaps from this complex scene into a musical number performed by actors on a stage. Although *Cradle Will Rock* was in production before November 1999, this could easily be a line taken from the Seattle protests, where crowds sang a song first used in the anti-Vietnam War protests of the 1960s and 1970s: 'there ain't no power like the power of the people and the power of the people is here'.

What is significant here are the relationships at play in the neat construction of the sequence. Mark has a relationship to the crowd, which affects his composition – he actually incorporates dialogue from the crowd scene into his lyrics. Mark and the crowd both have a relationship to the queue at the labour exchange. This is thematic – Mark is writing a play about poverty and workers, these are workers protesting in the park and those in the queue are unemployed workers. Or to put it another way, the theme is social class. The use of Mark's composition as score music for all elements of the sequence cleverly ensures that all elements are connected. Music alone in the cinema has this ability to move around the film and connect it up. What Robbins achieves through music in this sequence of *Cradle Will Rock* is the communication of several parts of a complex social whole with one another. *Cradle Will Rock* constructs a reality that is experienced collectively and in which the activity of a crowd of protesters becomes a collective response to the injustice of society. This collectivist social approach is the hallmark of the new generation of Hollywood progressives that emerged at the turn of the millennium.

These activists also want to make politically engaged films. Tim Robbins sums up the thrust of artistic endeavours by the more radical elements in Hollywood, when talking about *Cradle Will Rock*, 'I wouldn't have done it if there hadn't been a window into the present'.[113] Robbins makes this obvious in the final scene of the film, where a shot of actors in 1940s period costume expands into Times Square in the present day – full of sparkling adverts for trans-national corporations – takes over the frame. It is clear that Robbins wants his historical subject to reference modern-day America. This approach typifies the position of Hollywood's new progressive generation in the early years of the new millennium: politically active and making political films. They were not, however, the only political force to emerge on America's West Coast during the Bush era. Alongside the Hollywood left's growth there was an election for California governor that was won by a Republican and a movie star, an election that should have warned this new left of the potential for a Republican victory in the 2004 presidential race.

Hey! Arnie, the election

In 2003, action-movie hero and former body builder Arnold Schwarzenegger ran all the way to the governorship of California. The Austrian-born Arnold replaced Democrat Gray Davis after a campaign backed by a Republican millionaire had ousted the incumbent governor. This was, arguably, America's most high-profile election for a generation. Former Republican California Governor Pete Wilson was the mastermind behind Schwarzenegger's campaign, the success of which is not as straightforward as it might appear. There were over 30 candidates – knowing nothing about most of them, surely most people would pick a name they recognised? There was no left candidate with equal name recognition. People like Mike Farrell and Martin Sheen stayed away. Kate McArdle suggests that most progressives in Hollywood 'don't want a life in politics'.

The *LA Village Voice* and *The Nation* ran pieces that implied the electorate was both star-struck and apolitical when it elected Arnold, or Arnie as he is commonly known. You could easily believe that the man who monosyllabically played the robotic killer the Terminator just morphed into the Govern-ator, a shift of emphasis but not celebrity status. So fooled have so many been, that when George Bush turned up to a victory rally one press camera actually stayed on Arnie after the host announced 'Welcome the President of the United States' – until the station's journalist pointed out they were looking at the wrong guy.

Arnie's publicists, who predicted around the time Michael Moore invaded the Oscars in March 2003 that Schwarzenegger would guarantee extensive coverage of the race for governor, adopted Martin Sheen's notion that 'celebrity can bring publicity for your other concerns'.[114] They were right; Arnie's campaign became headline news in the UK, France, Australia, Norway and even Brazil. Immediately after the Oscars a number of stars were quick to back Michael Moore's position but Arnie was not. After speaking about the war at a post-Oscar party Brad Pitt instructed his publicist to contact journalist George Rush and make sure he distributed widely his article clarifying Pitt's anti-war position. According to commentary on laweekly.com, Schwarzenegger's bowels experienced a sudden movement at another Oscar party, forcing him into the toilet and away from journalists probing his opinion on the conflict in Iraq. This example betrays the contradictory nature of Arnie's position. Here is a man who is everything the American right needs him to be but who does not face the press during one of the most controversial and contested moments for Republicanism in recent years – the unilateral decision by President Bush to invade Iraq.

For some in the Republican Party Arnie is a rags-to-riches icon, an adopted American on whose shoulders the future of right politics now rests. Witness the mobbing he received on various walkabouts, pre- and post-election, as evidence of the basis of their belief. From the point of view of the Bush administration, Arnie makes a perfect candidate for a well-trodden political path. Both Richard Nixon and Ronald Reagan held the highest office in California before their succession to Washington. Arnie can't become president, however, as he was not born on American soil. There is an obvious parallel between the qualities of Arnie's onscreen persona and the mythology of Bush Jr's presidency. Schwarzenegger's brand is identified by physical dominance over adversaries. In films such as *Commando*, *Conan the Barbarian* and *The Running Man* he is a soldier, or a warrior or a former police officer with greater fitness, dexterity and more lethal moves then any opponent. He also has technological superiority in *Total Recall* and *Terminator 1, 2* and *3*, in which he is either in or from the future and possesses accurate and explosive firepower. All this is wielded in a relentless charge to victory in *Predator*, where he fights off a seemingly more powerful alien and in *Terminator*, where his robot is simply unstoppable. Meanwhile, Bush is responsible for immense mobilisations in Afghanistan and Iraq, for the nuclear missile defence programme and phrases like 'rest assured we will not be deterred from bringing our enemies to their knees'.

The 'just cause' of a Schwarzenegger screen character is taken as read. The only time he has ever played the enemy was in the first of the multi-billion dollar *Terminator* franchise. In dialogue Arnie rarely develops underlying themes. Compare the clichés of *Terminator 3: Rise of the Machines* to the narrow rhetoric employed by the Bush team over

Iraq. Questions of oil industry, the California energy crisis, economic stability, the degradation of Los Angeles' inner city or regional conflict were pushed to one side in his campaign. Arnie's patriotic credentials were affirmed in *True Lies*, taking on Arab assailants as an American secret agent, accent not withstanding. Likewise Bush and his administration stake a claim on patriotism of the highest order, burying the stories of Donald Rumsfeld's past bartering with and bolstering of Saddam Hussein. To complete the Americanisation of the Schwarzenegger brand Arnie exhibits wholesome family values as a naive brother to comedy actor Danny De Vito in *Twins* and as an undercover policeman with a sensitive side in *Kindergarten Cop*. By way of comparison, picture Bush walking his dogs on the lawn or surveying his ranch in denims and leather, with extended family beside him.

All this could have been said of the last actor of Republican ilk to govern California. Even if Schwarzenegger's abundant right-wing credentials on screen outweigh any predecessor, Ronald Reagan's patriotism, machismo and countless clichés were of equal volume. Yet Reagan never came out in support of gay marriage or adoption, never suggested that the children of illegal immigrants deserve equal educational rights, never lamented the damage caused by heavy industry to the environment, and never organised electoral house-to-house conferences in LA's poorest communities. Arnie employed each one of these before the real campaigning in 2003 even began. Reagan refused to bend to such moderate concessions. The fact that the Schwarzenegger brand is so demonstrably Reaganite and yet his early campaign utterances were moderate, underlines the changed political climate and current crisis of morale with which Republicanism grapples today. As Republican commentator Rush Limbaugh put it, the American right is 'so insecure in their own confidence of their belief system that they need it validated by celebrities or Hollywood types'. Or, to be more precise, they need it to be re-defined.

It is the context of change in Hollywood and American society at large that led Schwarzenegger to modify his rhetoric: the anti-Reagan movement in Hollywood, followed by the fraternity with Clinton, followed by the rise of the anti-capitalist movement with its new resonance in Hollywood and the runaway success that Michael Moore's documentaries have found at the box office. The cultivation of a pre-election softer Republican image for Arnie suggests that at least some Republicans recognise these developments. To some, Schwarzenegger is a dangerous chauvinist – articles were written during his election in the London *Evening Standard* exposing infidelity and groping of co-stars. He has been quoted as saying he'd love to support women's causes, especially the cause of those who are 'blonde and pretty'. To a new and recently more active Hollywood left, the man who made it in a film about body building called *Pumping Iron*, is pumping up fearful memories of Ronald Reagan. A sense of déjà vu is certainly justified – Ronald Reagan's first ventures in politics were also out of keeping with Republican rhetoric. In the 1940s Reagan was an activist in the Screen Actors' Guild, made anti-racist broadcasts and was involved with the left-wing 'Mobilization for Democracy'. Before he testified to the House Un-American Activities Committee that many of his friends were communists in 1947, providing an extensive list of names, studio chiefs labelled him a 'militant'. Yet Reagan's transition from popular Hollywood star, and moderate public speaker, to Republican moralist and even FBI informer was comfortable. Perhaps it is this distant memory that stirred Allan Mayer, of Strick and Co. publicists, to inform the *Washington Post*, 'we'll see some celebrity political activity' against Arnie.

If Michael Moore's *Fahrenheit 9/11* success is anything to go by then there has been a smouldering anti-Bush sentiment at home too, and beyond the Hollywood left. How long before the mask slips and Arnie begins to push home measures like Proposition 187, the anti-immigrant bill, with clauses removing all civil rights from Latin Americans who cross the border into California, that he had backed vehemently in 1994? Some fear an attack on the growing Latino population. Notably, actress and producer Salma Hayek, who stated during the election that she wanted to homogenise the Latino vote behind a future and as-yet unknown liberal candidate. How long before those who voted recognise that Arnie's economic policies do not reverse the state's energy crisis caused by the Enron scandal and the blackouts in 1991? Arnie's policy is in fact a copy of former governor Pete Wilson's, who is a close ally of the Bush White House and was personal friends with Enron's disgraced chief executive Ken Lay. Indeed, in the current crisis in Iraq, where the handover of power from a US occupation force to an 'elected' government has resulted in bombings on state buildings and street fighting, what happens when Arnie is forced out of hiding on the question of Iraq?

Arnie's ascension to the highest office in America's most important state did not happen simply because he's Arnie. His was a superficial appeal to an increasingly angry and discontented electorate that, in time, may just inspire the kind of alternative left challenge that the

Republicans fear the most. Such a challenge may in time find an equally recognisable bona fide star, inspired by opposition to Republican politics and global capitalism. What does that the anti-globalisation ferment, the rise of a new Hollywood left and the production of movies that capture an anti-system mood at the box office mean for Arnie's success? Certainly the course of the last 20 years in Hollywood, especially the early part of the new millennium, suggests that grass roots organisation over a host of issues will continue to interact with both movie production and American social life. Viewed in that way, Hollywood progressives can only continue to be active against the kind of agenda that Arnie and his party stand for. Perhaps one of those progressive Hollywood stars will follow Arnie's example and stand for election on a radical platform. However, they did not do so in California in 2003, nor did they do so when George W. Bush was re-elected president in November 2004, despite a first term in office that had included the Iraq war and the immense campaign against it.

Now the Hollywood left is faced with a confident right-wing president, who believes he has a mandate to continue with the plans he began to unveil in his first four years in the White House. Perhaps the Hollywood left and its allies in wider society will find that Arnie quickly affirms his commitment for the Bush agenda. That instead of the growing anti-globalisation mood sweeping aside war and exploitation, the anti-capitalist and anti-war movements will need to work harder and fight longer for the changes they desire. Certainly, Hollywood progressives will need to learn the lessons of Arnie's populist electoral success if they are to make a stand for their beliefs in California. In a wider context they need to recognise the failure of any alternative to Bush to oust him from the White House in 2004, and decide what role they will play in any future opposition.

Epilogue

Within days of the re-election of President George Bush Jr, in November 2004, Kate McArdle was able to summarise the mood among Hollywood progressives. 'It has been very, very sad for us',[1] she said. McArdle was then the key organiser for Artists United for a Win Without War, the coalition of celebrity activists formed in 2003. Artists United is supported by stars who have made significant contributions to the development of the Hollywood left over the last 25 years. These include veterans of anti-Reagan activity in the 1980s: Mike Farrell and Ed Asner, multi-issue campaigner Martin Sheen, Emmy-winning television producer Robert Greenwald and anti-capitalist film star Tim Robbins. This celebrity organisation, faced with a Republican president it fundamentally disagreed with, had become committed to removing him from office. That commitment, and a year of joint work with wider social constituencies, failed.

Artists United began campaigning against the president in late 2003 under the umbrella of the national Win Without War and MoveOn coalitions. In December 2003 they jointly published an advert in dozens of US newspapers, picturing Bush making a vitriolic speech, labelling him a 'mis-leader' and suggesting that 'young men and women were sent to die for a lie' in Iraq. As 2004 began, MoveOn were campaigning over a range of issues including electoral reform and environmental action. All these issues were linked back to the president's perceived mistakes, the biggest of which, as MoveOn's press releases throughout 2004 rarely failed to mention, was the Iraq war of 2003. MoveOn and their Artists United affiliates capitalised on the profile of their anti-war celebrity supporters and the memory of widespread protest during the Iraq war. As Kate McArdle pointed out in 2003, 'we hadn't succeeded in stopping the war but we had created a momentum about the issues connected to it'.[2]

The Iraq issue itself did not go away before the election. On 30 June 2004, American-led troops handed over power to the Iraqi authorities, or so it appeared. What followed was sporadic fighting across the country, with American troops unable to leave the battle scene. The engagement of American forces in Iraq that had caused such protest against Bush across the world, and which had forged a new coalition of activists in Hollywood, was still going on when the election took place on 2 November. Likewise, the momentum of the protests did not dissipate. Instead, that momentum was crystallised into electoral activity. MoveOn set up a sister organisation, the MoveOn Political

Action Committee (PAC), in early 2004. MoveOn PAC stated its aim as involving 'more than 10,000 Americans' in challenging 'national leaders [who] actively disregard public opinion and common sense'. 'Our only alternative', they argued, 'is electoral action'.[3]

MoveOn's election activity was eye catching, and often required much effort on the part of the creative community. A cacophony of television adverts were produced by Hollywood talent: director Richard Linklater interviewed disgruntled Texans; Donal Logue exposed the 9/11 terrorists to be Saudi Arabians, not Iraqis; actor Woody Harrelson hammered corruption in the decision to choose corporate oil giant Halliburton to rebuild Iraq; director Rob Reiner cut press conferences where Bush denied mistakes with evidence of his errors. On 11 July the biggest grossing documentary of all time, *Fahrenheit 9/11*, became a campaign tool. Fifty-five thousand volunteers organised house parties where *Fahrenheit 9/11* could be watched. In New York Edie Falco, star of HBO's hit series *The Sopranos,* joined movie actor Bill Pullman in the best-publicised of these events. Outside, popular musicians including Pearl Jam, the Dixie Chicks, Bonnie Raitt and R.E.M performed on the 'Vote for Change Tour', that peppered the country with politically charged gigs.

As the election drew near, many organisations and individuals sided against Bush. One of these was an organisation that, more than any other in America, represents the fruition of the developing social movement studied in this book. United for Peace and Justice (UFPJ) represents over 800 member organisations, including: the 9/11 Coalition founded by the families of victims of the World Trade Center attacks in 2001, dozens of Green Party chapters, several chapters of Veterans For Peace, over 80 faith-based organisations, progressive media magazine *In These Times*, the women's human rights organisation MADRE, of which Susan Sarandon had been president in the 1990s, multitudinous labour organisations from 20 American states and the country-wide Student Peace Action Network (SPAN). UFPJ's steering committee is conscious that its membership compares favourably with the collectives that organised anti-capitalist protests in Seattle in 1999, and several other locations since. They argue on the UFPJ website that 'corporate globalisation is central to the Bush Administration's broad empire-building agenda and a key cause of militarism and war'.[4]

Artists United is a UFPJ member, so are Znet, who backed Noam Chomsky's Not In Our Name coalition during the Iraq war. Norman Solomon has signed up his Institute of Public Accuracy, which took

Sean Penn to Iraq before the war began. UFPJ 'calls to action' during 2004 included a programme of election debates, vigils for American soldiers, voter recruitment drives, demonstrations at government meetings and the monitoring of polling stations to prevent electoral fraud. An indication of UFPJ's power was demonstrated in July when they mobilised 500,000 people to protest in New York at the Republican convention. There is no doubt from our exploration of the growing radicalisation of many Hollywood stars that their sympathies, inspired by their own engagement with anti-capitalism, would be with the approach of UFPJ. However, what they offered as artists more naturally fitted with the MoveOn style of organising. So, in an extension of the artistic verve shown in MoveOn's adverts, a body of fiction and non-fiction work emerged in 2004 that carried the flag of anti-Bushism into American cinemas.

John Sayles, the director who created *Sunshine State* with its distinct humanist anti-corporate message, was one of the first to enter the fray. In 2004 Sayles wrote and directed *Silver City*, a movie where the main character is incompetent Republican candidate Dicky Pilager. Sayles uses the device of a private investigation into the appearance of a body to peel back his plot like the layers of an onion, giving a spell in the limelight to each member of a supporting cast of wayward relatives, aggressive campaign managers, political and business associates, news people and environmentalists. The plot expands as if trying to fill the impressive background of the Colorado mountains with murky corporate associations and political corruption. Pilager fumbles through speeches whilst his manager Chuck Raven is the real brain behind his election, something that draws immediate comparisons with George Bush Jr's stumbling speech and his ever-present political strategist Karl Rove. This satirical approach and caricatured performances by the actors playing these parts is much less subtle than the complex exposition of social class through character development in *Sunshine State*. The way *Silver City* ends helps us understand why Sayles made such artistic choices.

As the final credits roll, no one has been brought to book for the Pilager family's crimes against democracy. Sayles says he believes that in Bush's America 'an awful lot is non-democratic',[5] and that *Silver City* was a direct intervention into the election. That Sayles fought his distributors to get a September 2004 release in the USA demonstrates just how determined he was to get the film to an audience before the election took place. This was Sayles's contribution to anti-Bush activism. David O. Russell – who made the Iraq war drama *Three Kings* – tried

11. Clear and present danger: John Sayles's message to the American public in *Silver City* concerned the problems posed by incompetent, corupt politicians (*courtesy of John Sayles and Maggi Renzi*).

something similar with *Soldier's Play* early in 2004. Unlike *Three Kings*, this was a factual film shot in a traditional documentary style, featuring interviews with human rights officials and Iraqi refugees about the unjust behaviour of American soldiers. Recognising the success of Michael Moore's documentaries, Russell proclaimed that the 'theatrical film is one of the last windows available to people on the left',[6] and consciously sought out Artists United founder Robert Greenwald to support his project. In fiction the same rule applies, according to David O. Russell, and in October 2004 he released the surreal, existential *I Love Huckabees*. This complicated, bizarre film involves a fireman-turned-ecologist, an environmental activist, an unscrupulous chain-store executive and two psychic detectives. *I Love Huckabees* does in a narrative sense what *Three Kings* does aesthetically, it mixes and matches styles, never letting the audience settle into a comfort zone of familiarity. Consequently, the meaning of the film is unclear, but it does present an obvious cross-section of city life, in which saving the planet is favourable to selling it. Those sentiments are in keeping with other progressive films of 2004.

Robert Greenwald also produced two films in the election year. The first, *Uncovered*, was a biting exposition of the failure of the American government to find weapons of mass destruction in Iraq. The film takes apart the Bush administration's justification for war, starting its story immediately after the events of 11 September 2001 and interviewing weapons inspectors, military strategists, United Nations officials and CIA analysts. Put together in classic television documentary style, the film nevertheless achieved a small cinema release. Produced with a similar aesthetic, Greenwald's other film, *OutFoxed*, was an aggressive assault on the imbalanced news coverage of billionaire Rupert Murdoch's Fox Corporation. The subtitle of the film, *Rupert Murdoch's War on Journalism*, encapsulates the outlook of progressives in the creative community during this pre-election period. This was a war with George Bush Jr and his cohort, including their corporate allies. The tactics of the anti-Bush army in Hollywood were aesthetic, utilising satire and drama, or exploiting the emergence of the new market for documentary to hold up mirrors to the administration. Outside the cinema this was equally true, where actor and director Tim Robbins produced a successful stage play, *Embedded*, which sharply satirised the government.

Despite this plethora of filmmaking, the position of Hollywood progressives in the 2004 election is perhaps best illustrated by the fact that Tim Robbins was not a visible supporter of any presidential candidate.

At the 2000 election Robbins, Susan Sarandon, Danny Glover, Bill Murray and activists like Medea Benjamin – who had been central to organising the Seattle protests in 1999 – united behind the Green Party nominee Ralph Nader. Radicalised by the anti-capitalist movement which had erupted on the Seattle streets, these Hollywood personalities were at home with the anti-globalisation rhetoric of Nader. He was an alternative to both the right-wing ideas of George Bush Jr and to the support for globalisation shown by the previous Democratic administration, in which the Democrat nominee Al Gore had been vice-president. However, by 2004 the immense anti-war movement had catapulted organisations without any commitment to Nader, like MoveOn, into the public eye. Furthermore, the Green Party chose not to back Nader, thus undermining his electoral credibility. Consequently Nader failed to draw enough support to make the ballot paper as an independent in many states, and Hollywood's most radical talent were without a mast to nail their colours to.

The MoveOn PAC website does not list political organisations and presents itself as a non-partisan initiative. One function of the PAC was to endorse candidates to Congress. Candidates were chosen because of their support for what the site calls 'progressive principles of national government'.[7] Yet despite the non-partisan approach most of MoveOn PAC's candidates were Democrats. This was a moment of unity of purpose between anti-Bush activists and anti-Bush movie-makers. However, with organisations like MoveOn at the head of this action and organisations like the UFPJ and the Greens providing no anti-capitalist electoral alternative, Hollywood progressives found themselves supporting the Democrats by default. On the question of the Iraq war this posed them a serious problem.

Democratic presidential nominee John Kerry was an unsatisfactory choice for anti-war activists. One of those dissatisfied with him was Danny Schechter, who had produced the Emmy-winning *Human Rights, Human Wrongs* television series in the mid 1990s. His *News Dissector* daily bulletin is read by hundreds of thousands of Americans via e-mail. His contribution to the anti-Bush body of filmmaking was *Weapons of Mass Deception*, which details the course of the Iraq war up to February 2004 and exposes key journalistic decisions made by the major media corporations. Schechter recognised that John Kerry was not the right man to challenge Bush on the anti-capitalists' behalf. After a detailed day-by-day study of the election campaign, Schechter concluded that Kerry 'tried to outflank Bush on the right. He would kill the terrorists that Bush didn't. He would escalate the war. He would bring more troops in … It was ultimately unconvincing.'[8] Kerry was, in fact, one of those Democrats shamed in *Fahrenheit 9/11*. Dissatisfied with Kerry, in the same way that Danny Schechter was, Hollywood's radical progressives seemed to retreat from supporting any candidate directly and left their non-partisan anti-Bush activities to be construed as support for Kerry. Ralph Nader summed it up when he wrote on his website that activists and progressives had 'sidelined themselves in this election [giving] silent support for a candidate who has become aggressive on the war.'[9] So, where does that leave the Hollywood left once Kerry was defeated and Bush re-elected?

Hollywood progressives have been a small high-profile element of much American progressive activism over the last 25 years. The era of Ronald Reagan inspired public opposition against a right-wing individual at the head of American society. In Hollywood this led to an individualistic form of action and a few bitter oppositional mainstream movies. Then Bill Clinton, a Democrat politician, appealed to Hollywood progressives for support. During most of the 1990s they responded positively, helping him fundraise. When Clinton betrayed their agenda of social justice, many of those progressives fell out with the Democrats. Consequently, they were won over to a radical anti-globalisation perspective and engaged in diverse activities outside mainstream political processes. In the first four years of the Bush Jr presidency, with its virulent support of the free market and warmongering, Hollywood progressives joined a widespread anti-war movement. The anti-war movement advanced the coalition-building tendencies of the anti-capitalist movement, and adopted much of its ideological outlook. It also threw up organisations that promoted cultural forms of activity and that attracted Hollywood talent, but which were not necessarily as radical as other coalitions.

The position of Hollywood's new left in the second term of a Bush administration and beyond depends on the capacity of organisations like UFPJ and MoveOn to recognise that a defeat for Kerry is not a defeat for the activists who built the movement. If the anti-Bush flame is re-ignited perhaps Hollywood's progressives will make movies that not only assault the Bush administration, but also explore the consequence of a two-horse electoral race between political animals who share the same rhetoric. If activists and organisations simply stand aside then perhaps the Hollywood left will also pack up their progressive ideas and cease making movies with the kind of socially charged aesthetics that this book has analysed. Either scenario is possible. What we can conclude is that in 25 years of recent history a variety of social eruptions have continued to interact with the life of the American cinema, and in that time Hollywood progressives have never yet left town.

Notes

Part one: The inheritance

1 Stone, Oliver, speech at Torch of Liberty Award, The American Civil Liberties Union Foundation, 17 September 1987

2 Dodson-Cobb, Shirley, 'Story of a Movie Mogul', *Sooner Magazine*, April 1984

3 Prince, Stephen, *A New Pot of Gold: Hollywood Under the Electronic Rainbow, 1980–89* (Los Angeles, 2000), p. 46

4 Prince: *A New Pot of Gold*, p. 75

5 'Salvador', *Variety*, 5 March 1986

6 'Platoon', *Variety*, 3 December 1986

7 'Mass Media Hearings', *Report to the National Commission on the Causes and Prevention of Violence*, (Washington, 1969), p. 193

8 Jacobson, J., *The Negro and the American Labor Movement* (New York, 1968), p. 220

9 Jacobson: *The Negro and the American Labor Movement*, p. 218

10 Georgakas, Dan, and Surkin, Marvin, *Detroit I Do Mind Dying* (London, 1998), p. 21

11 Bart, Peter, and Guber, Peter, *Shoot Out: Surviving Fame and [Mis]Fortune in Hollywood* (New York, 2000), p. 6

12 Stone: speech at Torch of Liberty Award

13 Asner, Ed, interviewed by the author, March 2004

14 *Washington Post*, 4 November 1991

15 Phillips, Kevin, *The Politics of Rich and Poor* (New York, 1990), p. 53

16 Asner: author interview

17 Wexler, Haskell, interviewed by the author, January 2004, February 2004 and March 2004

18 Garnett, Tony, interviewed by the author, July 2004

19 Speech to the National Press Club, 15 December 1983

20 Reagan, Ronald, press conference, March 1982

21 Reagan, Ronald, speech, 27 October, 1964

22 Landau, Saul, interviewed by the author, September 2003

23 *New York Times*, 18 November 1988

24 Oxfam, *Report*, 1984

25 Table information taken from Blum, William, *Rogue State: A Guide to the World's Only Superpower* (London, 2000)

26 Reagan, Ronald, speech to the National Association of Evangelicals, 8 March 1983
27 Prince: *A New Pot of Gold*, p. 46
28 Prince: *A New Pot of Gold*, p. 260
29 Cooper, Marc, 'Postcards from the Left – Under the Cloud of Clinton- ism', *The Nation*, 5 April 1999
30 Garnett: author interview
31 Walker, John, ed., *Halliwell's Film and Video Guide 2003* (London, 2003), p. 704
32 Walker: *Halliwell's Film and Video Guide 2003*, p. 342
33 Lyons, Charles, 'The Paradox of Protest', in Couvares, Francis G., *Movie Censorship and American Culture* (New York, 1996), p. 309
34 Garnett: author interview
35 McArdle, Kate, interviewed by the author, November 2003, January 2004, Feburary 2004 and November 2004
36 Cooper: 'Postcards from the Left'
37 Cooper: 'Postcards from the Left'
38 www.thecreativecoalition.org
39 Asner: author interview

Part two: The crisis of Hollywood liberalism

1 Biskind, Peter, 'On Movies, Money & Politics – Beatty, Baldwin, Glover, Robbins, Stone and Lear', *The Nation*, 5 April 1999
2 Smith, Sharon, 'Twilight of the American Dream', *International Socialism Journal*, 2:54, 1992
3 Jacobson, Julius, 'Pax Americana: The New World Order', *New Politics*, 11:5, 1991, p. 18
4 Phillips, Kevin, *The Politics of Rich and Poor* (New York, 1990), p. 53
5 'Joe Klein Discusses Claims that Bill Clinton Could Have Been Tried and Convicted for Perjury and Obstruction of Justice in the Monica Lewinsky Scandal', on *Morning Edition: National Policy Review*, 7 March 2002
6 Solomon, Norman, interviewed by the author, February 2004 and Octo- ber 2004
7 Freedland, Jonathan, 'Trying to Fill Bill's Shoes', *Guardian*, 16 August 2000
8 Mailer, Norman, 'Footfalls in the Crypt', *Vanity Fair*, February 1992
9 Ebert, Roger, 'The Matrix', *Chicago Sun Times*, 31 March 1997
10 Michael Harrison of *Talkers Magazine*, quoted in Harris, John F., 'As Term Wanes "Clinton Fatigue" Yields to Nostalgia', *Washington Post*, 1 May 2000
11 Asner: author interview

12 Klein, Joe, *The Natural: The Misunderstood Presidency of Bill Clinton* (New York, 2003)

13 Biskind: 'On Movies, Money & Politics'

14 Wexler: author interview

15 Klein, Joe, *Primary Colors* (London, 1998), p. 161 – this book was originally published anonymously, but Klein later accepted ownership of the text.

16 Baltake, Joe, 'Fact or Fiction? John Travolta Plays a Clintonesque Presidential Candidate in "Primary Colors"', *Sacramento Bee*, 20 March 1998

17 Quoted in Stiglitz, Joseph, *The Roaring Nineties, Seeds of Destruction* (London, 2003), p. 23

18 Woodward, Bob, *The Agenda: Inside the Clinton White House* (New York, 1995), p. 84

19 'Profile: Economic legacy of President Bill Clinton', on *Morning Edition: National Policy Review*, 12 January 2001

20 Schecter, Danny, interviewed by the author, December 2003

21 'Clinton Reflects on Victories, Regrets over nearly 8 Years', www.CNN.com, 8 October 2000

22 Landau, Saul, *Hot Air: A Radio Diary* (Washington, DC, 1995), p. 15

23 Solomon: author interview

24 Asner: author interview

25 Kapstein, Ethan B., 'A Global Third Way', *World Policy Journal*, 15, Winter 1998–9

26 Landau: *Hot Air*, p. 87

27 Hitchens, Christopher, *No One Left To Lie To* (London, 1999), p. 89

28 Wasko, Janet, *How Hollywood Works* (London, 2003), pp. 1–56

29 Schamus, James, 'A Rant', *Filmmaker Magazine*, Summer 2000; also published in Lewis, Jon, ed., *The End of Cinema As We Know It* (New York, 2001)

30 '2000 Review', at www.boxofficeguru.com, 5 December 2001

31 Cooper: 'Postcards from the Left'

32 Cooper: 'Postcards from the Left'; additional information found at www.commoncause.org/laundromat/stat/topdonors95.htm

33 Asner: author interview

34 FCC monitoring report, 1997

35 'Mergers and Acquisitions', *M&A Database*, (Washington, DC, 1990)

36 *Variety*, 24 February 1988

37 Sony financial report, *10-K* (Sony Corp, 1991)

38 Mike Figgis, author interview, November 2003

39 Prince: *A New Pot of Gold*, p. 69

40 Greene, Ray, *Hollywood Migraine, The Inside Story of a Decade in Film* (Dublin, 2000), p. 59

41 Greene: *Hollywood Migraine*

42 Seabrook, John, 'Why is the Force Still with Us?', *New Yorker*, 6 January 1997

43 Council of Economic Advisers, *Economic Report to the President* (Washington, DC, 1995), p. 164

44 Doherty, Thomas, 'Movie Star Presidents', in Lewis, *The End of Cinema As We Know It*, p. 156

45 Biskind: 'On Movies, Money & Politics'

46 Perren, Alisa, 'Sex, Lies and Marketing: Miaramax and the Development of the Indie Blockbuster', *Film Quarterly*, 55:2, 2001

47 Wood, Jason, *Steven Soderbergh* (London, 2002), p. 25

48 Perren: 'Sex, Lies and Marketing'

49 Johnson, Lynne D., 'The Distribution of Black Film', *Bright Lights Film Magazine*, April 2002

50 Greene: *Hollywood Migraine*

51 Greene: *Hollywood Migraine*, p. 272

52 Greene: *Hollywood Migraine*, p. 46

53 George Clooney, quoted in *LA Village Voice*, 2 May 1992

54 Walsh, Kenneth T., *US News and World Report*, 2 March 1992

55 Ridder, Knight, 'Will the Fire Last Time Be the Fire Next Time?', *Orange County Register*, 24 March 1997

56 Seymour, Gene, *We've Gotta Have It* (New York, 2002)

57 Study by Lori Dorfman (Berkley Media Studies Group) and Vincent Schiraldi (Justice Policy Institute)

58 Wexler: author interview

59 Greene, *Hollywood Migraine*, p. 46

60 Solomon: author interview

61 Johnson: 'The Distribution of Black Film'

62 Davis, Mike, *Ecology of Fear* (London, 1998), p. 48

63 Davis: *Ecology of Fear*, p. 52

64 Schlosser, Eric, *Reefer Madness* (London, 2003), pp. 215–18, and Ehrenerich, Barbara, *Nickel and Dimed* (New York, 2002), pp. 10–11

65 Kusnet, David, 'A Language for Change', *In These Times*, Winter 2003

66 Asner: author interview

67 Solomon: author interview

68 McArdle: author interview

69 'Profile: Economic Legacy of President Bill Clinton'

70 'Profile: Economic Legacy of President Bill Clinton'

71 Editorial, *Minneapolis Star Tribune*, 5 March 1997

72 Goldstein, Amy, and Harris, John F., *Washington Post*, 23 August 2000

73 McArdle: author interview

74 Biskind, 'On Movies, Money & Politics'

75 Fraser, Ian, *Sunday Tribune*, quoted on the cover of Stiglitz: *The Roaring Nineties*

76 Stiglitz: *The Roaring Nineties*, p. 25

77 Stiglitz: *The Roaring Nineties*, p. 52

78 Stiglitz: *The Roaring Nineties*, pp. 96–7

79 Schecter: author interview

80 Stiglitz: *The Roaring Nineties*, p. 11
81 Stiglitz: *The Roaring Nineties*, p. 53
82 Stiglitz: *The Roaring Nineties*, p. 53
83 According to the Institute for Policy Studies and Center for Urban Economic Development at the University of Illinois, November 1994
84 *The Economist*, 27 November 1994
85 Davies, Phillip John, 'Hollywood in Elections and Elections in Hollywood', in Davies, Phillip John, ed., *American Film and Politics from Reagan to Bush Jnr*, (Manchester, 2002)
86 Asner: author interview
87 Wexler: author interview
88 Landau: author interview
89 Moore, Michael, *Stupid White Men* (London, 2001); Moore, Michael, *Dude, Where's My Country?* (London, 2003)
90 Moore: *Dude, Where's My Country?*, pp. 165–6
91 Polan, Dana, 'The Confusions of Warren Beatty', in Lewis: *The End of Cinema As We Know It*, p. 148
92 Biskind: 'On Movies, Money & Politics'
93 Polan: 'The Confusions of Warren Beatty'
94 Biskind: 'On Movies, Money & Politics'
95 Biskind: 'On Movies, Money & Politics'
96 'Will The Real Progressives Please Stand Up', *Christian Science Monitor*, 10 September 2001
97 Steven Soderbergh, 'The Filmmaker Series', in *Premiere*, December 2000
98 Wood: *Steven Soderbergh*, p. 16
99 Wood: *Steven Soderbergh*, p. 15
100 Wood: *Steven Soderbergh*, p. 76
101 The former is evidenced in Biskind, Peter, *Easy Riders, Raging Bulls* (London, 1996), the latter in Biskind: 'On Movies, Money & Politics'
102 Lachman, Ed, director of photography on *Erin Brockovich*, quoted on the film's official website
103 Hudson, Jeff, *George Clooney: A Biography* (London, 2004)
104 Asner: author interview
105 Lapsley, Robert, and Westlake, Michael, *Film Theory: An Introduction* (Manchester, 1988), p. 184
106 Soderbergh, Steven, quoted on the official *Erin Brockovich* website
107 Soderbergh: official *Erin Brockovich* website
108 Massina, Philip, art director of *Erin Brockovich*, quoted on official website
109 Durgan, Andy, chief researcher on the film, told this story in summer 1997 at a special showing of the film in London
110 Lachman: official *Erin Brockovich* website
111 Corner, John, 'Television, Documentary and the Category of the Aesthetic', *Screen*, 44:1, Spring 2003, p. 96

112 Corner: 'Television, Documentary and the Category of the Aesthetic', p. 97
113 Figgis: author interview
114 Figgis, Mike, speaking at the North East Audio Visual Festival, November 2003

Part three: The next generation

 1 Klein, Naomi, *No Logo: Taking Aim at the Brand Bullies* (New York, 2001); Moore: *Stupid White Men*
 2 Cooper: 'Postcards from the Left
 3 McArdle: author interview
 4 Wexler: author interview
 5 Sheen, Martin, quoted on www.commondreams.org
 6 Wasko: *How Hollywood Works*, pp. 71–3
 7 Huberman, Jack, *The Bush Haters' Handbook: An A–Z Of The Most Appalling Presidency Of The Past 100 Years* (London, 2004)
 8 Asner: author interview
 9 Solomon, Norman, and Erlich, Reese, *Target Iraq: What the News Media Didn't Tell You*, (New York, 2003), p. 46
10 Walker, John, ed, *Halliwell's Film, Video & DVD Guide 2004*, (London, 2004)
11 McArdle: author interview
12 'West Wing Creator Blasts Reality West Wing', at www.imdb.com/name/nm0815070/news, 26 February 2002
13 www.humanitasprize.org
14 Robbins, Tim, *Cradle Will Rock: The Movie and the Moment* (New York, 1999)
15 Bohmer, Peter, www.zmag.org/CrisesCurEvts/Globalism
16 Soriano, Jennifer, www.zmag.org/Bulletins/pseaeven
17 Milner, Josh, www.zmag.org/CrisesCurEvts/Globalism
18 www.indymedia.org/seattle and Charlton, John, 'Talking Seattle', *International Socialism Journal*, 2:86, 2000
19 Danaher, Kevin, *Globalize This! The Battle Against the World Trade Organization and Corporate Rule* (New York, 2000), pp. 7–8
20 Pulver, Andrew, 'The Revolution Starts Here', *Guardian*, 28 August 2001
21 Eisenscher, Michael, at www.indymedia.org
22 Eisenscher, Michael, 'Director of Organizational Development for the University Council of American Federation of Teachers', at www.znet.org
23 'Nader et al. at the Rose Garden', at www.indymedia.org, 6 August 2001

24 Stiglitz, Joseph, *Globalisation and its Discontents* (New York, 2001)

25 Moore, Michael, *Downsize This* (New York, 1996)

26 Moore: *Stupid White Men*

27 www.znet.org

28 Krugman, Paul, *The Great Unravelling: From Boom to Bust in Three Scandalous Years* (New York, 2003), p. 6

29 Hedges, Steven J., 'The Colour of Money', *US World and News Report*, 16 March 1992

30 Begley: author interview

31 Steger, Manfred B., *Globalisation – A Very Short Introduction* (Oxford, 2003), p. 41

32 Steger: *Globalisation*, p. 49

33 Quart, Alissa, *Branded: The Buying and Selling of Teenagers* (New York, 2003)

34 Quart: *Branded*, pp. 281–8

35 Table sources: Bircham, Emma, *Anti-Capitalism: A Guide to the Movement* (London, 2001); Coates, Barry, at www.wdm.org.uk; Klein: *No Logo*; Steger: *Globalisation*; Stiglitz: *The Roaring Nineties*; Tibbet, Steve, *The Global Divide* (London, 1998); Tibbet, Steve, *Borderless Business* (London, 1998); www.asje.org; www.caat.org.uk; www.cnd.org.uk; www.eia.doe.gov; fzln-l@nopal.laneta.apc.org; www.globalisereistance.org.uk; www.nlcnet.org; www.oxfam.org.uk; www.stopwar.org.uk; www.utlanic.texas.edu; www.znet.org

36 Charlton: 'Talking Seattle'

37 Solomon: author interview

38 Asner: author interview

39 Bradshaw, Peter, 'The Pledge', *Guardian*, 16 August 2001

40 Pulver, Andrew, 'Actor Lays into "Trash Ethos" of US Films', *Guardian*, 24 August 2001

41 Kennedy, Patrick, 'One Deadly Summit', *Sight and Sound*, September 2001

42 Bircham: *Anti-Capitalism*, p. 351.

43 *SkyNews*, November 2000.

44 Bottorff, Tim, 'America, Apple Pie, Baseball ... and Censorship', at www.commondreams.org, 11 April 2003

45 Bottorff: 'America, Apple Pie, Baseball'

46 Robbins, Tim, 'Against Fundamentalism', *The Nation*, 18 October 2002

47 'Business Date for Mystic River', at www.imdb.com

48 Penn, Sean, in *San Francisco Chronicle*, 14 January 2004

49 With strong connections to Latin American non-governmental organisations, it is no surprise that MADRE adopted a title that means woman, or mother, in colloquial Spanish.

50 Cooper, 'Postcards from the Left'

51 Sommers, Dave, 'Lethal Lesson', at www.trentonian.com, 16 November 2001

52 Sommers: 'Lethal Lesson'
53 'Danny Glover Under Fire for His Anti-War Position', *Oakland Tribune*, 19 May 2003
54 Pattison, Mark, 'Has Martin Sheen's Activism Hurt his Career?', at www.horizonmab.com, July 1999
55 Kaplan, James, 'Give it up for Sean Penn', *Guardian*, 6 May 2001
56 Robbins, Tim, 'A Bully Can Be Stopped', *The Nation*, 15 April 2003
57 Biskind: 'On Movies, Money & Politics'
58 Wexler: author interview
59 Wexler: author interview
60 Solomon: author interview
61 Landau, Saul, author interview, November 2003
62 Clark, Mike, *USA Today*, 17 December 1999
63 Chastain, Jim, at www.rottentomatoes.com, December 1999
64 Turan, Kenneth, *LA Times*, 14 October 1999
65 Sanford, James, *Kalamzoo Gazette*, 5 November 1999
66 'Top 250 Movies as Voted by our Users', at www.imdb.com/top_25_films, 1 May 2002
67 www.imdb.com/title/tt0105236/boxoffice
68 Greene: *Hollywood Migraine*, p. 146
69 Dodona Research Publication, *Hollywood: America's Film Industry* (Leicester, 2001)
70 Wasko: *How Hollywood Works*, p. 212
71 Bart and Guber: *Shoot Out*, p. 259
72 Schamus: 'A Rant', p. 259
73 Wasko: *How Hollywood Works*, p. 62
74 *Producing, Financing and Distributing Motion Pictures* (New York, 1992), p. 53
75 Garnett: author interview
76 Bart: *Shoot Out*, p. 93
77 Bart: *Shoot Out*, p. 224
78 Biskind: 'On Movies, Money & Politics'
79 Garnett: author interview
80 www.imdb.com
81 Corliss, Richard, 'The World According to Michael; Taking Aim at George W., a Populist Agitator Makes Noise, News and a New Kind of Political Entertainment', *Time Magazine*, 12 July 2004
82 Greenwald, Robert, interviewed by the author, July 2004.
83 Garnett: author interview
84 'Now with Bill Moyers', *PBS*, 4 April 2003
85 Robbins: 'A Bully Can Be Stopped'
86 Huberman: *The Bush Haters' Handbook*, p. 250
87 Chait, Jonathan, 'Mad About You', *The New Republic*, 29 September 2003
88 Ali, Tariq, speech to demonstration in London, 15 February 2003
89 Polizeros, Bob, interviewed by the author, February 2004

90 Wypijewski, J, 'Workers Against The War', at www.counterpunch.org
91 Solomon: author interview
92 Pollack, Kenneth M., *The Threatening Storm: the Case for Invading Iraq* (New York, 2002)
93 *CNN Evening News*, October 2002
94 Asner: author interview
95 Campbell, Duncan, 'US Artists Damn War without Limit', *Guardian*, 14 June 2002
96 World Entertainment News Network, 4 October 2002
97 *Hard Talk*, BBC News24, January 2003
98 www.bbc.co.uk, 20 January 2003
99 Asner: author interview
100 McArdle: author interview
101 McArdle: author interview
102 'Letter from Sean Penn', *New York Times*, 30 May 2003
103 Robbins, Tim, 'Against Fundamentalism', speech to anti-war rally, New York Central Park, 6 October 2002
104 *History v Hollywood*, The History Channel, 2003
105 A Conversation', documentary on *The Last Samurai* DVD.
106 *History v Hollywood*
107 *History v Hollywood*
108 Hudson: *George Clooney*
109 Robbins: *Cradle Will Rock: The Movie and the Moment*
110 Radner, Hilary, 'Hollywood Redux', in Lewis: *The End of Cinema as We Know It*, p. 80
111 *Sight and Sound*, July 2003
112 Jone, Kent, 'Dogville', *Sight and Sound*, July 2003
113 Biskind: 'On Movies, Money & Politics', p. 10
114 Sheen, Martin, quoted at www.commondreams.org

Epilogue

1 McArdle: author interview
2 McArdle: author interview
3 www.MoveOnpac.org, August 2004
4 www.unitedforpeace.org, November 2004
5 Houpt, Simon, 'Anti-Bush Sentiment Busts Out All Over', *Canadian Globe and Mail*, 17 April 2004
6 Philip, Steven, 'Movie News', *Socialist Review*, October 2004
7 www.MoveOnpac.org, August 2004
8 Schechter, Danny, at www.News Dissector, 5 November 2004
9 Nader, Ralph, at www.votenader.org, 13 November 2004

Index